Here Shall I Die Ashore

Here Shall I Die Ashore

STEPHEN HOPKINS:
Bermuda Castaway, Jamestown Survivor,
and *Mayflower* Pilgrim.

Caleb Johnson

To order additional copies of this book, contact:
Xlibris Corporation
1-888-795-4274
www.Xlibris.com
Orders@Xlibris.com
32567

CONTENTS

Appendices

Acknowledgements

I would like to first thank my wife Anna, and daughter Athena, for sharing me with this book project. I know that I have given this book far more attention than it deserved, and them far less attention than they deserved. This book was made possible by their sacrifice.

I would also like to recognize Ernie Christensen, who exchanged numerous e-mails with me, gave his opinions, and opened his extensive research papers into Stephen Hopkins to me. He also generously provided permission to reproduce his own article on Stephen Hopkins' English origins, which can be found in Appendix II.

Several other researchers have at various points in time assisted me in researching Stephen. These include Leslie Mahler, who did some of the preliminary parish register and probate record searches that facilitated my initial Hopkins' discoveries; Simon Neal, who performed many detailed record searches for me in Hampshire and elsewhere; Paul C. Reed, who performed additional research that contributed to my initial Hopkins' discoveries; and John C. Brandon, who provided some valuable information with regards to Hopkins' apparent relationship to the Palmer family of Plymouth.

Thanks is also due to Patty Baker at the Pilgrim Hall Museum, for permission to use the photo of Constance Hopkins' hat; and to Ruth Leslie and the Kerry Cattle Society for providing some pictures of Kerry cows—the same or very similar breed to that which the Hopkins family owned at Plymouth.

Special recognition is also due to Mike Haywood, whose gorgeous paintings "The Main Beam Bowed and Cracked," and "Pilgrim's Landing," were collaged together to create the cover. Prints of his artwork are available on his website, http://www.mikehaywoodart.co.uk. Special thanks are likewise due to Ruth DeWilde-Major, whose wonderful and carefully-researched portrait of Massasoit Ousemequin is found on the reverse cover. A descendant of John Howland, she has done a large number of Plymouth, Wampanoag, and Pilgrim-themed works, a part of a series of paintings entitled "New England Images, 1605-1635," all critiqued for accuracy by museum experts, archaeologists, historians and researchers.

Thanks also to my father, Frank Johnson, who created the fantastic illustrations of the various churches of Stephen Hopkins' life, including All Saints Upper Clatford, St. Thomas Winchester, St. Swithin's Upon Kingsgate, and All Saints Hursley, as well as the street scene of Upper Clatford, all based on period artwork, descriptions, and 19th century photographs. Frank is a descendant of the same *Mayflower* passengers that I am, namely the Aldens' and Mullins', Myles Standish, George Soule, Edward Doty, Henry Samson, and Richard Warren.

Preface

Back in the winter of 1996, while compiling research for my Mayflower Web Pages (now MayflowerHistory.com), I made a stop at the local LDS Family History Center, where they had a CD-ROM version of their International Genealogical Index—back then, it was not available on the web. I sat there for hours doing search after search, just to see what tidbits and clues I could find on any of the *Mayflower* passengers. One odd record I noticed was the baptism of "Constancia Hopkyns," daughter of Stephen, in the parish of Hursley, co. Hampshire, England. The baptism was dated 11 May 1606, and the source was a parish register abstraction, not some less reputable "user submission." I knew that the *Mayflower* passenger Constance Hopkins, the daughter of Stephen, was born about 1606, so it seemed like a promising entry. But every book and article on Stephen to that point had, without fail, indicated that the *Mayflower* passenger and his family were from Wortley, co. Gloucester. I did a brief search for Constance's brother Giles, to see if he was also listed there, and did not find him. Thinking it must have just been a name coincidence, I filed it away and forgot about it for about a year.

At some point the following year, as I was reviewing my notes, I started to think about it a little more. The Wortley, Gloucester origin that had been widely published was not based on any strong evidence, it was merely based upon the fact that the name Stephen showed up in that family. There was no hard evidence—despite the elaborate family structures that genealogists had developed around the Gloucester family—to show with any certainty that this was the right family. And the name Constance and Stephen are not the most common in the world—when combined with the birth year (1606) that should have been expected, this record was starting to look much more interesting.

I asked a research associate of mine who I had worked with on many occasions, Leslie Mahler, to take a look at the Hursley parish registers, to see if there was anything interesting there. Indeed, there was! Giles' baptism was there, right at the year it should have been expected—he was just listed under the Latin variant of Giles, namely Egidius, which is why my cursory initial search had failed to turn him up. Stephen Hopkins and his family were not from Gloucester as had long been assumed and oft-published: he was actually from Hampshire. The mythical wife Constance Dudley, and the brother William, and the whole cast of characters that had been developed around his supposed Gloucester origins, were simply wrong. The family history had to be rewritten.

This discovery led to a series of additional insights into the family, which are found in my article published in the July 1998 issue of *The American Genealogist* (the full text of which is included as Appendix I of this book). It is from this discovery that my special interest in Stephen Hopkins developed. Ernie Christensen followed this research up and in 2004 discovered Stephen's own baptism at Upper Clatford, Hampshire, which he published with additional research in a subsequent issue of *The American Genealogist*—this article is reproduced, in full and with permission, as Appendix II.

I am a descendant of nine *Mayflower* passengers myself, but Hopkins is not among them—though I can come up with a few distant connections to the biography: I am a descendant of Hopkins' troublesome manservant, Edward Doty; I am a descendant of Captain Myles Standish, who worked with Hopkins frequently in early Indian affairs and who administered Stephen's estate when he died; and I am a descendant of Kenelm Winslow, who was a witness against Stephen in a price-fixing court case.

Little has been written on Stephen Hopkins, and only within the last decade have the details of his life become fully apparent. His adventures are extraordinarily fascinating, making him a fun and enjoyable character to write about. He just seems to have been everywhere and experienced everything, whether it was a shipwreck in Bermuda, a near shipwreck on the shoals off Cape Cod, a shallop-wreck on Clark's Island, a hurricane or a water spout, a death sentence, or a fine for selling beer too expensively, meeting Pocahontas, or housing Squanto, signing up for the Pequot War, or heading off on a diplomatic mission to the great Wampanoag sachem Massasoit Ousemaquin. My only hope is that I can achieve some semblance of justice to his exciting life.

Following the biography, I have included a substantial amount of material in the appendices, which I strongly encourage those who are interested to read. Appendix I and II contain the full text of the original peer-reviewed

The American Genealogist articles, from 1998 and 2004, discovering Stephen Hopkins' origins in England. The first article is my own, and the second article is a follow-up by Ernie Christensen. These more academic treatments on the subject will be of particular interest to genealogists, and to those who may not yet be convinced of the illegitimacy of the Gloucester origins, the fictional "Constance Dudley," and the other biographical aspects once assigned to Stephen.

Appendix III and Appendix IV contain the only two surviving primary source accounts of the *Sea Venture's* shipwreck in Bermuda: the first written by William Strachey, and the second by Silvester Jourdaine. Since Stephen Hopkins was onboard and participated in all the events described, these works will be of particular interest to those who want more day-to-day details than are provided in my biography itself. Strachey's account, in particular, is a very enjoyable first-hand account to read. Silvester Jourdaine's account was the first one published, in 1613—perhaps just early enough that Stephen's wife Mary may have had a chance to read it.

William Strachey's account was actually a private letter written to an unspecified "Noble Lady," which was not formally published until 1625. It is interesting to note that William Brewster, Plymouth's church Elder, actually owned a copy of the book in which this account was first published (Samuel Purchas, *Purchas His Pilgrimes*), and Governor Bradford cited this book in his *History* as well: meaning Stephen Hopkins very well may have read this personal letter, that describes him, his mutiny, his death sentence, his pleas and moans for forgiveness! One wonders what the other leading men of Plymouth must have thought, upon reading this account for the first time. I wonder if it matched with the stories Stephen had told them on the *Mayflower*, or if it was a surprise revelation the first time they read it?

Appendix V contains a chapter "A Journey to Pokanoket," from the 1622 book, *A Relation or Journal of the Beginnings and Proceedings of the English Plantation Settled at Plymouth*, which was essentially the journals written by the Pilgrims, covering their arrival, exploration, settling, and first year at Plymouth. "A Journey to Pokanoket," written by Edward Winslow, describes in great detail all the events surrounding Winslow and Hopkins' journey and visit to Massasoit in 1621. Those who are interested in reading the entire journals, along with William Bradford's own history *Of Plymouth Plantation*, should get a copy of my edition of *William Bradford's Of Plymouth Plantation: Along with the full text of the Pilgrims' journals for their first year at Plymouth* (Xlibris 2005, ISBN 1-4257-0576-6), available on my MayflowerHistory. com website.

Appendix VI contains a brief genealogical summary of the first three generations of Stephen Hopkins' descendants. For anyone interested in a more detailed genealogy, and one that extends to the fifth generation, consult volume six of the General Society of Mayflower Descendants' *Mayflower Families* series.

Introduction

Enter Stephano, singing, with a bottle in his hand.

STEPHANO. I shall no more to sea, to sea;
   Here shall I die ashore.

William Shakespeare
"The Tempest," Act II, scene ii.

Stephen Hopkins had stepped ashore at many places throughout his life, and each time he did, there were new, adventurous, and dangerous experiences awaiting him. He stepped ashore as a castaway on the Isle of Devils, after shipwrecking in a Bermuda Triangle hurricane. He stepped ashore at Jamestown, Virginia, to witness the few survivors there starving to death. He stepped ashore at Cape Cod in the middle of winter, to search out with the *Mayflower* Pilgrims a place to build a colony. He stepped ashore at night on Clark's Island in Plymouth Harbor, following a storm and near shallop-wreck. And he stepped ashore at Plymouth, no doubt crossing the famous Plymouth Rock numerous times as the colonists unloaded their cargo and began constructing their plantation.

Stephen's first steps, though, were not off a shipwreck, but rather were taken in the small country parish of Upper Clatford, in Hampshire, England.

Chapter 1

THE EARLY YEARS

Spring was in full bloom, with May just one day away, as John and Elizabeth Hopkins made their way along the wide and open bank of the gently flowing Anton river, through the green fertile meadows lined with willows and pollard lindens, that lead to the little village of Upper Clatford's main architectural feature—the Church of All Saints. Originally built during the reign of King Henry I, the church still had its original Norman-era doorways and isles, and recently-constructed low, square church towers. Two singular arches divided the nave and chancel, and rested on a heavy central pier. The road to the church was leafy and pleasant, and the river—flowing gently southeast from the larger town of Andover, just a short stroll away on the opposing bank—was beautiful to look upon: an angler's paradise.

John and Elizabeth, with young children William and Alice in tow, were bringing their newborn baby, Stephen, to the parish church for his baptism.[1] By the Church of England's custom, infants were baptized as soon as practicable after their birth, often the Sunday following; infant mortality

---

[1]   Stephen Hopkins' baptism at Upper Clatford was first reported in Ernest Martin Christensen, "The Probable Parentage of Stephen[1] Hopkins of the *Mayflower*," *The American Genealogist* 79(October 2004):241-249. Descriptions of Upper Clatford and the parish church are based on the following sources: Christensen, ibid., pp. 243, citing Arthur J. Willis, ed., *Winchester Consistory Court Depositions 1561-1602* (Winchester, 1960), pp. 20-21; George A. B. Dewar, et.al., *Dent's County Guides: Hampshire: With the Isle of Wight* (London: E.P. Dutton & Co., 1901), p. 81; and Henry Rider Haggard, *Rural England: Being an Account of*

The parish church of All Saints, Upper Clatford, where Stephen Hopkins was baptized in 1581. William Palmer, who came to Plymouth Colony in 1621 onboard the ship *Fortune*, also appears to have been baptized here that same year.

was very high, and failure to baptize an infant before he or she died was believed to rob Christ's flock of one of its lambs.[2]

Children William, age six, and Alice, age three, had been born to John's first wife, Agnes Borrow. Agnes, John's wife of five years, died in 1578. It is quite probable that she died as a result of complications from the birth of their daughter Alice: childbirth, or complications stemming from it, was the leading cause of death for women during this time period. John Hopkins married his current wife, Elizabeth Williams, at the same Church of All Saints, on 28 July 1579, not long after Agnes' death; baby Stephen was their first child together.

The Hopkins' and Williams' families had been in Upper Clatford for a couple generations at least; they had been raising crops on a farm with three common fields, called Norman's Court Farm. One field was for growing wheat, the second for barley, and the third was reserved for a "summer field." Back in 1553, the Williams family sued the Hopkins family over a dispute about tithes for the crops grown in common fields.[3] Obviously the legal dispute of 26-years before was settled long before John and Elizabeth were married, uniting the families.

A little over three months after Stephen's birth, the family of William and Alice (Knight) Palmer came to the same parish church in Upper Clatford to baptize their first son, William, on 13 August 1581. William Palmer and Stephen Hopkins were quite probably childhood companions. These two toddlers could never have guessed that forty years later they would be related to each other, and sharing a house on the other side of the world![4]

Agricultural and Social Researches Carried Out in the Years 1901 & 1902 (London: Longmans, Green, and Co., 1906), 1:53, 290, 347.

2   Richard Clyfton, one of the original founders of the Pilgrims' church back in Scrooby, argued this point in his book *A Plea for Infants and Elder People Concerning their Baptism* (Amsterdam, 1610).

3   Christensen, ibid., at pp. 243, citing Arthur J. Willis, ed., *Winchester Consistory Court Depositions 1561-1602* (Winchester, 1960), pp. 20-21.

4   John C. Brandon deserves credit for first having recognized the possible connection between Stephen Hopkins and William Palmer, in an e-mail to me back in late 1998. So it is highly interesting to find William Palmer baptized just a few entries away from Stephen in Upper Clatford—exactly the right age to have been the early Plymouth resident (and Hopkins relative) of the same name.

One of the main streets of Upper Clatford, as it looked during the
time young Stephen was growing up.

Three years after Stephen's baptism, the Hopkins family was back at All Saints for another: newborn sister Susanna. Susanna would be Stephen's only full-blooded sibling, at least as far as parish records reveal to us more than four hundred years later.

John and Elizabeth Hopkins and their family of four children did not remain in Upper Clatford much beyond the birth of Susanna. By the time Stephen was five or six, the family moved about ten miles south to the bustling city of Winchester. Once the capital of England back in the 10th century, the city was still a large and active trading center when the Hopkins' family arrived. The city's most famous landmark, Winchester Cathedral, was built in 1079. At 556 feet in length, it still holds the record as the longest cathedral in all of Europe. William II, son of William the Conqueror, was buried there in 1100. Another dominating landmark, Winchester Castle, with its 110' x 55' x 55' Great Hall, was built by King Henry III around 1230.

John Hopkins first shows up in the parish of St. Thomas, Winchester, in 1586, where he was assessed a lay subsidy—a tax that Queen Elizabeth used primarily to subsidize the English navy. Although war had not been formally declared, the English navy was, for all practical purposes, at war with Spain. In 1587, Spain prepared a fleet to sail against England, but thirty-seven of the ships were caught in a surprise attack led by Sir Francis Drake, setting back the invasion date by a year. In 1588, however, the Spanish Armada, consisting of 130 Spanish warships, set sail for England with the intention of supporting a full-scale land invasion. The English navy managed to intercept and scatter the fleet in the battle of Gravelines, and then picked off the individual ships one-by-one until the Armada was decimated; the small remainder of the fleet was forced to circumnavigate England to return home.

John Hopkins paid additional lay subsidy taxes, usually about £4, in subsequent years as well. England and Spain did not formally end hostilities against one another until King James came to power a decade and a half later. John not only supported England by paying his lay subsidies, but he also appears to have been an archer in the local militia. In a little chamber room in his Winchester house, he kept his militia equipment: a bow, a sheaf of arrows, a sword and dagger, and some body armor including arm and leg plates and a helmet.[5]

---

[5]   These items are listed in John Hopkins' probate record, which is reproduced in full in Ernie Christensen's article, found in Appendix II

St. Thomas, Winchester, the parish church of Stephen Hopkins' youth. The Hopkins family attended Sunday services here from about 1586 through 1594

Given the state of war and the recent invasion attempt, it seems entirely probable that by 1593, John was giving his sons William (age 18) and Stephen (age 12) some lessons on fighting and archery. But John Hopkins died unexpectedly around August of that year. The surviving records do not indicate what the cause of death was, but John died intestate—meaning he did not make out a will—and he was only in his mid-40s, so it was probably a sudden illness or accident of some kind.

Elizabeth Hopkins, now a widow, had some very difficult decisions to make. She and William were granted administration of her husband's estate, and on September 4, an inventory of the family's goods was taken by three local residents, John Paye, Henry Greene, and William Colson. The estate totaled £37, 9s, 8d. John owned no real estate, no livestock, and had no reportable amount of cash. There was not enough estate for Elizabeth to live on while supporting her family. Since women could not simply go out and get a job in 16th century England, her options were very limited. She could quickly remarry, and her new husband could support the family's financial needs. Or she could apprentice out her children to relatives, church members, or neighbors, and then rely on the remaining estate, charity of family, neighbors, and the church, for her own subsistence.

The inventory of the family's household goods, taken on 4 September 1593 shortly after John's death, is a virtual tour of the house they lived in and the material goods the family owned. As the three assessors made their way around the Hopkins' household, they took inventory of the following[6]:

In the hallway
A table board, frame, joined stools, a chair, and cupboard full of clothes.

In the parlor
A joined bedstead, truckle bedstead, a featherbed, a feather bolster and coverlet, a flock bed and flock bolster and coverlet, a square table with frame, two chests, nine cushions, five pairs of sheets, three pairs of canvas sheets, six canvas tablecloths, two diaper

---

[6]   The estate inventory of John Hopkins was first published by Ernest Christensen, ibid., at pp. 247-249, citing Hampshire Records Office 1593 AD/42. Christensen's article, including the complete estate inventory, can be found, in full, in Appendix II.

cloths with towels, two dozen napkins, five Holland pillowcases, and John's wearing apparel (which included a pair of breeches, two pairs of stockings, one hat, two doublets, two cowls, and one old gown.)

In the fore-chamber
A joined bedstead, a trockel bedstead, two featherbeds, coverlet, rug, a pair of blankets, a pair of curtains and curtain rods, and a table board with frame and forms.

In the second chamber
A table, form, and side table, a chair, joined bedstead and trockel bedstead, one featherbed and bolster, a pair of blankets and one old cover, a let of arras (a tapestry fabric used especially for wall hangings), a flock bed and feather bolster, seven feather pillows, three quilts, and various clothes.

In the little chamber
Two old bedsteads and one old side table.

In the kitchen chamber
Two old bedsteads, one flock bed, one old chest full of torn valance, a torn bolster, a hand basket, a bow and sheath of arrows, a sword, dagger, and body armor including a skull (helmet), greaves (for lower legs) and warbrace (for arms).

In the kitchen itself
Two table boards, one old cupboard, one old stool, two basins and one ewer (a pitcher), eight platters, three porringers (bowls) and six saucers, four water pots, three saltshakers, three white candlestick holders, four flour pots, a drinking cup, two pewter pots, two brass pots, three kettles, a posnet (small basin), two little pans, a skillet, chafing dish, braise mortar, a skimmer, a frying pan, two andirons, two fire dogs, another frying pan, a pair of tongs, a dripping pan, two pair of cottrels (hooks to hold a pot over a fire), a pair of pothooks, a gridiron, an old trivet, an old bowl, a well bucket, a chain, two baking tubs, three covers, a soap bowl, a grain mortar, and a chopping board. Also, near the fireplace, there was a cord and a half of wood, a load of hay, and a great kettle.

The Hopkins' were not a wealthy family by any means; but they certainly appear to be living comfortably enough, and they seem to have owned all the normal and necessary household items needed to sustain a small family. One interesting tidbit brought out in the inventory is the fact that the family, consisting of John and Elizabeth, and their four children, had about fifteen beds in their house. Why the family owned so many beds is unknown. Perhaps there were some more distant family members or apprentices living with them.

Exactly what happened to the family following John's death is unclear. The widow Elizabeth was taxed twice in 1594. Her first lay subsidy that she was assessed was for £1.[7] Since the tax was based on 10% of the value of her personal goods, this would indicate she owned goods valued about £10 in total. She was then assessed an additional 4 shillings subsidy on a landholding that was valued at 20 shillings.[8] So it would appear that Elizabeth received the traditional dowry of one third of her husband's £35 estate, or about £12 total, and that she then used a couple of those pounds to purchase a small landholding for herself. The remaining two-thirds of John's estate would traditionally have been divided for the benefit of his children, with the eldest son William receiving a double share.

Since there is no indication that Elizabeth remarried, she probably was forced to apprentice out her youngest children Stephen and Susanna. Eldest son William, who had just turned eighteen, was probably able to take his double portion and begin to make a way for himself without undergoing an apprenticeship so late in his teenage years.

Exactly where twelve year old Stephen Hopkins ended up is not made clear by any surviving record, but there is an interesting clue. St. Swithins-Upon-Kingsgate, Winchester, is an odd parish church located near St. Thomas. It is built right on top of Kingsgate, an entry-gate to the city. Underneath the church passed foot and horse traffic through several archways. Churchgoers climb up a set of stairs to reach the small church-built-on-top-of-a-gate. It was here, about a year and a half before John Hopkins' death, that a William Hopkins and Constance Marline were married—on 16 April 1592. Since Stephen's older brother William was then only seventeen years of age, and Constance Marline was the widow of Reynold Marline, a barber who had

---

7   Christensen, ibid., p. 244, citing Douglas F. Vick, *Central Hampshire Lay Subsidy Assessments, 1558-1603* (Farnham, Surrey, 1987), p. 66.

8   Public Records Office E179/174/415A.

Interior of St. Swithin's Upon Kingsgate, the church where William and Constance (Marline) Hopkins were married in 1592. If Stephen did indeed live with this Hopkins family, then this is likely the church Stephen attended as a teenager.

died the year previous[9], it seems highly improbable that this is the marriage of Stephen's older brother; but it is quite likely this is a close relative, perhaps an uncle. As will be seen shortly, when Stephen became an adult, he named his first daughter Elizabeth (after his mother, no doubt—er, . . . in honor of Queen Elizabeth, no doubt), and his second daughter was given the quite distinctive name of Constance. So perhaps William and Constance (Marline) Hopkins were Stephen's adoptive parents during his teenage years.

---

[9] The 1591 will of Reynold Marlyn, Winchester (Hampshire Records Office 1591/A094). In the will, Reynold mentions he is a barber; that he had a wife named Constance and two sons John and Timothy; and that he had a tenement in the parish of St. Thomas, Winchester.

Chapter 2

HURSLEY

The parish of Hursley, Hampshire, neighbors Winchester to the southwest, and it is in this parish that Stephen Hopkins emerges as an adult, from the black hole that was his teenage years. Merdon Castle, built there in 1138 by Henry de Blois, Bishop of Winchester, had been abandoned a few decades before Stephen arrived, but its ruins, on top of a high, southern, gently-sloping hill surrounded by large yew trees, were still a very prominent landmark. The Merdon manor had been owned by the church until the time of King Edward IV, at which point it was granted to Sir Philip Hoby, Knight, one of King Henry VIII's privy councilors. The manor descended through several generations of the Hoby family, and was in the possession of Sir Giles Hoby when Stephen Hopkins took up residence there.[10]

One of King Henry VIII's Gentleman of the Bedchamber, Thomas Sternhold, also took up residence in Hursley, and died there in 1549. Sternhold was famous for having written thirty seven psalms in English verse, which were later expanded upon by John Hopkins of Oxford University—no known relation to Stephen—and published as the Sternhold and Hopkins psalter: the psalm book used throughout the next few centuries by the Anglican church.

---

[10]   This brief history of Hursley is based on Rev. John Frewen Moor, Jr., *The Birth-Place, Home, Churches, and Other Places Connected with the Author of 'The Christian Year,'* Second edition (William Savage: London, 1867), pp. 107-110, and Charlotte Yonge's *John Keble's Parishes: A History of Hursley and Otterbourne* (McMillan: London, 1898).

Stephen Hopkins' first appearance in the parish records of Hursley, Hampshire, occurs on 13 March 1605, when his first child, a daughter named Elizabeth, was baptized at the local parish church of All Saints. Stephen was married to a woman named Mary, but the record of their marriage is unfortunately not found in the parish registers, making her parentage and maiden name uncertain. What little circumstantial evidence there is hints that she might have been the daughter of Giles Machell of Hursley—but that identification is far from conclusive at this point.[11]

Stephen and Mary's marriage would have likely occurred around 1602 or 1603, based on Stephen's age and the baptism date of eldest daughter Elizabeth. Little more than a year after Elizabeth's baptism, on 11 May 1606, Stephen and Mary baptized their second daughter, Constance—the child that was perhaps named in honor of Constance (Marline) Hopkins of Winchester. And on 30 January 1608, Stephen and Mary baptized their first son, whom they named Giles. If my suspicions are right about Mary's identity, then their son was named after Mary's father, Giles Machell.

On 19 May 1608, when baby Giles was just four months old, a dramatic change in the Hopkins family occurred. On that date, Stephen Hopkins' lease at Hursley's Merdon manor, where the family had apparently been residing for the past several years, was turned over to a "widow Kent."[12] Exactly why is unclear from the manorial record; a marginal note seems to suggest Stephen was fined or penalized. The Hopkins family either moved out, or was forced out. The lack of any landholding may have significantly affected the family: Stephen would not hang around Hursley for much longer. Whether for lack of money, some business or trading prospect, out of some sense of adventure or religious zeal, or more likely because Stephen needed some land to support

---

11   The will of Robert Machell of Hursley, dated 24 January 1575 (Hampshire Records Office 1575/P06), mentions (among others) his wife Joan and his son Giles. This Giles would have been an appropriate age to have been the father of a hypothetical Mary Machell, who would have been born sometime around 1585. Unfortunately the Hursley parish registers do not commence until 1599. Aside from the fact the name "Giles" runs in the Machell family, another indication the Machell family had some connection to the Hopkins family comes from the estate inventory of Mary Hopkins in 1613, where one of the inventory-takers was William Toot, whose wife was Alice Machell, potentially another daughter of Giles Machell.

12   Hampshire Records Office, Court Book of the Manor of Merdon, 63M84/21.

The parish church of All Saints, Hursley, as it looked at the time when Stephen and Mary Hopkins baptized their first three children Elizabeth (1605), Constance (1606), and Giles (1608). The church was completely rebuilt in 1848, so looks much different today.

his growing family, he somehow managed to get himself associated with a group of investors and colonists headed for the newly-founded Jamestown Colony in Virginia.

Stephen signed on as a minister's clerk for Rev. Richard Buck, an Oxford-educated minister described as an "able and painful preacher." The fact that an Oxford-educated minister would choose Stephen Hopkins from Hursley to read a psalter written by Hursley-buried Thomas Sternhold and co-authored by Oxford minister John Hopkins, . . . it all seems so bizarrely coincidental. But then again, maybe it was.

On 2 June 1609, Hopkins boarded the *Sea Venture* in Plymouth, England, the flagship of a fleet of seven ships and two pinnaces headed for Virginia, to start his new life. Wife Mary, two daughters Elizabeth and Constance, and young son Giles—then barely a year old—were left behind in Hursley to fend for themselves until he would return, or send for them to come: seven years later, by contract. Mary may have gone back to lease a place from, or perhaps just near, her parents or siblings; perhaps some neighbors or fellow church members helped to support the family. There is some indication that Mary may have had a side business as a shopkeeper—perhaps she was just continuing a small business that Stephen had helped to establish before he left.

It must have been an agonizing and horribly difficult time for Mary. Life without a husband present in 17th century England was tough indeed, especially with three young children. And knowing her husband was on a treacherous sea voyage, and would then live for seven years in a harsh and primitive colony continually plagued by disease, Indian attacks, famine, and mismanagement, must have taken a severe toll on her both mentally and physically. But even her worst fears may not have prepared her for what was *really* going to happen.

THE
WHOLE BOOKE
OF PSALMES.

COLLECTED INTO ENGLISH MEETER,

by THOMAS STERNHOLD, IOHN HOPKINS, and
others, conferred with the Hebrew, with apt Notes to
Sing them with all.

Set foorth and allowed to bee Sung in all Churches, of all the
people together, and after Morning and Euening Prayer, as also
before and after Sermons: and moreouer in priuate Houses, for their
godly folace and comfort, laying apart all vngodly Songs and
Ballads, which tend onely to the nourifhing of
vice, and corrupting of
YOVTH.

COLOSSIANS. III.

*Let the word of God dwell plenteoufly in you in all wifedome, teaching and exhorting one
another in Pfalmes, Hymnes, and fpirituall Songs, and Sing to the Lord in your
hearts.*

IAMES. V.

If any be afflicted, let him Pray; if any be merry, let him fing Pfalmes.

LONDON
Printed for the Companie of Stationers. 1618.

The title page of a Sternhold and Hopkins psalter, used by the
Church of England. First published in 1562, it went through many
reprinting, including this one in 1618.

Chapter 3

VOYAGE OF THE *SEA VENTURE*

The *Sea Venture* was the flagship of a fleet that consisted of seven ships and two pinnaces that were headed to resupply the Jamestown Colony and deliver a new governor.[13] The passengers and crews readied themselves at the port of Plymouth, England, loading the ships with livestock, food, drink, work tools, weapons and ammunition, and personal goods like clothing and books.

As the flagship, the brand new 300-ton *Sea Venture* was well outfitted, well armed, and would transport the more eminent passengers, including Jamestown's next governor Sir Thomas Gates; the fleet's Admiral, Sir George Somers; and ship's captain, Christopher Newport, who had led the first fleet of ships to Jamestown back in 1607. Also onboard was Jamestown's future minister, Rev. Richard Buck. Stephen had signed onto the voyage as minister's clerk for Reverend Buck, and would read the psalms and Biblical passages during the Thursday and Sunday services; so he too got the privilege of being transported on the fleet's flagship.

The fleet departed Plymouth, England, late in the evening on Friday, 2 June 1609. The weather and wind were with them as they headed out across the Atlantic. The fleet would use a more northerly route than past voyages to Virginia, in an attempt to avoid the shipping routes and regions more frequented by the Spanish around Dominica. The Spanish were a continual threat to English ships and colonies—Spain, after all, claimed the Virginian

---

[13] Two published first-hand accounts of the *Sea Venture*'s voyage were written: one by William Strachey, and one by Sylvester Jourdaine. Both accounts are reproduced, in full, as Appendix III and IV.

region too, and considered the English to be trespassing and invading their territory.

A month and a half into the voyage, everything was going well for the fleet. The weather and winds had been in their favor most of the voyage. All seven ships had managed to maintain sight one of another; and Virginia, they estimated, was only a week or so away. It almost seemed too good to be true . . .

Indeed, the situation took a dramatic turn on St. James Day, July 24. The previous night, the clouds had begun to gather, and by morning the wind was "singing and whistling most unusually." The crew cast off the pinnace they had been towing, so that the two vessels would not collide and damage each other during the storm that had so suddenly arose from the northeast.

It was no ordinary storm, however: it was a hurricane. The couple surviving accounts of the events that transpired onboard the *Sea Venture* provide a rare glimpse into what must have been the most dreadful, exhausting and fearful event in the lives of everyone onboard:

> [A] dreadful storm and hideous began to blow from out the northeast, which, swelling and roaring as it were by fits, some hours with more violence than others, at length did beat all light from Heaven; which like an hell of darkness, turned black upon us, so much more the fuller of horror . . . the ear lay so sensible to the terrible cries and murmurs of the winds and distraction of our company as who was most armed and best prepared was not a little shaken.
>
> For four and twenty hours the storm in a restless tumult had blown so exceedingly as we could not apprehend in our imaginations any possibility of greater violence; . . . fury added to fury, and one storm urging a second more outrageous than the former . . . . Sometimes shrieks in our ship amongst our women and passengers not used to such hurly and discomforts made us look one upon the other with troubled hearts and panting bosoms . . . . Prayers might well be in the heart and lips, but drowned in the outcries of the officers.

The storm raged on with such violence that the crew could not utilize any sails, and the seas were so rough it took as many as eight men just to hold the whipstaff in the steerage room, making it nearly impossible to control the ship's direction. As one passenger noted, "[I]t could not be said to rain:

the waters like whole rivers did flood in the air . . . . [W]inds and seas were as mad as fury and rage could make them."

As scary as riding out a hurricane might seem, it was not an impossible task. Ships, even 17th century sailing ships, could normally survive even the most severe storm at sea, if the crew was on their feet and able to respond to the various emergencies that were bound to arise during the intensive battering. So the situation would not have been quite so dire with the *Sea Venture*, if it were not for one unfortunate problem: less than a day into the storm, they had sprung a leak; and not just any leak, a "mighty leak." Being a brand new ship, the oakum that sealed the joints of the ship was still somewhat fresh, and not as hardened and solid as it might have been on an older ship. The intense shaking and pounding caused one of the most dreaded conditions: the ship began to "spew her oakum," making the ship leaky throughout many of her seams.

By the time the crew first discovered the leak, the ship had taken on so much water that the ballast below deck was already five feet underwater. One passenger could not help noting the irony: "[W]e almost drowned within, while we sat looking . . . to perish from above." He went on to note: "This imparting no less terror than danger, ran through the whole ship with much fright and amazement, startled and turned the blood and took down the braves of the most hardy mariner of them all." It was a desperate situation: they were leaking, and sinking, in the middle of a hurricane.

The danger was critical, and the ship's crew had to take immediate action: they had to find the leak. "[M]aster, master's mate, boatswain, quartermasters, coopers, carpenters, and who not, with candles in their hands, creeping along the ribs viewing the sides, searching every corner, and listening in every place if they could hear the water run." Many small leaks were found and patched, but the main leak remained elusive.

The ship had several pumps that the men could work, up and down, up and down, . . . in an endless struggle to rid the ship of some of the water. But the efforts only slowed down the inevitable: the ship was still leaking faster than it could be pumped out. And the pumps were being continually clogged with soggy biscuit as the waters rose high enough to cover the ten thousand pounds of hardtack that was being stored in the bread-room.

By the second day—Tuesday—the waters overtook much of the ship's supply of food and drink. The hundred and forty men, and ten women, would mostly go without victuals from that point forward. With the water level still rising, the governor divided the men and boys into three groups. One group went to the ship's forecastle; one went to the waist; and one went to an area near the binnacle (the compass box). Their job: bail water with large six gallon buckets, or kettles, or whatever was available to use. Each man was to bail water continuously for one hour. Then he could rest an hour; then back to bailing again. It was a 24-hour a day job. The men soon found their clothing waterlogged and difficult to work in, so most of them ended up stripping naked.

While the men focused on bailing water from the sinking ship, they could not turn their backs on the hurricane either:

> Once so huge a sea brake upon the poop and quarter upon us as it covered our ship from stern to stem like a garment or a vast cloud; it filled her brim full for while within, from the hatches up to the spardeck. The source or confluence of water was so violent as it rushed and carried the helmsman from the helm and wrested the whipstaff out of his hands, which so flew from side to side that when he would have seized the same again it so tossed him from starboard to larboard as it was God's mercy it had not split him . . . . Our governor was at this time below at the capstan . . . It struck him from the place where he sat and groveled him and all us about him on our faces, beating together with our breaths all thoughts from our bosoms else than that we were now sinking. For my part, I thought her already in the bottom of the sea.

Tuesday turned into Wednesday. Wednesday turned into Thursday. The storm raged on. The men, cold, wet, naked, and without food or drink, continued their shifts. One hour bailing water, and one hour resting. The days were as black as the nights, they could barely tell the difference between the two.

Thursday night, some of the men saw an apparition. A little, round light, like a faint star "trembling and streaming along with a sparking blaze, half the height upon the main mast and shooting sometimes from shroud to shroud, tempting to settle, as it were, upon any of the four shrouds." The mysterious light, known to mariners as St. Elmo's Fire, continued to dance around half the night. The Greek's called the apparitions Castor and Pollux, because two lights were usually seen dancing together. If only one appeared, as was the case here, it was considered a bad omen—a sign of a great tempest.

The passengers and crew on the *Sea Venture* did not need any warning of a great tempest, they knew that already! The ship was slowly sinking, in spite of the fact that the passengers had managed to bail thousands and thousands of gallons of water. It was a losing battle, and they all knew it. In desperation, the passengers and crew also began dumping overboard anything that was unnecessary, in an effort to lighten the ship. Luggage, chests, trunks, the starboard cannon; they even debated the merits of cutting down the main mast.

Thursday turned into Friday. That morning there was a general but mostly unspoken feeling amongst everyone: they could not take the suffering any longer. That night, if their situation did not change, they would just shut the hatches, commit their souls to God, and let the ship sink. Silvester Jourdaine, one of the passengers, described the situation:

> [O]ur men stood up to the middles, with buckets, barricos, and kettles, to bail out the water, and continually pumped . . . without any intermission; and yet the water seemed rather to increase, than to diminish: in so much that all our men, being utterly spent, tired, and disabled for longer labor, were even resolved, without any hope of their lives, to shut up the hatches, and to have committed themselves to the mercy of the sea (which is said to be merciless) or rather to the mercy of their mighty God and Redeemer (whose mercies exceed all his works) seeing no help, nor hope, in the apprehension of man's reason, that any mother's child could escape that inevitable dagger, which every man had proposed and digested to himself of present sinking. So that some of them having some good and comfortable waters in the ship, fetched them, and drunk one to another, taking their last leave one of the other, until their more joyful and happy meeting in a more blessed world.

But just as everyone had given up all hope, as morning was transitioning into the afternoon, the storm cleared just a little.

"Land!"

The excited cry from Admiral Somers came across as a dream to many of the weary men. Was it some kind of cruel joke? "It being better surveyed, the very trees were seen to move with the wind upon the shoreside."

There was a problem, however. Normally a ship would pull up some distance offshore, anchor in deep water, and then the passengers and crew would disembark using the ship's longboat. But the *Sea Venture* was sinking, she could not be anchored. The decision was made to bear full speed ahead, in an attempt to drive the ship aground. If all went well, the passengers and crew could then ferry themselves off the wrecked ship to shore. If all went awry, the ship would split open, flounder, and capsize, leaving those onboard (most of whom could not swim) to drown.

The *Sea Venture*'s crew put the plan into action, and surprisingly managed to wedge the ship securely between two large rocks about half a mile offshore. For the rest of the afternoon and evening, they used the ship's longboat and skiff to bring ashore all the passengers, crew, and what little was left of the ship's cargo and livestock. The ship was wedged in so tightly, they were even able to make later return visits to the wreck to salvage wood, iron, rigging, and other useful items. Even more miraculously: not a single person lost their life through the whole ordeal; they had all been brought safely ashore.

Chapter 4

ISLE OF DEVILS

Friday evening, 28 July 1609, the sun began to set upon the hundred and fifty men and women who just hours earlier had thought they were all going to be dead. The men had been endlessly pumping and bailing water for five days and four nights, expecting every moment to meet their maker. Now they lay exhausted on a sandy shore, as the red glow of the sunset reflected off their wrecked ship.

The question had not occurred to anyone during all the hubbub and frenzy to get ashore and save their lives; but now that they had a moment to think about it, . . . just where were they? Word quickly spread around: they were on the most feared islands in the world, the Isle of Devils, so named because they were thought to be haunted, enchanted, and bedeviled by spirits and apparitions. Mariners tried to avoid these islands more than any other place in the world. Even today, the paranormal superstitions live on—they had shipwrecked on Bermuda, in the infamous Bermuda Triangle. It must have been an eerie night, full of all kinds of strange noises, lightning flashes from the distant storm, haunted cackling of the cahow birds, and remnant storm winds whistling through the leaves of the palm trees.

As Saturday dawned, it was time to make an assessment of the situation. There were upwards of 150 people onshore, including ten women, who now needed food, water and shelter. First up was to figure out who was in charge. Sir George Somers was the fleet's Admiral, whereas Sir Thomas Gates was the colony's appointed governor. Since they were not at sea, Sir George Somers was not really in charge any longer. But since they were not at Jamestown, Sir Thomas Gates was not really in charge either. Luckily for everyone involved, there was no power struggle to speak of—that could have doomed

23 Such as in ships or brittle barks
   into the feas defcend :
Their Merchandize through feárefull flouds
   to compaffe and to end.
24 Thofe men are forced to behold
   the Lords works, what they be :
And in the dangerous deepe the fame
   moft marueilous they fee.

25 For at his word the ftormie winde
   arifeth in a rage,
And ftirreth vp the furges fo,
   as nought can them affwage.
26 Then are they lifted vp fo hie,
   the clouds they feeme to gaine :
And plunging downe the depth, vntill
   their foules confume with paine.

27 And like a Drunkard to and fro,
   now here, now there they reele :
As men with feare of wit bereft,
   or had of fenfe no feele.
28 Then did they crie in their diftreffe
   vnto the Lord for aide :
Who did remoue their troublous ftate,
   according as they praide.

29 For with his word the Lord did make
   the fturdie ftormes to ceafe :
So that the great waues from their rage,
   are brought to reft and peace.
30 Then are men glad when reft is come,
   which they fo much do craue :
And are by him in hauen brought,
   which they fo faine would haue.

A section of Psalms 107, from a Sternhold and Hopkins psalter.
We can certainly imagine Stephen reading this appropriate passage
to the *Sea Venture* castaways at a Sunday service soon after they
came ashore.

the group from the very start. Gates took charge, and Somers remained a strong ally sharing in that authority, as did Christopher Newport, the *Sea Venture's* captain.

They had wrecked on the northern side of Bermuda, and had established themselves inside a bay that they dutifully named Gates' Bay. The castaways promptly got to work exploring the island looking for resources. Finding food and water enough for 150 people was no small task; they also needed to build themselves cabins, and they wanted to begin making preparations for an escape or rescue from the island.

As they began to explore the island during their first week, Bermuda quickly lost its haunting reputation. The weather was hot, yet pleasant, with frequent thunder and lightning, and most importantly—frequent rain showers that allowed everyone to gather and collect more than enough drinking water by digging pits and wells. There were large groves of cedar, which could be used for framing houses, and the cedar berries were boiled and made into a pleasant tea. There were palm trees aplenty, whose leaves made excellent thatch for their cabin roofs, "for they being stiff and smooth, as if so many flags were knit together, the rain easily slideth off." The soft top of the palm tree was roasted and stewed, and was eaten like a cabbage—apparently it was less gassy, though, and tasted like roasted melon.

The Governor squared off a garden and planted some melon, peas, onions, radishes, lettuce, and various salad herbs, from seeds that had been saved from the shipwreck. Unfortunately, they did not do that well, and most were parched by the sun little more than ten days after emerging. Although they were not sure what the problem was, they suspected the dark red, sandy and dry soil had something to do with it. He also tried planting sugar cane, which seemed to do much better; but alas, several of the ship's surviving hogs broke into the garden and finished them off.

They found a native blueberry bush that was "much eaten by our own people, . . . to stay or bind the flux, which the often eating of the luscious palm berry would bring them into, for the nature of sweet things is to cleanse and dissolve."

The Bermudan bays were full of fish, so they built a flat-bottomed gondola out of cedar, and "daily hooked great store of many kinds, as excellent angelfish, salmon, peal, bonitos, sting ray, cabally, snappers, hogfish, sharks, dogfish, pilchards, mullets, and rockfish, of which be divers kinds." And luckily for everyone, they had managed to preserve some salt from the shipwreck, so the excess catch could be salted and preserved for future need. They also had preserved a large net, which they dragged through the various sea coves, collecting even more fish. One passenger remembered "I may boldly say we have taken five thousand of small and great fish at one hale, as pilchards, breams, mullets, rockfish, etc. and other kinds for which we have no names." Shellfish were caught and gathered as well, lobsters, oysters, crabs, and whelks.

Sea turtles also proved an important food supply for the colonists. Not only were the sea turtles enormous and could feed as many as fifty or sixty people, but the oil ("as sweet as any butter") was used for frying and baking. Later in the winter, the female sea turtles would come ashore and lay hundreds of eggs—yet another food source, "sweeter than any hen's egg." Silvester Jourdaine, one of the passengers, recalled that they once had taken forty sea turtles in a single day.

On shore, the castaways found another surprising source in seemingly endless supply: wild hogs. The *Sea Venture* had not been the first ship to wreck on Bermuda, nor would it be the last. The island proved to be full of wild hogs, descendants of swine that had been released over the past century of Spanish visits to the island—intentional and unintentional. "[O]ur people would go a-hunting with our ship dog and sometimes bring home thirty, sometimes fifty boars, sows and pigs in a week alive." When the supply of seafood was low, they would eat some of their hogs; when their supply of food was otherwise good, they would simply keep the hogs fat, feeding them twice daily with the berries of the cedars and palms.

As everyone was building their cabins and learning how to best gather and preserve their water and food, Sir Thomas Gates also did not ignore their ultimate goal: escaping the island. Towards the end of August, as everyone was finally settling into a more established and civil routine, an escape plan was being finalized. The ship's longboat—the one that had rescued everyone off the wreck and ferried them ashore—would be outfitted with a small deck and sail. A small group of about eight men would then sail the ship west to Virginia, which was thought to be only a week or so away, to inform the Jamestown colonists of their current whereabouts, and to send a rescue ship to them at the next new moon—when they would light a large bonfire on the highest point of the island to help direct the ship in.

Henry Ravens, the *Sea Venture's* master's mate and pilot, was volunteered to lead the voyage, and accepted. He, along with cape merchant Thomas Whittingham and six other sailors, set sail on August 28, little more than a month after their shipwreck, headed for Jamestown. The group unexpectedly returned two days later after failing to get around the island. They set off a second time on September 1, this time successfully making it out into the open ocean.

At the first new moon, the colonists all went to the highest point on the island, and for several nights created a large bonfire signal to bring in the rescue ship. But no matter how hard or how carefully they monitored the horizon, no ship came. Perhaps it was too soon, they thought; or perhaps the Jamestown colonists had trouble organizing the rescue mission. So a month later, at the next new moon, they all gathered once more upon the promontory and lit up their bonfire signal for several more nights. "But two moons were wasted upon the promontory before mentioned and gave many a long and wished look round about the horizon, from the northeast to the southwest, but in vain, discovering nothing all the while, which way soever we turned our eye, but air and sea." The eight men were never seen or heard from again.

The abundant food and fresh water, and the pleasant weather, would seem to have been an extraordinary benefit to the large group of marooned men and women, and indeed it was. But the blessing ended up being a double-edged sword. After several months living in comfort and paradise, several people began to openly wonder . . . why should we go to Jamestown, where we know there have been famines, brutal Indian attacks, disease, political corruption, and where we would be expected to labor far more intensively than anything we have had to do in Bermuda?

So even as Governor Gates and Admiral Somers were pursuing plans to organize an escape from the island, there were others who began to actively subvert their efforts. If they did not want to go to Jamestown, who had the right or authority to force them? Governor Gates was the governor of *Jamestown*, not of Bermuda; and Admiral Somers only had authority over them when they were at sea, but now they were on land. The dissention started first with the *Sea Venture's* crew, since unlike the other castaways, they had less contractual obligations to the Virginia Company.

Even as they were awaiting Henry Raven's return from Virginia, Governor Gates had begun employing a group of men to build a small pinnace that could be used to transport some of the colonists to Virginia, in case he did not return. At that time, six men (John Want—a suspected Brownist, Christopher Carter, Francis Pearepont, William Brian, William Martin, and Richard Knowles) had conspired together to refuse to labor or in any way assist those in building the small escape ship. Why should they be forced to labor on a ship that would take them to the hellhole that was Jamestown, when they were perfectly happy in Bermudan paradise? If they ever got tired, they would just build their own ship and get themselves over to Virginia at their own convenience. The men threatened to remove themselves to a separate island that they could claim for themselves and take possession of—so Governor Gates sentenced them to exactly what they wanted: banishment to a Bermudan island all their own. Discovering their newfound island lacked the Company's store of supplies, equipment, and food reserves, the six men began to want those "comforts" they had come to relish. They were soon sending messages humbly apologizing and begging to be allowed back. Needing manpower to expedite their escape plans, Governor Gates eventually acceded to their request.

The mutiny was not the only civil dispute the Governor had to deal with. Another sailor, Robert Waters, in the course of a heated dispute, took up a shovel and struck another sailor, Edward Samuel, just under the ear—a wound that ended up being fatal. Robert Waters was apprehended, tried for murder, and sentenced to be hanged the following morning; but that night, with the assistance of some fellow sailors, he escaped custody and fled to the woods.

On October 1, the castaways celebrated their first Communion, with Rev. Richard Buck giving a godly sermon, and Stephen Hopkins reading the psalms. They would celebrate another Communion on Christmas Eve as well.

In November and December, a new food supply began arriving, in the form of nesting waterfowl. Several of the small islands—those without hogs on them—were nesting grounds for many birds. One of those birds, a now extinct variety of shearwater nicknamed the cahow for its "strange hollow and harsh howling," proved an invaluable and easily gathered commodity. William Strachey, one of the *Sea Venture's* castaways, recalled them thus:

> I have been at the taking of three hundred in an hour, and we might have laden our boats. Our men found a pretty way to take them, which was by standing on the rocks or sands by the seaside and holloing, laughing, and making the strangest outcry that possibly they could. With the noise whereof the birds would come flocking to that place and settle upon the very arms and head of him that so cried, and still creep nearer and nearer, answering the noise themselves; by which our men would weigh them with their hand, and which weighed heaviest they took for the best and let the others alone. And so our men would take twenty dozen in two hours of the chiefest of them; and they were a good and well-relished fowl, fat and full as a partridge.

Silvester Jourdaine, another of the castaways, recalled once collecting a thousand eggs in a single morning from another species of nesting sea fowl that was "about the size of a pigeon."

In late November, after the two new moons had passed and it had become clear that Henry Ravens would not return with a rescue ship, Admiral Somers proposed to Governor Gates that he be allowed to take some men to an adjacent island, and begin construction of a second pinnace, because the current pinnace then under construction would not have been big enough to have allowed everyone to get off the island together. Governor Gates agreed, so the colonists split into two groups, each working to construct a small ship with which they could sail everyone to Jamestown. They used local materials, and any scraps they could harvest from the shipwreck. Stephen Hopkins remained in the group working on Governor Gates' ship.

On 26 November 1609, the usual routine was broken, as the company celebrated the marriage of Sir George Somers' cook, Thomas Powell, to a maidservant, Elizabeth Persons. It was the first recorded marriage in Bermuda.

As winter approached, the weather turned somewhat cooler, although not uncomfortably so. There was a pretty large hail storm in December, and a sharp northerly wind throughout the season. One passenger described the winter months as "heavy and melancholy." The cedar berries were mostly expired, but their loss was countered by the arrival of more palm berries.

Christmas Eve was celebrated with a communion service held by Rev. Buck, with assistance from psalm-reader Hopkins. Governor Gates and Master James Swift brought in the New Year with a bang, killing a couple of large swans that morning. In the evening, the colonists went out and gathered a large number of eggs from the nesting birds.

Progress on Governor Gates' and Admiral Somers' pinnaces was also moving right along. The keel had been laid on Governor Gates' pinnace back on August 28, and on January 2 they towed her out from the wharf, but she was still green, and even the slightest breeze would nearly capsize her; her knees were not set and her joints not yet firm; so they brought her back in. They also needed a steady causeway built from stones to break the violence of the tide. It would be another couple months before they would put her feet in the water again.

As January continued on, Stephen Hopkins began to grow more and more discontented with the colony's situation, or as Secretary William Strachey put it, Hopkins "more subtly began to shake the foundation of our quiet safety." He continued:

[T]herein did one Stephen Hopkins commence the first act or overture—a fellow who had much knowledge in the Scriptures and could reason well therein, whom our minister therefore chose to be his clerk to read the psalms and chapters upon Sundays at the assembly of the congregation under him; who in January, the twenty-fourth, brake with one Samuel Sharp and Humphrey Reed (who presently discovered it to the governor) and alleged substantial arguments both civil and divine (the Scripture falsely quoted) that it was no breach of honesty, conscience, nor religion to decline from the obedience of the governor or refuse to go any further led by his authority (except it so pleased themselves), since the authority ceased when the wreck was committed, and, with it, they were all then freed from the government of any man, and for a matter of conscience it was not unknown to the meanest how much we were therein bound each one to provide for himself and his own family. For which were two apparent reasons to stay them even in this place: first, abundance by God's providence of all manner of good food; next, some hope in reasonable time, when they might grow weary of the place, to build a small bark, with the skill and help of the aforesaid Nicholas Bennett, whom they insinuated to them, albeit he was now absent from his quarter and working in the main island with Sir George Somers upon his pinnace, to be of the conspiracy, that so might get clear from hence at their own pleasures. When in Virginia, the first would be assuredly wanting and they might well fear to be detained in that country by the authority of the commander thereof and their whole life to serve the turns of the adventurers with their travails and labors.

Unfortunately for Stephen, denying the authority and undermining the Governor was mutiny; and the customary English penalty for mutiny was death. Hopkins was arrested and brought before the whole company in manacles, where, at the tolling of a bell, the *corps de garde* assembled. The court asked Stephen to give an answer to the accusations. Stephen, full of sorrow and tears, answered by pleading simplicity and denial. In the end, the court found him guilty, and being "generally held worthy to satisfy the punishment of his offense with the sacrifice of his life, our governor passed the sentence of a martial court upon him, such as belongs to mutiny and rebellion." Stephen had been sentenced to death.

Secretary Strachey recalled what happened next:

But so penitent he was, and made so much moan, alleging the ruin of his wife and children in this his trespass, as it wrought in the hearts of all the better sort of the company, who therefore with humble entreaties and earnest supplications went unto our governor, whom they besought (as likewise did Captain Newport and myself) and never left him until we had got his pardon.

Back in Hursley, Mrs. Mary Hopkins and children Elizabeth, Constance, and Giles, were just struggling to make it through. They had not heard anything from Stephen in almost a year, and may even have received word or heard rumors that the *Sea Venture* had been lost at sea. She may have even thought she was a widow at that point. Little did she know that her husband was shipwrecked in Bermuda, or that she and her children had just managed to save his life!

Stephen appears to have learned his lesson well. He fades quickly into the background, keeps his mouth shut, and is never heard from again. A month and a half later, yet another mutiny was uncovered, this time led by Henry Paine. Stephen was not involved in any way, and kept on the sidelines. Paine was not so lucky; Governor Gates sentenced him to death, and this time the execution was carried out that evening, Secretary Strachey noting "the sun and his life setting together."

Admiral George Somers' group, who were still diligently working on their pinnace on a neighboring island, received word of the execution several days later, and this caused several of his men to flee into the woods, fearing they had been "exposed" by the last confessions of Henry Paine. Some would refuse to return to work, and ultimately were left behind in Bermuda.

The month of February saw the birth of the first baby: Bermuda Rolfe, daughter of John Rolfe, was baptized on February 11. Another baby, this time a boy named Bermudas, was born to Edward Eason and baptized March 25.

As spring arrived, the sea turtles began to come ashore with their loads of eggs; new palm fronds were emerging; the birds were breeding; and the weather was warming up, with fresh spring rains and the occasional lightning storm.

By the end of March 1610, the two pinnaces were nearing completion. Caulking on Gates' pinnace had begun on February 26, and on March 30 they towed her out again and launched her, unrigged, to carry her to an island closer to where she would need to embark. At her launching, Governor Gates named the 80-ton ship the *Deliverance*. Towards the end of April, Sir George Somers launched his pinnace as well, which he named the *Patience*, and brought her to the same mooring place as the *Deliverance*.

The castaways had been living on Bermuda now for nearly ten months, but now the time had come to depart. With both ships basically ready to go, all they had to do was wait for a good westerly wind. They waited about ten days for their desired wind, which finally made its appearance on May 10. After nearly crashing into a rock, the two ships finally made it out to the open ocean, and with a good breeze they sailed for seven days until they spotted a change in the water, with more rubbish, indicating they were close to shore. That night they thought they could smell the coast, "strong and pleasant, which did not a little glad us." At the break of dawn, land was sighted, and they then navigated themselves up the coastline for a day, eventually pulling into the Chesapeake Bay, where James Davies, the English captain at Point Comfort, the fort guarding the bay and the Jamestown Colony that was somewhat up river, shot off a warning cannon. At long last, they had arrived!

Chapter 5

JAMESTOWN AND POCAHONTAS

Home Sweet Home, it was not. The joy of finally arriving at their ultimate destination was quickly doused. Even the Bermuda mutineers had vastly underestimated the truly horrific condition of the Jamestown colony. The fort was in ruins: the gates were off their hinges, the ports were all open, and the palisades had been torn down. Only a small handful of men had managed to survive the famine, disease, and frequent Indian attacks. All the livestock, including the work animals such as horses, had been long since killed and eaten. Even the few women in the colony were not safe: one night, Henry Collins killed and ate his pregnant wife—a crime for which he was later executed.

Outside the fort had become a killing field—anyone going beyond its bounds were targeted by the ever-present Indians, killed as they went to collect firewood, pick strawberries, or do their "natural duties." Because of the eminent dangers of leaving the fort, many began harvesting the houses of the deceased for firewood, rather than risk a trip into the woods. Many performed nature's duties inside the fort too, such that it had become an extraordinarily stinky place to live.

It was the wrong time of year to have any crops to harvest—if they had actually had some corn seed remaining, it would have just been ready to go into the ground. The bay and rivers were nearly empty of fish and their nets had rotted away.

Now there were about 140 more people to feed. The Bermuda castaways had been so intent on escaping the island, they had never even considered to lade their ships with food and supplies beyond what they needed for the voyage itself. Oh, what the starving and sickly Jamestown colonists would have given for some fresh Bermuda pork, tortoise eggs, fish, and roast cahow!

When Stephen saw these things, like everyone else his stomach must have sunk. He had been right all along: they never should have left Bermuda, full of so many plentiful resources and so much potential. Now he and all the others would either starve, get sick, or be killed.

The newly arrived Governor Thomas Gates marched into the fort to the little chapel that had been built, and caused the bells to be rung, signaling everyone in the town to gather at the church—at least those who were well enough to actually walk. Reverend Richard Buck, perhaps with Hopkins' assistance, delivered a "zealous and sorrowful prayer, finding all things so contrary to our expectations, so full of misery and misgovernment." Following the prayer and service, Gates formally took his commission as president from George Percy.

Just how had Jamestown deteriorated so quickly?[14]

Back in December 1606, Captain Christopher Newport departed London in the 120-ton flagship, the *Susan Constant*, the head of a fleet of three ships sent out by the Virginia Company of London, to establish a colony. The company had seen all the gold that the Spanish were bringing out of the New World from places in the former Aztec, Maya and Incan empires in Central and South America, and they wanted a piece of the action too. Certainly there was silver and gold in them thar' Virginia hills! They could trade with the Indians for it, or they could locate mines and extract it themselves. London investors and speculators went wild for the idea and poured money into the company in the hope of great returns.

Newport was himself no stranger to Spanish riches—he was a former pirate, and was responsible for capturing and bringing in the Spanish ship *Madre de Dios* in 1592, one of the biggest plunders ever for an English privateer: a large ship full of gold, silver, gemstones, and spices.

Onboard the *Susan Constant* with Captain Newport was, among others, Jamestown's first president, Edward Maria Wingfield; councilors George Kendall and John Martin; and the not-yet-famous John Smith. The other two ships in the fleet were the 40-ton *Godspeed*, captained by Bartholomew Gosnold, who had about five years before explored the New England coastline,

---

[14]   Information on early Jamestown for this section was derived primarily from two sources: the works of John Smith; and David A. Price, *Love and Hate in Jamestown: John Smith, Pocahontas, and the Heart of a Nation* (Alfred A. Knopf: New York, 2003).

leaving behind place names such as Martha's Vineyard and Cape Cod; and the 20-ton *Discovery*, captained by John Radcliffe. In all, the fleet brought 105 passengers and 39 crewmembers—only men and boys—to establish Jamestown.

The colonists got off to a rocky start. Just days after landing, they had a brief skirmish with some local Indians. They ultimately decided to settle on a marshy peninsula they thought would be easy to defend: but unfortunately the spit of land isolated them from mainland resources such as food and timber; and the marshy ground made agriculture more difficult and readily bred mosquitoes.

Nonetheless, they decided it was the safest place to settle, and built a fort . . . or not. Actually President Wingfield decided that any sign of defense would be the wrong sign to send to the Indians. A walled fort with cannons and every man a gun was not a sign of friendship that would encourage neighborly relations, he reasoned. It took less than a month for the Indians to attack the defenseless colonists, who probably would have been massacred had an enormous cannon from the *Susan Constant* not startled the attackers. Only then did Wingfield authorize the building of the fort and the carrying of weapons.

Meanwhile, the company needed to seek out the gold mines it had been sent to find, so Captain Newport set out with John Smith, a few other Jamestown colonists, and eighteen of his own sailors, to explore upriver. They travelled as far as modern-day Richmond, with the assistance of a few friendly native guides, before returning to Jamestown. Captain Newport and his ship of hard-working sailors departed a month later, leaving the much less competent Jamestown colonists—half of whom were gentlemen that had not spent a day working in their lives—to fend for themselves. Newport planned to be back later that year with a resupply and additional colonists, and this too gave them an excuse not to pursue their own self-supporting subsistence with as much vigor as they might have had otherwise. President Wingfield was eventually voted out of office and replaced by President Radcliffe, but the situation did not change much.

Unwilling to work for their own subsistence by farming, hunting and gathering, John Smith was sent out on expeditions to trade for food from the neighboring Indian groups; he returned with nearly 30 bushels of corn and other foodstuffs—an enormous boost to the withering colony. When all that was eaten up, they sent him out again to trade for more food. And again. And again. The Indians in the area had become familiar with Captain Smith, and he was learning their ways, customs and language, so he could better negotiate and trade.

Seeing that John Smith had been so successful in his trading activities, and perhaps fearing his rising status, the colony's leadership sent him out to further explore the rivers, resuming their original task of trying to locate navigable rivers that might lead them to gold or other trade riches beyond simply corn—some even thought the Pacific Ocean (with its valuable trade links to China and India) was only a few days further upriver. It was on this expedition, after travelling about 50 miles up the Chickahominy, that he was ambushed, taken captive, and ultimately brought to Powhattan, the great Indian leader of the region, where—as the story goes—he was sentenced to execution but was, at the last second, saved by the persuasion of Powhattan's daughter Pocahontas. While the American legend typically implies some kind of infatuation between Pocahontas and John Smith, the historical record suggests she was more infatuated with English bells, beads and copper—she was, after all, a ten-year old girl.

Smith was freed and returned to Jamestown, where he quickly got himself into conflict with Jamestown's leadership. In an effort to dispose of Smith once and for all, President Radcliffe held Smith responsible for the deaths of two of his men on his last exploratory voyage (they had been captured and killed by the Indians). John Smith was sentenced to be hanged the next day. It was the third time John Smith had been sentenced to die—twice by the English and once by Powhattan! And, once more, he managed to get out of it, as the evening before his execution Captain Christopher Newport arrived with the colony's resupply, and overturned Smith's death sentence: quite interestingly, that's the same man who several years later would help Stephen Hopkins overturn his own death sentence.

The desperately needed resupply was greatly welcomed, and Newport also brought sixty additional colonists. Unfortunately, one of those new colonists accidentally caught his house on fire—and it quickly spread throughout the colony, ultimately burning down all the houses, including the storehouse where much of the colony's food and supplies were housed. Once again, they would have to rely on trade with the Indians to feed themselves.

Smith and Newport took a voyage up to visit Powhattan, where they also traded, and then Newport continued with the company's true task at hand—searching for gold. Newport had gold fever; Smith, on the other hand, realized already there was none—if there had been gold, he would have encountered it on his many trading expeditions with the natives. In April 1608, after three months at Jamestown, Captain Newport headed back to England with his ship full of worthless dirt samples.

After Newport's departure, John Smith continued leading explorations for the Jamestown colony, taking one expedition up the Potomac as far as modern day Washington, DC, and up the Rappahannock. It was on this expedition that the famous John Smith, adventurer and survivor who had escaped death on so many occasions, a man most everyone imaged was invincible, was nearly killed by a freak encounter . . . with a stingray. His arm swelled up so large, and he was in so much pain, that he was sure he was going to die very shortly—so he had his men dig his grave and prepare his funeral on the banks of the river, which they did. But the poison eventually wore off, and Smith survived the ordeal.

On 10 September 1608, John Smith took over the presidency of the colony from John Radcliffe, and was only in charge for a few weeks before Captain Newport returned again with further men, resupplies, and the colony's first two women: a wife and a maidservant. Newport stayed long enough to make another visit to Powhattan, spoiling him with gifts, before departing again that December. Newport's next voyage to Jamestown would be as captain of the infamous *Sea Venture*.

Following Newport's visit to Powhattan, which was apparently not well received, the Indians promptly stopped trading with the Jamestown colonists, and relations soured—probably because Newport also paid a visit to Powhattan's enemies, the Monacans. With the Indians unwilling to trade, on orders from Powhattan, and the Jamestown colonists unable to supply their 200 surviving colonists with food for the winter, John Smith took to using strong-arm tactics and threats to obtain corn from the neighboring Indian tribes. But the Indians themselves had little corn to begin with, so even when it was extorted away from them, Jamestown still did not have what it needed. Smith thought the best thing to do was to attack and steal it from Powhattan's storehouses directly, but the idea was not approved by the rest of Jamestown's council.

Shortly thereafter, Powhattan sent the colony word that he would trade corn and other food in exchange for the English building him an English-style house. Desperate, Jamestown agreed. Smith sent about sixteen men to work on Powhattan's house, and after work was underway he traveled there for a visit and to check up on the construction. His first night, while visiting Powhattan in his house, Smith became suspicious and foiled an apparent ambush; but Powhattan insisted it was just a misunderstanding, and lured Smith to stay another night.

As their second evening fell, a fearful Pocahontas made a secretive appearance and warned Smith that her father was planning to have them killed at dinner. When dinner arrived, Smith and his men were especially on guard; the would-be attackers never found the moment they needed to initiate their "surprise" ambush. Smith and his men left the next day with their supply of corn they had received in trade. They stopped to trade with several additional tribes, with only mediocre success, only to learn that one of the barges carrying much of the corn supply had capsized, for a substantial loss. Two of the remaining three council members were also drowned in the accident—and since the president had a double vote, John Smith was now in complete command of Jamestown and could not be overruled by the surviving councilman. He decided to return to raid Powhattan's corn supply per his originally-rejected plan, but found Powhattan had been tipped off and had moved his storehouses to an unknown place.

John Smith returned to Jamestown. Food was scarce, and trade had not brought in what they would need to survive the winter. He had attacked and extorted corn from all the neighboring Indians, so they were none too friendly. Powhattan had more than a dozen of Jamestown's men in his custody—hostages in a sense. A number of the colony's tools and weapons had also been stolen by a few Jamestown traitors, who abandoned the colony to live with the Indians—fearing, quite justifiably, that they would be much less likely to starve to death if they were servants to the Indians rather than of the Virginia Company.

Smith then formulated a clever plan. He would divide the colonists up into small groups, and each group would move out to a different location around the bay, to live off local resources plentiful there, such as oysters and fish. In small groups, they were more likely to be active and less slothful, more intent on helping one another, and would be able to watch each other more closely. And it was easier for small groups to live off the land. Back at the fort, Smith also instituted a policy of "no work, no food," effectively ending the laziness of many of the elite and gentlemen who had been consuming but not producing. No matter anyone's rank or status, everyone was expected to labor.

As their modest fields of corn were growing, a ship arrived, captained by Samuel Argall. Captain Argall informed Smith that the Virginia Company was sending a very large resupply of goods and men, as well as a new governor. Despite having turned the colony around from desperation to some level of productivity, Smith's time as president was limited. A month later, the ships started arriving. The first four ships came in on August 11, and unloaded several hundred new colonists, and a small supply of provisions. Three more ships trickled in over the next few days, unloading still more passengers. But the majority of the provisions, not to mention Admiral Somers, Governor Gates, and Captain Newport, were onboard the largest ship in the fleet—the *Sea Venture*—that nobody had seen since the hurricane separated the fleet.

When John Smith's term as president expired the following month, and realizing the new leadership was inept and incompetent in the ways of the New World, he negotiated himself passage back to England. Jamestown and its 500 colonists were on their own. Stephen Hopkins and the others, marooned in Bermuda, would never see Captain John Smith at Jamestown.

Several letters went back to England in the ship with John Smith, with the bad news that the *Sea Venture* went missing in a hurricane and was presumed lost at sea. No doubt this news would eventually reach Mrs. Mary Hopkins, who must have assumed her husband was dead, while undoubtedly holding onto some little hope that the news was wrong. It would have been an extremely difficult and stressful time for Mary. Without a husband, she would not have any way to support her three young children. But without confirmation of his death, she couldn't remarry either. For now, she was stuck relying on family and friends for support, and holding out hope that by some miracle he might still be alive.

With John Smith dead (so the Indians were told anyway—he'd really just gone back to England), the native's attitudes toward Jamestown quickly changed. They stepped up attacks and began killing large numbers of colonists, starting with some of the smaller outposts that Smith had originally established outside Jamestown's fort. The new Jamestown leadership failed to establish a food supply (perhaps still hoping resupplies from England would end their wants), and they had failed to ensure that their equipment was in good working order. They fell back to the custom of the gentlemen lazing around, rationing provisions where needed to the demoralized and uninspired working class. Even the fishing nets had been allowed to spoil for lack of attention. John Smith had been adept at negotiating with the Indians and carefully avoiding their traps and ambushes, but the new leadership was completely lacking in this department. John Radcliffe led an expedition back to Powhattan to trade for food, and was ambushed, captured, and executed by being dismembered and burned alive by the women of the tribe. Only sixteen of the fifty men on the expedition returned to Jamestown alive—and with no corn.

George Percy, the new governor, then sent out another trading expedition led by Francis West, to some Indian groups he hoped would be more peaceful. The men attacked and decapitated several natives, before forcing the rest to load up their ship with food. It was a large amount of corn, and would have been an enormous benefit to the nearly starving colonists—but they all watched helplessly from shore as Francis West and his men sailed right on past Jamestown, past the fort at Point Comfort, and out into the Atlantic. They escaped back to England, taking with them Jamestown's trading ship, and the large supply of food they had gathered in "trade." All they left for Jamestown was yet another group of angry Indians.

Winter hit hard. With no ships, no trade, no crops, and no nets, finding food was next to impossible. Anyone who dared to step outside the walls of the fort was a potential target of Indian ambushes. Men were dying right and left, either from starvation or Indian attacks. Rats, mice, starch, and shoe leather were not off-limits as a food source. Dead Indians and Englishmen were not off limits either—even after they were buried. That winter over 400 died. The sixty survivors were malnourished, walking dead, just surviving one day at a time.

Then, on 24 May 1610, the *Patience* and *Deliverance* arrived, with Governor Gates, Captain Newport, Admiral Somers, Reverend Buck, Stephen Hopkins, and the 140 or so others who had managed to "escape" their shipwreck in Bermuda. What they found at Jamestown was absolutely not what they had expected!

Chapter 6

STUCK IN VIRGINIA

Governor Thomas Gates had a very difficult task ahead of him. He assumed the governorship of a colony of around two hundred men and a few women. The colony had no food and no crops, low morale, no hope of trade, and very few tools or supplies. Governor Gates made a speech to the colonists, telling them that if he should find it not possible to supply them, he would find a way to transport them all back to England. That was the biggest morale booster the famished Jamestown colonists had ever heard!

Governor Gates sent out fishing expeditions all around the bays, but the men came back with only a few token fish, not even worth the labor. The Indians were not willing to trade, and likely did not have any excess to spare anyway, it being planting season. When Gates took inventory of his food supply, he calculated there was only about sixteen days left. It was just enough to last them to Newfoundland, where they could barter passage back to England on the fishing vessels that frequented there.

After taking a little more than a week to analyze the situation and investigate options, Gates made his decision: it was time to abandon the colony and save everyone's lives. The colonists were overjoyed! Stephen probably saw himself back at home in Hursley with his wife Mary, and the young children he had not seen in nearly a year.

On June 7, less than two weeks after arriving, everyone packed up and boarded the ships. They made it upriver that evening and anchored off Hog Island; the next morning they continued on to Mulberry Island where they anchored for the afternoon tide. While anchored there, they spotted a ship's longboat off in the distance, heading their direction. It was Thomas West, Lord De La Warr (i.e. "Delaware"), the new governor of Jamestown, with three ships full of food and supplies (enough for an entire year), along with 150 more healthy colonists. While the prospect of fresh food and supplies was certainly welcomed, the surprising change of events disheartened and frustrated many who had come so close to getting themselves back home to comfortable England.

Stephen Hopkins would not see England again for five or six years: Jamestown was now home. Reverend Buck gave a sermon welcoming the new governor, and then Lord De La Warr went right to work, ordering the cleaning up of the fort. Admiral Somers was appointed to return to Bermuda to bring back a supply of wild hogs to supplement the provisions brought by the resupply ships. And Sir Thomas Gates returned to England to supply a report to the Virginia Company.

Governor De La Warr sent out a message to Powhattan to return the stolen tools and weapons he had, along with any Englishmen he was still holding. When Powhattan responded he would not do so, an expedition of seventy men led by George Percy was sent out to capture and burn a town loyal to Powhattan—a brutal expedition that even captured and executed the village's "queen" and her children. Whether Hopkins was on this expedition, or remained behind working on cleaning up the trash heaps in Jamestown, is not recorded.

Admiral George Somers did make it back to Bermuda, but died there from exhaustion, failing in his mission to return hogs to Jamestown. His crew returned his body to England, after burying his heart on the island that he had come to love.

Despite the substantial turnaround at Jamestown, it proved to be not to the liking of Lord De La Warr, who less than ten months into his life-appointment as governor, decided to head home to England, leaving George Percy—the man many held responsible for Jamestown's collapse—back in charge until Sir Thomas Dale arrived three months later, in May 1611, and took over as governor.

Sir Thomas Dale was a tough and severe governor, sent by the Virginia Company in the hopes of establishing some sense of order and discipline. He implemented strict laws akin to what John Smith had done, but even more severe. The penalty for stealing a small grain of corn from the company's storehouse, or from a neighbor's garden, was death. Execution was the punishment for many other crimes as well, including unauthorized trade with the Indians, and leaving the colony without authorization (to live with the Indians, or in an attempt to escape back to England). Minor crimes, such as being late to work, were punishable by whipping. And Dale's punishments were not idle threats—he executed perhaps a dozen colonists over the course of a few years. Many of the executions were not simple hangings either, some were tortuous sentences that involved burning at the stake, or being tied to a tree and left to die from the elements.

Stephen Hopkins must have looked on all these severe punishments and executions with some empathy for the victims, and with some trepidation—if it had not been for leniency and mercy, he would have been executed back in Bermuda. Governor Dale had no leniency or mercy—there was no opportunity for a mistake. Stephen, and everyone else, had to be on their best behavior.

The same year that Sir Thomas Dale was taking control of Jamestown, back in England, William Shakespeare was premiering his latest play, "The Tempest." No doubt playing to the English population's fascination with stories of explorations and shipwrecks, such as the *Sea Venture*, the play starts with a dramatic storm and shipwreck on an enchanted island inhabited by spirits and devils, including Ariel:

> ARIEL.
>> From the still-vexed Bermoothes, there she's hid;
>> The mariners all under hatches stowed,
>> Who, with a charm joined to their suffered labor,
>> I have left asleep; and for the rest o' the fleet,
>> Which I have dispersed, they all have met again, . . .

Accounts of the *Sea Venture's* shipwreck on the "Isle of Devils" in Bermuda had reached Shakespeare, who had contacts within the Virginia Company, from which he gained some level of knowledge about the then-unpublished events. In fact, many of the descriptions and details in "The Tempest" seem to have been taken almost directly from William Strachey's written account, which even includes the statement that may have led to the very premise and title of the play itself: "The superstitious seamen make many constructions of this sea fire [St. Elmo's Fire], which nevertheless is unusual in storms, the same (it may be) which the Grecians were wont in the Mediterranean to call Castor and Pollux, of which if only one appeared without the other they took it for an evil sign of great tempest."

Shakespeare's description of Ariel matches very closely to Strachey's description of the mysterious light that danced around the rigging during the storm. William Strachey also comments briefly on a book entitled *The General History of the West Indies*, written by Gonzalus Ferdnandus Oviedus, which would seem to be the origin of "The Tempest" characters Gonzalo and Ferdinando. Strachey mentions how they picked, boiled and strained the berries of the Bermuda cedars to make a drink; Shakespeare's character Caliban states "When thou cam'st first, thou strok'st me and made much of me; wouldst give me water with berries in't." Strachey mentions how the castaways went hunting birds by moonlight; Shakespeare's character Sebastian mentions "bat-fowling," hunting birds with clubs by moonlight

And then there is the mutinous character named Stephano—a suspicious-sounding name indeed: a character whom Shakespeare describes as "a drunken butler," who unsuccessfully but mutinously plots to become King of the island, taking as his allies the gullible and deformed slave Caliban, and a court jester, Trinculo.

Back in Hursley, about seventy-five miles east of Whitehall, London, where "The Tempest" was playing in late 1611, Stephen's wife and children were struggling to maintain the family in his absence. They must have learned by now that he had survived the shipwreck in Bermuda and made it safely to Jamestown. But Jamestown was a dangerous place, and Mary Hopkins no doubt was expecting to hear the worst from Stephen any day.

The continual stress and fear may have gotten the best of her: she died and was buried at Hursley on 9 May 1613, only in her very early thirties. Although the parish church's burial record calls her "Mary Hopkines the wife of Steeven Hopkines," her probate record, dated May 10, refers to her as "Mary Hopkins of Hursley in the Countie of South[amp]ton widowe deceased." For the purpose of probate, because Stephen was so far absent and his condition was unknown, she was considered a widow, which made the estate available for the benefit of the children. Robert Lyte administered the estate, and Thomas Syms became the supervisor of children Elizabeth (then nine years old), Constance (seven years old), and Giles (five years old). Whether the children all lived with him, or whether he placed them with other families, is not recorded, nor is it known exactly what relation Thomas Syms had to Stephen and Mary Hopkins. Nine year old Elizabeth disappears from the historical record following her mother's death, and may well have died shortly after her mother.

On May 10, an estate inventory was made of the Hopkins' household in Hursley. The estate consisted of "certain beams in the garden and wood in the back side"; a beerhouse; "certain things in the kitchen"; a table and cupboard in the hallway; "six small vessels" in the buttery; some brass and pewter; two beds and a table in the chamber over the shop; a featherbed, three chests and a box in the chamber over the hall; linens and wearing apparel; a shopboard and plank; and a lease to the house. She also had over £17 in cash and debts owed to her.

It was a very modest estate to be sure, but there are some interesting aspects to be noted. First is the beerhouse, and the mention of a shop and a shop-board (a sales counter) and plank (probably for seating customers). This would seem to indicate that Stephen and Mary Hopkins had at one time been shopkeepers, and perhaps Mary had even kept up the business in some manner in Stephen's absence. As will be seen, Stephen returns to shopkeeping later in his life, selling wine, beer, and spices within the Plymouth Colony.

Chapter 7

BACK TO LONDON

With the death of his wife Mary, Stephen's children were effectively orphaned in England. While it is unclear whether this would have constituted a situation in which the Virginia Company would have recalled him back to England before his seven-year contract was up, it is interesting to note that on 20 September 1614, a letter was written up for Sir Thomas Dale, Marshall of the Colony of Virginia, requesting that he send home, by the next ship, "Eliezer Hopkins." The original letter no longer exists; all that survives is a brief abstract of the letter, in what was essentially a log-book or calendar of Virginia Company correspondence.[15] Could the scribe have simply misread "Steeven" for "Eliezer" when he was quickly jotting down a summary of it for the logbook?—the two names do look surprisingly similar when written out in the flowery 17th century handwriting in use at the time. There is no known Eliezer Hopkins living at Jamestown during this time period, and I have been unable to find any example of this name occurring in England during the 16th or early 17th centuries.[16] The timing does seem to be appropriate for recalling Stephen home so that he could support his orphaned children.

Exactly when the letter would have reached Jamestown, and exactly when the next ship returning to England would have departed, is only a matter of speculation. But one of the next ships to return to England

---

[15] Public Records Office, State Papers Colonial, SP 38/11, 20 September 1614.

[16] The earliest occurrence of the name that I have seen in England is the baptism of an Eleazer Hopkins on 30 September 1661 at St. Dunstan, Stepney, son of Edward Hopkins.

departed Jamestown in the spring of 1616, with three interesting passengers onboard: John and Rebecca Rolfe, and their baby son Thomas. Rebecca, more commonly known by her native name, Pocahontas, was joined by an entourage of about a dozen Powhatan Indians. John Rolfe, who would later be known for developing tobacco into a viable commercial enterprise at Jamestown, was a fellow *Sea Venture* castaway with Stephen, and in April 1614 he was married to Pocahontas—a marriage that was performed by Rev. Richard Buck, and quite probably attended by Hopkins himself. And perhaps, just perhaps, Stephen even returned to England with them in 1616, spending a couple of months in very close quarters at sea with a couple of American history's most interesting figures. What a fascinating voyage that must have been!

After returning to England sometime around 1616, Stephen took up residence just to the east of London proper. The first record of Stephen back in England is his marriage, at St. Mary Whitechapel, on 19 February 1618, to Elizabeth Fisher. Elizabeth's identity has not been conclusively established, but there were Fisher families in the area, including an Elizabeth Fisher that was baptized at St. Mary's on 3 March 1582. However, given it was Stephen's second marriage, it is entirely possible it was also Elizabeth's second, in which case she would have been baptized under a different surname. About a year later, presumably still in London, the couple had their first child together, a daughter they named Damaris.[17]

---

[17] The unusual name Damaris may also be a valuable clue to Elizabeth's origins. The only Damaris that I have found at St. Mary Whitechapel was Damaris Holloway, daughter of Reynold and Joan (Hynde) Holloway, baptized there in 1599. There is also a Damaris Fisher baptized at Great Coates, Lincolnshire in 1585, who might also be worthy of further investigation.

Chapter 8

THE VOYAGE OF THE *MAYFLOWER*

The voyage of the *Mayflower* was being organized by a group of religious Separatists, the core of which had fled their secret meetinghouse in Scrooby, co. Nottingham, England, for the religious toleration of Holland, in 1608 and 1609. The congregation, which ultimately located itself in Leiden after spending a short time in Amsterdam, grew over time, as additional Separatists from Sandwich, Canterbury, Norwich, Colchester, Yarmouth, London, and a few other areas in England, were drawn to their church by word-of-mouth.

By 1617, just as Stephen was establishing himself in London, the congregation made the decision to relocate to Northern Virginia under the auspices of the Virginia Company of London; but unable to come up with the financial support necessary, they were lured into a joint-stock venture led by some London merchants headed by Thomas Weston, an ironmonger and savvy merchant who seemed to have as many get-rich-quick schemes as he had contacts with wealthy investors.

Weston lived in the Aldgate ward of London, the parish immediately to the southwest bordering St. Mary Whitechapel. As business negotiations continued between Weston and the Pilgrims, several members of the Leiden congregation, including Edward Southworth, Edward Mitchell, Robert Cushman, George Morton, and maybe even for a short time John Carver and William Bradford, periodically took up residence at the Heneage House, also in Aldgate. It is thought that the separatists used the parish of Holy Trinity, embedded within Aldgate, as a refuge, because at the time the parish did not have an active parish church, allowing them to avoid the requirement to attend services in the Church of England. St. Mary Whitechapel, where

Stephen was married, was also the home parish of one of the leading Leiden congregation members, Randall Thickens, who was married to pastor John Robinson's sister.

St. Dunstan's, Stepney, the parish bordering on the east of St. Mary Whitechapel, also had a number of connections to early Plymouth colonists: Thomas Clarke (who came to Plymouth on the *Anne* in 1623), and Stephen's future son-in-law Nicholas Snow, were both baptized there; and it appears *Mayflower* passenger John Howland also may have had a connection to this parish.[18]

Stephen, who himself may have had some Brownist-Separatist tendencies, and who also must have had some contacts within the Virginia Company after nearly seven years of service, probably at this time made acquaintance with some of the men the Leiden congregation had sent over, or with some of the merchants who were helping fund the company and organize the adventure. He was, after all, living in a parish right in the midst of their activities.

The Leiden separatists, and the joint-stock company, had difficulty obtaining enough laborers to make the investors happy, so they opened up spots on the ship to Londoners willing to exchange seven years of labor for one share of the joint-stock company, along with a grant of land. One share of the company had an initial par value of £10, but of course it was hoped that by the time the company was liquidated in seven years, the value of those shares would be substantially greater. Children between the ages of 10 and 16, such as Giles and Constance, would receive half a share; those under 10 years of age, such as Damaris, would only receive a token land grant of fifty acres—but that was still fifty acres more than they could ever hope to have in England.

Basic needs such as food, clothing and housing would be provided by the company—of course, using the labor of their "employees," the colonists, to provide for those needs. Profits would be sought from local resources, namely from lumber, fur, trade with the Indians, and fishing. After the seven years were up, the company would liquidate, and the shareholders would (hopefully) get a substantial return, as well as their share of all the company's assets, including land and houses.

---

[18]   The Pilgrim John Howland Society has possession of an original indenture, signed by a John Howland "citizen and salter of London," that mentions Stepney, Middlesex, as well as Leiden congregation member Randall Thickens and his brother Ralph.

It was a deal Stephen Hopkins could not pass up. Despite having endured a shipwreck, starvation and disease, Indian attacks, and harsh governors, he still had the New World bug, and this time he wanted to bring his whole family with him. If he brought himself, his wife, and his three surviving children Constance, Giles, and baby Damaris, he would get £30 worth of company stock—a substantial sum of money (after all, Stephen's entire Hursley estate had only been valued at £25 when his wife Mary had died). That £30 could grow substantially if the company made good profit, and on top of that he would receive land—something he could never afford in England.

Stephen brought with him two manservants, Edward Doty and Edward Leister, both young men in their early twenties that he had likely come into contact with while living in London. He would get an additional £20 worth of stock (two shares) for bringing them. There are Doty and Leister families at St. Dunstan's, Stepney, although no Edwards have been identified as yet amongst them. Most likely, Edward Doty and Edward Leister's fathers had died before the boys had reached adulthood, so they were placed with Hopkins, who, by contract, would feed, clothe, and house them, in exchange for their labor. Contracts such as this normally lasted until the servant or apprentice turned twenty five, at which point they were given some additional compensation (whatever the apprenticeship contract specified, sometimes land, sometimes clothing, sometimes money), and they could then begin to make a life for themselves. Now Stephen could essentially turn around and give their labor over to the company, in exchange for the two shares—Stephen clearly had high hopes for his investment.

The joint stock company's terms and conditions were finalized on July 1. The company's intention was to have sailed shortly thereafter, but money shortfalls, bickering over the terms and conditions, and delays in purchasing provisions caused the departure date to continually slip from early July, to mid July, to late July . . .

The Leiden congregation, still in Holland, finally embarked for Southampton, England, about July 22, onboard the 60-ton *Speedwell*. At Southampton, the *Speedwell* met up with the larger 180-ton *Mayflower*, which had come down from London earlier in the month. Stephen Hopkins and his family were likely already onboard the *Mayflower*, just waiting for the Separatists to arrive from Holland so that the voyage could get underway.

Christopher Jones was the master of the *Mayflower*, a ship that had spent the past decade primarily hauling wine and Cognac from Bordeaux and La Rochelle, France, to London. His mates, John Clark and Robert Coppin, were hired because they had both been to the New World before. In fact,

John Clark had been at Jamestown in 1611, when Stephen had also been there; Clark was kidnapped by a Spanish ship that visited the harbor, and held for a time in Havana, and later Madrid, before finally being released to the English in a prisoner exchange. He had made a voyage to Jamestown in 1618 as well, onboard a ship delivering cattle.

As Hopkins and his family remained aboard the *Mayflower*, the newly-arrived Separatist church members began debating, consulting and complaining about various changes to the company's contracts that were made without their knowledge or approval. This, along with additional time spent loading provisions and getting the new arrivals settled onboard ship, and some poor winds, delayed the voyage another two weeks. It was not until August 5 that the *Mayflower* and *Speedwell* finally pulled up anchor from Southampton, and headed off on their voyage to America. They did not get far, however. The *Speedwell* was leaking, so the two ships pulled into Dartmouth to await repairs. The repairs took two weeks to complete, so it was not until August 23 that the two ships were again ready to embark for America. This time, both ships made it almost 300 miles out into the Atlantic, before again the *Speedwell* was leaking at an alarming rate.

By this time, tempers and frustrations were at a peak. The two ships returned to the western port town of Plymouth, England, where they made the decision to abandon the *Speedwell* altogether. A couple dozen passengers, including the Cushman, Ring, and Blossom families, disembarked. The remaining *Speedwell* passengers crammed themselves onto the already tight *Mayflower*, bringing the passenger count up to 102, and transferred over the additional cargo.

The voyage was supposed to have begun in mid-July, but it was now early September. Many of the passengers had been living onboard the ship for more than a month already—and they had not even left England yet! Finally, on September 6, the *Mayflower* departed Plymouth, England, and this time there would be no stopping her.

All these delays had a significant impact on the Hopkins family, perhaps more than any other. That was because Stephen's wife, Elizabeth, was pregnant. When the voyage started back in July, she was only six months pregnant. With a voyage expected to take between one and two months, this gave the family time to spare. But now she was eight months pregnant, and the voyage had just begun.

Giving birth at sea was not exactly what Elizabeth and Stephen had in mind when they signed up for the voyage. With 102 people crammed into a living space no bigger than 50 feet by 25 feet, privacy was not exactly something that could be had. And it is probable she did not have any friendships or associations with the Leiden Separatists prior to the voyage, which meant that a complete stranger would have to fill in as midwife. But she had little control over the circumstances; Stephen had made the decision to bring his family to Northern Virginia, and there was no turning back now. And give birth during the *Mayflower's* voyage she did—to a young son that the couple named, quite appropriately, Oceanus. Perhaps Stephen had memories of John Rolfe's daughter, Bermuda.

With 103 passengers now, the *Mayflower* continued on its voyage—a voyage that would ultimately last sixty-six days, more than two full months. That was a long time to sit, stand, and walk around. To entertain themselves, the passengers must have talked, sang, read, and told stories. And if anyone onboard had some stories to tell, it was Stephen Hopkins! None of the other passengers had ever been to the New World, so they must have listened with intent fascination to everything Stephen had to say. What did an Indian look like? What was Jamestown like? What kind of animals and trees are there? How often did the Spanish show up? Did you know Pocahontas?—What was she like? What was it like to be shipwrecked for nearly a year on the Isle of Devils? How did you escape the island? Did you like Bermuda? What does sea turtle taste like? Did you ever see a bear, or lion? How do the Indians live? What does their language sound like? Did you know Captain John Smith? How bad are the winters? Did you see Master's Mate John Clark get kidnapped by the Spanish?

As the *Mayflower* passed the halfway point, the seas began to get rougher, as the October storms began a-brewing. During one storm, a young man named John Howland was swept overboard, but somehow managed to grab hold of the topsail halyards, and was then rescued by a boathook. In another storm, the main beam cracked, causing great concern among the passengers and crew alike. Eventually the crack was braced, but the ship was leakier than ever, and the passengers were now living in a damp, cold, leaky, drippy environment. One of the crewmembers (remembered as being quite a profane man) came down with a "grievous disease," and died. Then one of the passengers, a young boy named William Button, also got sick and died. Their bodies were wrapped, weighted, and thrown overboard, as was the maritime custom.

Finally, after two months at sea, land was within reach. It was first sighted on November 9, and identified as Cape Cod, in New England. Since the Pilgrims had intended to establish their colony at the mouth of the Hudson's River, in modern-day New York State (back then, this region was considered

Northern Virginia), the *Mayflower* turned and headed south, . . . right into Pollock's Rip, a treacherous stretch of sea just off southern Cape Cod. They nearly shipwrecked, but after several hours of tense and dangerous maneuvers, Master Jones managed to break the *Mayflower* free and get the ship turned around headed north again.

Rather than risk another pass through Pollock's Rip, Master Jones and the Pilgrims decided instead to just check out Cape Cod and see what was there. There was just one small problem with that decision: the company held patents granting them the right to establish and govern an English colony in Virginia; but these patents were no good for New England. Many of the passengers—especially the Londoners who had no previous ties to the Pilgrims' church in Leiden, had signed onto the voyage for the land they would get when the company was liquidated. How could the company hold to its promise to give them land, if they settled in an area to which they did not have legal title? And worse yet, the patents gave the company the right to govern a colony in Virginia, but it did not give them the right to govern a colony in New England. If they did not have the authority to govern a colony, what would stop the colonists from picking up and leaving? Without the right to govern the company and the colony, they could not move forward.

Stephen Hopkins must have had some serious déjà vu when this began to unfold! When he was shipwrecked in Bermuda, he expounded his opinion that the governors there only had the right to govern in Virginia, not in Bermuda, and he denied their authority to govern those individuals who wanted their freedom—at which point he was sentenced to death for mutiny. And now, here were the Pilgrims, settling themselves in a place where they had no right to govern. No doubt Stephen could see the problems that this would cause, and understood the serious implications. Any time anyone had any disagreement with the new colony's leaders, there would be mutinies, as groups and individuals denied the authority of the colony's and company's leaders.

With Stephen's consultation no doubt, the Pilgrims arrived at a very novel solution. Since their authority to govern could not be securely established by the rights granted to them by the English crown, they would draw up a legal contract that every adult male in the colony would sign, in which they acknowledged and authorized their governors and government. They would individually agree and sign off to establish a government, and agree to recognize that said government. Then, nobody could deny the authority of the colony's elected governor and council. This document has come to be known as the "Mayflower Compact."

In ye name of god Amen· We whose names are underwriten,
the loyall subjects of our dread soveraigne Lord King James
by ye grace of god, of great Britaine, franc, & Ireland king
defendor of ye faith, &c

Haueing vndertaken, for ye glorie of god, and aduancemente
of ye christian faith, and honour of our king & countrie, a voyage to
plant ye first colonie in ye Northerne parts of Virginia· doe
by these presents solemnly & mutualy in ye presence of god, and
one of another; couenant, & combine our selues togeather into a
ciuill body politick; for ye our better ordering, & preseruation & fur=
therance of ye ends aforesaid; and by vertue hearof to Enacte,
constitute, and frame shuch just & equall Lawes, ordinances,
Acts, constitutions, & offices, from time to time, as shall be thought
most meete & convenient for ye generall good of ye Colonie: vnto
which we promise all due submission and obedience· yn witnes
wherof we haue here vnder subscribed our names at Cap=
Codd ye ·11· of Nouember, in ye year of ye raigne of our soueraigne
Lord king James of England, franc, & Ireland ye eighteenth
and of scotland ye fiftie fourth, An: dom ·1620·]

The handwritten copy of the Mayflower Compact written by
Gov. William Bradford into his history, *Of Plymouth Plantation*,
sometime around 1630. The original Compact no longer survives.
Nathaniel Morton, in 1669, published the first record of the names
of the signers, and on his list Stephen Hopkins was the 14th signer,
and Hopkins' servants Edward Doty and Edward Leister were the
last to sign.

The original document has not survived. The names of the signers of the Mayflower Compact were first published by Nathaniel Morton in 1669, in his book *New England's Memorial*. If the order he reports is true to the original, then Stephen was the 14th signer of the document, following John Howland. Stephen's servants, Edward Doty and Edward Leister, were the last two signers of the document, leading some to speculate that they may have been responsible for some of the "mutinous speeches."

The legality of the government having been established by formal agreement by the people themselves, the only remaining issue was the fact that they did not have legal English title to the land upon which they were going to settle, and as such they could never make a distribution of it to the shareholders at the company's liquidation. To remedy that situation, they would send letters back to their business partners in England, to have them take out new patents for the area of New England that they would decide upon settling.

With the legal details and decisions taken care of, and with everyone having signed the Mayflower Compact on November 11, the would-be colonists were ready to tackle their next big decision: where exactly would they choose to build their colony?

Chapter 9

EXPLORING CAPE COD

What the Pilgrims needed to find was a piece of ground that would best support their future colony. They needed some place that was near enough to a bay or ocean to facilitate easy anchorage of ships, to make trade and shipping back exports to England much easier. They needed a place that was defensible from the Spanish, French, and Dutch, and from privateers, with some high ground to mount their defensive cannons. It needed to be an area where the soil could support crops, and that could be cleared with reasonable ease. There needed to be running fresh water nearby, preferably a river or very large stream—not only for drinking, washing and irrigation, but also for access to food (primarily fish), boat moorage, and for eventually building mills to grind corn and wheat.

Finding that "perfect spot" would not be easy. The country was big, rugged, and difficult to survey; its native populations were mostly unknown; and the November weather was a wintery, blustery mess. To make matters worse, Master Jones and the *Mayflower's* crewmembers wanted to go home as soon as possible, and they were not shy to speak their minds about it either.

The passengers were also running low on food, and their primary beverage—beer. The distillation process killed water-borne parasites, making beer, wine, and hard liquors such as aqua-vitae, far safer to drink than water; so beer was the primary beverage of choice for everyone: men, women and children alike. On sea voyages, an adult was usually rationed a gallon of beer per day. That means the adults onboard the *Mayflower* would have consumed nearly 5,000 gallons (that's about 325 kegs!) of beer during the two month voyage: and now they had nearly run out, making a source of fresh, clean water of even greater importance.

The *Mayflower* anchored inside what is now Provincetown Harbor, right at the very tip of Cape Cod. The harbor was plenty big enough for ships, so the area passed one of their criteria at least. They noted lots of waterfowl, and forests of oaks, pines, and juniper. There were whales in the bay, but unfortunately the company was too short of funds to supply the colonists with any means to hunt them.

As soon as they could get organized, the passengers—then governed by John Carver, one of the Leiden Separatists—organized a group of about 16 men to make a quick trip ashore just to see what was there, and to gather some firewood, which they had run out of onboard the ship. They found the forests full of trees, mostly oak, pine, and juniper, the latter of which they gathered to burn onboard the ship because of its fragrance—after two months at sea, it was no doubt fairly rancid and foul smelling. It was also thought that burning juniper helped drive away "venom and corruption of the air . . . it is good to be burned in a plague time, in such places whereas the air is infected.[19]" They found the ground to be generally sandy with a small layer of good black crust.

The following day was Sunday. Since the Pilgrims did not work on Sunday, they just sat there onboard ship and held their church services. On Monday, it was back to work. The women were taken ashore, and got right to work on the laundry—which had been piling up for two months! There can be no doubt that everyone was just a little smelly . . .

The men went ashore, some to begin exploring the tip of Cape Cod in more detail, and others to start reassembling their main water transportation: a shallop they had disassembled and stored between the decks on the *Mayflower*. Some of the passengers had actually taken up residence inside the dismantled ship, and after two months of having people living in her, the boat was in need of quite a lot of repairs, on top of just needing to be reassembled.

The poor condition of the shallop and the extent of repairs she would need, was an unexpected delay. Without the ship, the Pilgrims had no way to conveniently coast the shorelines of the Cape to seek a place to settle. They had access to the much smaller longboat that belonged to the *Mayflower*, but it did not have a sail, and could not hold anywhere near as much cargo or people.

---

[19] Rambart Dodoens, *New Herbal, Or History of Plants* (London, 1586). There were at least two copies of this book onboard the *Mayflower*, one owned by Myles Standish and another owned by William Brewster.

After taking a day to "refresh themselves" and get organized, and after realizing their shallop would be weeks, not days, in repair, the Pilgrims decided to head out on their first exploration on foot. About sixteen men volunteered, led by Myles Standish, a former lieutenant in Queen Elizabeth's army that the Pilgrims had hired to be the captain of the colony's militia. Governor John Carver appointed three other men as advisers to Standish on their first exploration of Cape Cod: William Bradford and Edward Tilley, both Leiden separatists; and Stephen Hopkins. They were set ashore on Tuesday, November 15, and had only marched south about a mile along the beach sands when they spotted six men and a dog off in the distance. They initially assumed it was Christopher Jones and some of his men, but as they got closer they quickly realized the men were Indians. At that same moment, the Indians came to a similar realization, and took off into the woods.

What the Pilgrims did not know at this point was that the Indians on Cape Cod were not particularly fond of Europeans. In 1614, Captain John Smith (the same man more famous for his Jamestown exploits and his adventures with Pocahontas) was exploring and mapping New England, and stopped in at Cape Cod for a short time before moving on. He left behind an associate, Captain Thomas Hunt, to continue trading with the Indians. Captain Hunt, however, had other ideas: he lured twenty-seven Nauset and Patuxet onboard his ship under the guise of trading, and then sailed away with his captives—selling them off as slaves in Malaga, Spain. In 1617, three years later, a French ship unwittingly stopped by Cape Cod to trade with the Nauset, and was promptly attacked in retaliation for the kidnappings; the entire crew were killed or enslaved.

The Pilgrims, seeing the Indians on the beach, and desiring to find a native village to establish communications and ultimately trade, ignorantly give chase. The Indians, of course, saw something entirely different: a group of armed Englishmen giving chase, presumably in retaliation for the massacre of the Frenchmen, or perhaps to kidnap additional Indians. The Pilgrims followed the Indians' footprints for more than ten miles, before night fell. They picked up the trail the next morning, until they reached the Pamet River and lost the track.

The explorers spent the remainder of the day exploring the saltwater mouth of the Pamet River. Unfortunately the inexperienced group of would-be explorers had forgotten to bring with them anything to drink, and after a day of hiking through thickets and meadows, dying of thirst, they quickly turned their attention away from chasing Indians, and towards their more immediate emergency: finding fresh water. After hours of searching, they finally encountered some small freshwater ponds, and drank "with as much delight as we had ever drunk drink in all our lives."

Finally refreshed, the gang then turned their attention back to looking for Indians. What they found were some fifty acres of corn stubble from a previous season. Moving on, they found a mound of dirt with a mortar on top, which they dug into, and found some arrows and pots; suspecting it might be a grave, they covered it back up and moved on. They later came across an abandoned Indian house, where they found an old European kettle inside, which they took. Outside they found another mound of sand, which they dug into and found a large cache of corn seed. The Nauset, and other native groups in the region, preserved the next year's corn seed in large woven baskets that they buried in the ground for the better preservation of the seed. The Pilgrims did not have any native seed for themselves, and with no present way to get any in fair trade for the next planting season, they decided to take what they found. It was not stealing, they justified to themselves, because they promised to repay the owner, if he or she ever made themselves known. But for now the Pilgrims did not know who the owner was, so they could not pay them. What they got was 36 ears of corn, and a bunch of loose seed as well, amounting in total to a couple of bushels.

The Nauset, of course, saw things a little bit differently. The armed men who gave chase to them, had now dug into one of their graves, and then stole a family's entire supply of seed for the upcoming planting season. The Pilgrims were not making any friends at this point.

That night, it rained profusely, so the Pilgrims built a sturdy rendezvous to ride out the stormy night. The next morning, they started their march back from where they had come, but promptly got lost in the thick woods. As they were aimlessly wandering around trying to get their bearings, the group encountered a bizarre-looking manmade contraption. What was it? The group looked to Stephen Hopkins, the only man who had spent any time with Indians. Hopkins immediately recognized what it was: a deer trap. As everyone began to gather around to admire the handiwork and comment on the excellent rope work, William Bradford stumbled in from the rear wondering what everybody was looking at, stepped on and triggered the trap, and up he went with a jerk! Everyone but William got a good laugh out of it.

Finally the men returned to the vicinity of the *Mayflower*, shot off their guns to signal they were ready to be picked up by the ship's longboat, and delivered their corn into the company's store. In a sense, this was the first "income" the joint-stock company would get from the New World—some

Corn Hill in modern-day Truro, with the Pamet River in the foreground. This was the location where the Pilgrims first discovered mounds of buried corn, which they took to use as seed for the upcoming planting season. It would be more than a year, but the Pilgrims eventually did repay the natives for what they had "borrowed."

"borrowed" corn. The Pilgrims, who believed that God blessed enterprises based on the godliness of their carriage, might look back to this event for a possible explanation as to why their business venture would be ultimately unsuccessful. On the other hand, the Pilgrims may well have been right: had they not "borrowed" this corn, they probably would not have had enough food to survive the upcoming year—the English wheat, barley, peas, and other seed they brought, did not meet with much success, so it was the Indian corn that would sustain the colony in its earliest years.

For the next couple weeks, the Pilgrims worked on finishing up the shallop, and making and fixing up the tools they would use for exploring and later constructing their residences. But first things first: they needed to find a place to actually settle. In late November, with the shallop patched up enough to be functional, thirty-six men were organized to head out on the next exploration—most in the shallop, but some in the longboat too. They decided to return to the Pamet River to survey it more carefully to establish its possible suitability as a place to establish their colony; they also wanted to dig for more corn there, as the two bushels they found would not be enough.

The large group, consisting of nearly half the adult male passengers, in addition to nine crewmembers, were led (honorarily) by the *Mayflower's* master, Christopher Jones, with Captain Standish as the practical man-in-charge. While the names of the men that went on this exploration are nowhere specifically stated, Stephen Hopkins was undoubtedly amongst them, since he participated in all the other explorations, many of which had far fewer people: no doubt the Pilgrims wanted to take every advantage they could of his first-hand knowledge of the New World and the Indians.

The exploration started out uncomfortably enough—it rained and snowed, and the winds were so strong they had to sail to the nearest shore. Looking back, many of the Pilgrims who got sick and died the first winter blamed it on this expedition because of the freezing weather and exposure to the elements that everyone had to endure.

It was not until the middle of the following day that they managed to get back to the mouth of the Pamet River. Surveying the area more carefully, they determined the river could not support ships, although it was deep enough for boats. They hiked about five miles up the two main creeks, finding steep hills and deep valleys, which tired everyone out. More than six inches of snow had fallen by the end of the day. They built a small shelter out of pine trees, and killed three geese and six ducks, which they roasted, and served as a very welcome (and warm) meal to the wearied wanderers.

By morning, everyone had pretty much come to the conclusion that the area was not suitable for their future colony. The harbor was not very good and the ground was too hilly. So they decided to just return to Corn Hill, dig up any more corn they could find, and head back to the *Mayflower*. The ground was now covered with snow and frozen hard, so they had to cut into the ground with their swords (they forgot to bring any tools); at least this time they had enough people to carry back their spoils. They found three more large baskets of corn seed, nearly ten bushels in all; and they also found some oil in a bottle, and a bag of beans for seed as well. But the weather continued to worsen, and Master Jones did not want to leave the *Mayflower* unattended, so he returned to the ship with himself and fifteen others, leaving eighteen men to continue exploring.

The following day, the remaining eighteen men set out to see if they could meet with any Indians. They followed some game trails for about five miles until they stumbled across what appeared to be a grave. Wondering what it really was, they dug into it. They found mats, then a bow, then another mat, and some carved and painted boards, then some bowls, trays, dishes; then another mat, some fine red powder, and then finally . . . the bones and skull of a man, and a little child. Since the corpse still had some blond hair remaining, and some iron tools and a sailors' cassock were in the grave, the Pilgrims concluded it might be an Englishman or Frenchman that the natives had buried, but they could not be sure. Someone, presumably Stephen Hopkins, commented that Indians only had black hair, not blond.

As the Pilgrims nonchalantly note in their journals, "we brought sundry of the prettiest things away with us, and covered the corpse up again." The chronicler goes on to say, "After this, we digged in sundry like places, but found no more corn, nor anything else but graves." Continuing on their journey, they encountered two Indian houses that appeared to have been recently inhabited. Guns ready, the explorers entered the houses, rummaged around, "took out some things," and then departed. "[S]ome of the best things we took away with us, . . . it growing towards night, and the tide almost spent, we hasted with our things down to the shallop, . . . intending to have brought some beads, and other things to have left in the houses, in sign of peace, . . . but it was not done."

Returning all to the *Mayflower*, they had a large discussion and debate. Was this the place to settle? Some thought the location was just fine. The harbor was good for boats, albeit not for large ships. The ground seemed to be very productive as far as corn-growing was concerned. The bay seemed to be full of fish and whale. The hills made the area defensible. And anyway,

John Smith's map of New England, made in 1614. The Pilgrims used this map, and had access to Smith's other books and maps. Cape Cod is located at the bottom left of the map (and is shown enlarged). It is labeled "Cape James" on the map—a name which did not stick. One place name applied by Smith did stick: "Plimouth."

their provisions (food and drink both) were dwindling low. They would need all the food and drink possible for the heavy labors involved in constructing buildings and houses in the middle of winter, so they needed to get going as soon as possible. Those opposed to settling themselves at Pamet felt that there were other known places along the main coastline, not on the Cape itself, where there was better land—just look at John Smith's map of New England, which the Pilgrims had available to them.

Some of the sailors also spoke of a place known as Anguum (now Boston Harbor) that they thought was a far better place than the puny little Pamet. Others argued that they had barely explored the area, and by next spring they may discover a beautiful harbor just a few miles away—and by that time, it would be a great hindrance to move the colony. Still others pointed out there was no running fresh water, only the saltwater Pamet marshes, and a few stagnant ponds that might even dry up in the summer for all they knew. And the steep hills would make hauling water much more laborious.

In the end, it was concluded that the Pilgrims would send out one final expedition to circle all of Cape Cod by sea and land, to see if there were any other better harbors or rivers; but it was also agreed they would not go as far north as Anguum: they would stick to the area around Cape Cod. Eighteen men were organized, including Stephen Hopkins, and one of his two manservants, Edward Doty. They set off on December 6, now a full month after Cape Cod had first been sighted by the *Mayflower*.

Winter was now in full force. When they finally got the shallop out to sea, they found the wind so powerful that it blew up the sea spray and covered their clothes in sheets of ice "like coats of iron." Several of the men on the shallop were already "sick unto death" with coughs and colds, making travel all the more uncomfortable. After sailing along the coastline for what they thought was about twenty miles, they arrived in the evening at a bay that is today known as Welfleet Harbor. On shore, off in the far distance, they could see some Indians cleaning a large black fish, but they ran off long before the expedition could get anywhere near the beach. They set up camp for the night onshore, and built a small barricade and a fire. They could see the Indians' fires about five miles distant; no doubt the Indians saw the Pilgrims' fire too.

The next morning they set off to explore Welfleet Harbor, which they nicknamed Grampus Bay, after the large black fish they had seen the Indians cleaning onshore. They did not find any freshwater rivers or streams of any significance, so they then turned their attention to seeing if they could meet up with any of the Indians they had seen the day previous. They made their way to the location where the Indians had been cleaning the fish on shore, and followed their trails into the woods to a large pond. After hiking into the woods, they found some corn stubble from several years past, and what appeared to be a graveyard. This time they did not dig anything up, but continued on their way. As evening approached, they got themselves back to the shore, and rejoined the shallop just as night fell. They ate what little they had brought with them for food, built a small barricade and fire near modern-day Eastham, and quickly fell asleep, posting—as they always did—several sentinels to keep watch.

About midnight, the explorers were startled awake by some strange cries coming from the surrounding woods—"a great and hideous cry," as one of them described it. Scrambling to their muskets, they fired a couple shots into the air, and the noise subsided. One of the *Mayflower's* sailors who had been to Newfoundland on a previous voyage, thought the noise sounded like wolves howling; everyone went back to sleep.

About five in the morning, the men began to wake up. They shot off their matchlock muskets to make sure they had not gotten too damp during the night, had a group prayer, and then began to make some breakfast, when they were suddenly startled to hear the same voices from the previous night, which they now thought sounded like "*Woath woach ha ha hach woach*"; one of the men in the distance came running in, yelling "They are men, Indians, Indians!" Within seconds, the arrows were flying into their barricade. Some of the men took up a defensive position inside the barricade, while others were separated off near the shallop and had to make their own separate defense. Unfortunately, those at the shallop had been caught off guard by the sudden attack and did not have any fire with which they could light their matchlock muskets—they had little more than swords to fight with. So one brave man from the barricade grabbed a burning log from the fire and ran it out to the men near the shallop.

The Pilgrims managed to get off a few musket shots, and then held off firing until they could find a target with which to take better aim. One Indian, whom they thought might have been the leader of the attack, fired three arrows into the barricade, but all were avoided; he managed to avoid three musket shots taken at him as well, but a forth shot came too close for comfort and he gave a loud yell and the attackers retreated back into the woods. Not wanting to give the impression they were afraid or discouraged, Standish and a few men gave a half-hearted chase for a quarter mile, fired off their muskets into the air, and made a few triumphant yells for good measure.

Amazingly, for a surprise attack between about thirty Indians and eighteen Englishmen, with a large number of arrows and musketballs exchanged in the early twilight, there was not a single injury on either side. The explorers gathered up about eighteen arrows they found strewn about the leaf-litter, to send back to England as curiosities, and then headed off for the next day's exploration.

The group planned to explore the mainland next, hoping to find a place known as "Thievish Harbor" by Robert Coppin, one of the Master's Mates. As they rounded Cape Cod and headed towards what is now Plymouth Harbor, they encountered more snow and rain; as the afternoon approached, the winds and seas picked up. The waves became so violent, the hinges that held the rudder on were ripped off—so the only way to steer it was for several men to use oars. Then a large gust broke the mast into three separate pieces, and it too fell overboard. But as luck (or rather God's Providence) would have it, they saw an island within reach. Master's mates John Clark and Robert Coppin helped guide what was left of the shallop aground. They named the island Clark's Island—a name the island still carries today—in recognition of John Clark's heroic efforts to get the craft safely grounded on the rocky shoreline.

One has to wonder what Stephen Hopkins must have been thinking about at the moment they drove the shallop aground. After all, this was the second time he had been aboard a crippled vessel in the middle of a violent storm, which had to be deliberately run around on an island!

The shallop would need only minor repairs—a new mast and rudder—which was done the following day. They explored by foot around the island on Saturday, and the following day—the Sabbath—they rested, prayed, worshipped, and honored God by doing no work.

Monday, December 12, it was back to business. The weather had cleared up, the shallop had been mended, and the island had been explored to everyone's content. It was now time to coast around the rest of the harbor to see what was there. And what they saw, they liked. The harbor was good and big, deep enough for ships. The ground was generally level; there were cleared areas of abandoned cornfields; and there were freshwater streams. This was the best they had yet seen, and they were out of time to look for anything else. They returned to the *Mayflower*, still anchored off the tip of Cape Cod, with the good news: they had found a suitable harbor within which to locate their colony.

On December 15, the *Mayflower* raised her anchors and departed from the tip of Cape Cod and headed across to Plymouth Harbor, but the winds did not cooperate, so she was forced back. The following day they tried again, and this time successfully entered Plymouth Harbor and there anchored, giving everyone onboard a first glimpse of their new home. It was too late in the day to organize any expeditions ashore, and the next day was the Sabbath, so the Pilgrims rested.

Plymouth Rock: the rock that, by tradition, the *Mayflower* passengers used to step ashore. If the legend is true, then Stephen's feet must have crossed this stone many times, while helping to bring ashore the colony's food, tools, weapons, and other supplies. The stone was cracked in 1774 during an attempt to move it and put it on patriotic display in the lead-up to the Revolutionary War. The date "1620" was carved into it in 1880, when the rock was returned to its original location.

Finally, on December 18, they set ashore various parties of men to begin looking for the ideal spot to situate their township. They found no Indians or Indian houses, but did find some cornfields from several years previous. The following day they explored up one of the creeks several miles. They liked the mainland because of the abundant resources, but were disappointed there were no large navigable rivers. The woods were nearby, which they feared could hide the "savages," and they were concerned they were too far from the fishing grounds of Cape Cod—fishing was one of the ways they thought they could generate a profit, though for now the company had been too short of funds to supply any fishing equipment. Others thought that Clark's Island was better because it would be easily defensible, and it was very close to the mouth of Plymouth Harbor so the fishing grounds would be much more convenient. But the soil of Clark's Island was thought by some to be too rocky, and there was no reliable source of fresh water—no streams or creeks, only a few ponds that would probably dry up in summer.

Chapter 10

THE FOUNDING OF PLYMOUTH

After much debate, the Pilgrims held a vote the next day to see which place—mainland or Clark's Island—that they would settle. The majority of passengers voted for the mainland. The area on the mainland that was chosen was labeled "Plimouth" on Captain John Smith's map of the region made in 1614. Since Plymouth was also the name of the last city they stopped at before departing England, the name seemed appropriate, and it stuck. One of the passengers described the area shortly after they had viewed it for the first time:

> [W]e came to the conclusion, by most voices, to set on the mainland, on the first place, on a high ground, where there is a great deal of land cleared, and hath been planted with corn three or four years ago, and there is a very sweet brook runs under the hillside, and many delicate springs of as good water as can be drunk, and where we may harbor our shallops and boats exceeding well; and in this brook much good fish in their seasons: on the further side of the river also much corn ground cleared, in one field is a great hill, on which we point to make a platform, and plant our ordinance [cannon], which will command all round about. From thence we may see into the bay, and far into the sea, and we may see thence Cape Cod. Our greatest labor will be fetching our wood, which is half a quarter of an English mile, but there is enough so far off. What people inhabit here we yet know not, for as yet we have seen none.

With the decision to settle at Plymouth made, all that was left to do was to go ashore, and start building. But that was easier said than done. The next two days, December 21 and December 22, were so stormy, windy, rainy, and dark, that the Pilgrims could not safely get to shore. During the storms, Mary Allerton went into labor and gave birth to a stillborn son—adding further to the already depressing situation.

Finally, on December 23, the Pilgrims managed to make it ashore, for their first full day of labor. Most of the day was spent chopping down and hauling timber from the nearby forest, so that they would have the raw materials necessary to begin constructing their houses and other buildings. The labor was extremely difficult and tiring, but it must have been an enormous relief for everyone to see that construction on their colony had finally begun.

Today, school children are told that the Pilgrims' voyage lasted sixty-six days, and are amazed at how a hundred people could live for so long in such a small, cramped, damp and smelly place. But what is often forgotten is that many of the Pilgrims, like Stephen and Elizabeth Hopkins and their young children, had boarded the *Mayflower* way back in July—and by January, the Pilgrims had not even managed to build a single house or structure onshore, so everyone was still living onboard the ship, just as they had been for six months already!

Work progressed at a snail's pace. December 24 was the Sabbath. December 25 was a workday—Christmas was an invention of the Catholics and the Pope and was not honored—though the *Mayflower's* crew, who were not Separatists, did break out a small store of beer for the occasion. December 26 was too stormy to work. December 27, it was back to chopping and hauling trees.

December 28 they laid out where the houses would be built, dividing up 19 plots of land based upon family size, deciding to have two rows of houses and a street separating them. The lots were about 50 feet in depth, by 8 feet per family member in width. The Stephen Hopkins household probably consisted of himself and his wife, his four children Constance, Giles, Damaris, and Oceanus, and his two servants Edward Doty and Edward Leister; so Stephen's family was likely allotted an initial house and garden plot of 64 feet in width and 50 feet in depth.

The settlers collectively joined together to build a 20 foot by 20 foot common house, which would serve as a storehouse for their goods, as well as a temporary hospital for the sick—of which there were more and more every day. It was completed by mid January. They also collectively built a small storage shed for some of their supplies. After that, the individual families were responsible for constructing their own houses—a tactic the Plymouth leaders felt would lead to greater productivity.

Unfortunately in the productivity department, there were two significant problems: weather and health. The weather continued to be stormy, with rain, sleet, snow, and heavy winds. Many days the men found themselves unable to get any work done due to the weather: January 12, January 14, January 15, January 30, January 31, and February 4 through 9—all unproductive because of foul weather. In fact, on February 4, the winds were so strong, they significantly damaged a number of the houses that were then half-built, causing even more work to need to be done. Then there was the Sabbath, when the Pilgrims also did not work—January 7, January 14, January 21, January 28, and February 4.

In the health department, the situation was going from bad to worse. In November, only one person had died. In December, there were six. During the colony's construction, most of which occurred in January and February, there were 25 deaths. By the end of March, half the *Mayflower's* passengers—and half of the crew as well—had died. The exact medical cause of the deaths is not known, but presumably it was a combination of colds that turned into pneumonia, and scurvy from lack of vitamin C.

Those who did not die were not immune from being sick and weak. Of all the passengers, it was reported that only about seven made it through the first winter without having become seriously ill. Of those seven, we know of only two names for sure: William Brewster and Myles Standish. The Hopkins' household appears to have lost two members during the first winter: toddler Damaris, and infant Oceanus. But Stephen, wife Elizabeth, children Giles and Constance, and even Hopkins' servants Edward Doty and Edward Leister, seem to have been untouched by the widespread illness.

Others were not so lucky. On January 11, William Bradford was at work, when he was "vehemently taken with grief and pain, and so shot to his hucklebone, it was doubted that he would have instantly died, he got cold in the former discoveries, especially the last, and felt some pain in his ankles bytimes." Those were scurvy-like symptoms. The next day, Peter Brown and John Goodman got lost in the woods for the night; by the time they found their way back home, Goodman's feet were badly swollen and frostbitten—so much so that his shoes had to be cut off his feet and he was lame for many weeks thereafter.

Yet another productivity killer was fire. With the cold winter weather, a fire had to be going at all times inside the storehouse to keep everyone warm, and to cook food and boil water. But on occasion, a spark would fly into the roof, and catch the thatch on fire, as happened on January 14 to the storehouse where the sick (John Carver and William Bradford among them) were being housed. Another small house being used as a hospital caught fire on February 9.

It was not until March 21 that everyone was finally brought ashore and began permanently living at Plymouth—by that time, some people had likely been living onboard the ship for about nine months.

Chapter 11

MEETING THE INDIANS

As the Pilgrims continued to chop and haul timber, and gather thatch for roofing, one thing was always on their mind: the Indians. Since coming into Plymouth Harbor, they had seen none—unlike Cape Cod, where they had seen Indians on several different occasions. Once (back on December 24), they thought they heard some Indians yelling—but the noise subsided soon thereafter and there was no sign of anyone. On January 3, they saw some Indian fires about five or six miles distant, and the following day Captain Myles Standish led a group of men to the area to see if they could meet with anyone. All they found were long-abandoned houses and cornfields from several years prior. On January 8, thirteen year old Francis Billington and one of the *Mayflower's* sailors hiked inland together, and stumbled across some abandoned Indian houses—at which point they realized the two of them might be a little safer back at Plymouth and hightailed it out of there.

On February 16, the Pilgrims would have their first confirmed sighting of an Indian at Plymouth. One of the settlers, whose name was not recorded, was out near a creek, hiding in some reeds hunting waterfowl, when he looked up to see twelve Indians walking past him towards Plymouth. He froze stiff until they had passed, and then he ran to Plymouth by a different route to give the alarm. When the alarm sounded, the men in the woods dropped their tools and hurried back to Plymouth to take up their weapons, and waited. And waited some more. But no Indians ever came. When they returned later that day to their workplaces in the woods, they found some of their tools had been taken.

The next day, during the middle of a ceremony to formally establish their militia and appoint Myles Standish as captain, two Indians appeared on top of a neighboring hill about a quarter of a mile away, and made signals to the gathered colonists to come to them. The Pilgrims returned the signals, asking the Indians to come to them instead—while simultaneously grabbing their muskets in case there was an impending attack.

Seeing the Indians would not come to them, they decided to send two men across the brook to the hill, to meet them. The men that were chosen were Captain Standish, for his military prowess; and Stephen Hopkins, because of his knowledge and previous interactions with the Indians at Virginia. As Hopkins and Standish approached, they laid down their weapons in a peaceful gesture, and tried to approach, but the Indians were too skittish and eventually disappeared back into the woods.

The incident put the colonists on edge. They promptly cancelled all their other labors, and went straight to work collectively building a platform and fort. On February 21, they brought ashore their biggest cannon, which they hauled up and mounted on the top of their hill. Three other smaller cannon were also brought ashore and mounted in different defensive locations around the town.

Nearly a month had passed, without any further sightings of the Indians. Spring was approaching; one of the Pilgrims recalled that on March 3, "the birds sang in the woods most pleasantly," and on March 7, they planted some of their garden seeds, probably lettuce and peas.

On March 16, the Pilgrims decided to have the military ceremony that had been previously interrupted by the sudden appearance of the Indians back in February. And, once more, the ceremony was suddenly interrupted, as a lone Indian walked right into Plymouth, down the street, and right to the fort. He was intercepted before he could reach the fort itself, at which point, to everyone's great surprise, he spoke: "Welcome Englishmen."

His name was Samoset, and he was a native from Mohegan. He had learned some broken English from the ships that traded with his people there. He was a sagamore, or chief, from that area, and had been visiting the Wampanoag for about eight months. One of the Pilgrims described him as follows:

> He was stark naked, only a leather about his waist, with a fringe about a span long, or a little more; he had a bow and two arrows, the one headed and the other unheaded. He was a tall straight man, the hair of his head black, long behind, only short before, none on his face at all.

Portrait of Captain Myles Standish, from a painting made in 1625. The whereabouts of the original are unknown. This drawing, based on the now lost original, was done for Justin Winsor's *Memorial History of Boston* (1881).

Samoset informed the English that they were living at a place known as Patuxet, and that all the inhabitants had died about four years previous from a devastating plague. They learned that their nearest neighbors were the Wampanoag, led by a man called Massasoit, who had about sixty men under his immediate command. And they learned that the Indians who attacked them on Cape Cod were Nauset, and they had about a hundred men.

As night grew closer, the Pilgrims tried to hint to their new guest that he should leave, but apparently the hints were not received. Samoset had every intention of staying for the night. The Pilgrims, however, were still concerned about their safety, being rather afraid of the Indians, so they decided the safest place for him would be aboard the *Mayflower*. The weather and tide, however, prevented that option from being carried out.

Finally they concluded to allow Samoset to stay the night—in Stephen Hopkins' house. Guards were appointed to watch Samoset all night, expecting some kind of treachery, but the only thing the night watchmen got to see was Samoset sleeping. One wonders if Stephen and his family got any sleep though!

The next morning, Samoset returned to the Wampanoag, with various messages from the Plymouth colonists, and with promises to return in a day or two, with some natives interested in trading beaver skins.

Samoset followed the Pilgrims' instructions, and returned the next day with several Wampanoag men, interested in trading their beaver skins for some of the Pilgrims' trade goods, or "trinkets," as the Pilgrims often called them. These were likely pieces of copper, mirrors, small tools and knives, beads, and other similar items.

Unfortunately, there was a slight miscommunication: the five Indians and Samoset arrived for trading on the Sabbath, so the Pilgrims refused to do business. They had a cordial visit, gave them a few freebies and gifts, and then sent them away, insisting they come back in the next few days with even more skins to trade. Confused by the Pilgrims' refusal to trade, the five Indians began to suspect it was a trap, and slinked away. Samoset, however, claimed he was too sick—he wanted to stay with the Pilgrims again. So he took up residence, no doubt still in Hopkins' house, for the next few days, as everyone awaited the return of the men and their beaver skins.

On Wednesday, March 21, they sent Samoset away to find out why the Indians had not returned to trade, and conveniently decided this would be a good day to resume the ceremony that the Indians had interrupted on February 16, and then again on March 16. As if by clockwork, right in the middle of the ceremony again, three Indians came to the top of the nearby hill, and started making gestures at the Pilgrims—this time, the gestures did not seem quite as friendly. Again, two men—Captain Standish and probably Stephen Hopkins—were sent to initiate contact. The Indians whetted and rubbed their arrows and strings, but as the armed Standish and Hopkins got close, they ran off.

Having been interrupted, the meeting was rescheduled again for March 22—when it was promptly interrupted for the fourth time. Captain Standish, no doubt, must have been wondering if God did not want him to be formally named Captain!

Samoset had returned, and this time he brought with him an Indian named Tisquantum (conveniently nicknamed "Squanto" by the English, who no doubt had difficulty saying his full name). Squanto, it turned out, spoke even better English than Samoset. He was one of the twenty-seven Indians that had been kidnapped in 1614 by Captain Thomas Hunt. He was brought to Malaga, Spain, where he was rescued from slavery by some local friars, who somehow got him on a ship to England, where he lived for a time with the treasurer of the Newfoundland Company, John Slaney. About 1619, Squanto was dispatched to Newfoundland, where he met with an English captain by the name of Thomas Dermer. Captain Dermer was in the employ of Sir Ferdinando Gorges, Plymouth Company founder and president of the Council for New England, and recommended to his boss that he take Squanto to explore the coast of New England. Gorges agreed.

Captain Dermer, with Squanto's assistance, explored along the coastline of New England from Maine south, and eventually returned Squanto to his homeland at Patuxet (Plymouth). Squanto's triumphant and joyful return home was not to be, however—he returned to Patuxet to find his entire home town wiped out by a plague that had occurred a year or two earlier. With everyone dead, Squanto moved further inland to reside amongst the surviving Wampanoag at Nemasket and Sowams.

So there stood Samoset and Squanto, with three other Indians, holding a few skins and some dried herring. But more important than their few trade items was the message they brought: Massasoit himself was just across the brook, along with his brother Quadequinna. They had trouble delivering their message—both were rather rusty with their English. But as they were struggling to get their words together, across the brook and at the top of the hill appeared the great Wampanoag sachem, Massasoit Ousemaquin. He had sixty men with him. And he wanted to speak with the Pilgrims' governor—then John Carver.

Town Brook, Plymouth. The brook was central to early Plymouth's survival, providing fresh water, fish, and later waterpower for a grist mill. It was only a few paces away from their houses, which from this view would have been just up the slight hill to the right. It was this stream that Stephen Hopkins crossed when leaving Plymouth with Myles Standish on their first attempt to meet with the Indians.

There was a little problem, however: the Pilgrims had no desire to send their beloved Governor off into the waiting hands of sixty armed "savages," whose intentions they could not at this point discern. And Massasoit had no intention of heading into the Pilgrims' fort where there were twenty five Englishmen armed with cannon and muskets, metal armor and swords, and what other technology and magic he knew not.

This time, it was Edward Winslow who must have drawn the short straw, so he went out of the fort with Squanto, to meet Massasoit and deliver a message from Governor Carver. The message was basically that the Pilgrims' wanted to consider the Wampanoag friends and allies, and wanted to trade with them. Massasoit promptly offered to trade for Winslow's sword and armor, which he had to awkwardly reject. Eventually Massasoit was satisfied enough with Winslow and their message and conversation, that he appointed his brother Quadequinna to watch over Winslow, while he went down to visit the Plymouth settlers. Bringing an entourage of twenty men with him, Massasoit made his way across Town Brook, and there was met by Captain Myles Standish, Elder William Brewster (who in the primary source is referred to under the pseudonym "Master Williamson"), and six musketeers.

Massasoit was escorted to a house, where he was seated, and Governor Carver then arrived, to drum and trumpet, escorted by several musketeers. They kissed each other on the hand as a salutation, and then sat down to a drink—some "strong water" that made Massasoit "sweat all the while after." Massasoit was given some meat, which he shared with some of his men, and then they got down to business drafting a peace treaty.

As a formal treaty, it seems rather one-sided. The treaty required that (1) Massasoit and his people would not injure or harm the Pilgrims; (2) If any of his men did hurt the Pilgrims, he should turn them over to Plymouth for punishment; (3) If the Indians stole from the Pilgrims, Massasoit should cause those items to be returned; and vice-versa, if the Pilgrims stole from the Indians, the Governor would see to it that the items got returned to their rightful owner; and (4) When the Indians visit Plymouth, they should lay down their bows and arrows before arriving; and the Pilgrims would lay down their guns when they came to visit the Indians.

But the key and critical component of the treaty was the last and final item: "If any did unjustly war against him [Massasoit], we [Plymouth Colony] would aid him; if any did war against us, he would aid us." This mutual aid pact bound the Pilgrims and the Wampanoag together in a way that few other English and Indian groups would ever manage to do. It was a bold but very risky agreement. Massasoit, for his part, got allies with guns, cannon, and superior technology, which would keep his enemies at bay while also tying his allies even more closely to him. And the Pilgrims, for their part, got friendly neighbors not only willing to engage in trade, but also watching their backs. Of course, if the Wampanoag were attacked by a neighboring tribe such as the Narragansett, the tiny Plymouth colony of twenty-five weakened men would have likely found themselves little more than pawns in a potentially bloody regional war.

One of the Pilgrims, watching the signing of the treaty, remembered Massasoit thusly:

> [I]n his person he is a very lusty man, in his best years, an able body, grave of countenance, and spare of speech; in his attire little or nothing differing from the rest of his followers, only in a great chain of white bone beads about his neck, and at it behind his neck hangs a little bag of tobacco, which he drank [smoked] and gave us to drink [smoke]. His face was painted with a sad red like murrey, and oiled both head and face, that he looked greasily: all his followers likewise, were in their faces, in part or in whole painted, some black, some red, some yellow, and some white, some with crosses, and other antic works; some had skins on them, and some naked, all strong, tall . . . . one thing I forgot, the king had in his bosom hanging in a string a great long knife; he marveled much at our trumpet.

Samoset and Squanto both stayed the night at Plymouth, presumably again in Stephen Hopkins' house, while the remaining Wampanoag (who had their wives and children with them) spent the night in the woods on the other side of Town Brook. The next morning, many of the Wampanoag men and women came to visit their new friends at Plymouth—the Pilgrims suspected they just wanted some free food more than anything else. But it was not the time to ruffle any feathers, so the colonists went along with it. Several of the visitors mentioned that Massasoit wanted the English to come visit him too, so Captain Standish and Isaac Allerton were sent across the brook to pay him a cordial visit, which was well received by Massasoit, who gave them some ground nuts and tobacco as gifts.

Over the coming months, the Plymouth colonists found Massasoit to be true and faithful to his promise. It was not long before the English and Wampanoag were crossing paths in the woods and encountering each other while hunting and fishing—and they never had an ill encounter. Samoset soon returned to his home in modern-day Maine, but Squanto took up residence in Plymouth.

Exactly where Squanto lived in Plymouth is not recorded, but it would not be unreasonable to speculate he was living in the Hopkins household, where he and Samoset had been lodged on earlier occasions. Squanto was a Godsend for the Pilgrims. He acted as an ambassador and translator between the Pilgrims and Wampanoag; he relayed cultural, political, governmental and geographic intelligence, allowing the Pilgrims to better understand their nearest neighbors and the area in which they had settled. He was a teacher as well, instructing the Pilgrims on the correct time and season to plant various crops, how to properly prepare the Patuxet soil for the all-important corn crop (by fertilizing it with fish caught in the brook), and even how to catch the "fat and sweet" eels in the mud.

With the situation at Plymouth finally stabilized—the winter was over, the sickness and death had come to an end, the weather was improving, and peaceful relations had been tentatively established—it was time for the *Mayflower*, the Pilgrims only lifeline back to Old England, to depart. The *Mayflower* was never intended to spend the entire winter at Plymouth, and Christopher Jones, a savvy and well-experienced businessman, had undoubtedly written demurrage fees into his contract, as he had done in previous charter-party contracts in the past when hauling freight. Keeping the *Mayflower* there all winter was quite expensive for the already financially strapped company, but at the same time it was (from the settlers' point of view) a necessary expense.

Investors in the company back in England eagerly awaited the ship's return. If the *Mayflower* were loaded full of furs, timber, fish, and other commodities, the return would increase the value of their stock, and encourage additional investors to come onboard, funneling much needed money into the company so that they could purchase additional goods with which to trade with the Indians, purchase fishing equipment and salt, purchase additional tools, and hopefully even a boat so they would not have to pay exorbitant freight charges to get their returns back to England.

The *Mayflower* departed for England on April 5, and arrived back to the anxious investors in London on May 6. She was empty. There were the few beaver skins of token value that they had traded for with Samoset and Squanto a short time earlier; a bunch of letters full of sorrows, bad news, and complaints; a few wills and probate-related papers; and some Indian artifacts (like the arrows they had collected from Nauset). The company's stock value plummeted. There would be no funds with which to purchase trade goods, fishing equipment, tools, or even resupply the colony with food.

With what little money was left, the company back in London decided the best thing to do was send another shipment of laborers—clearly what the colony needed was more productive people willing to do hard work, not these religious separatists who debate, pray, and consult their days away. The company sought out and found a group of willing laborers from in and around London—most of whom were not particularly compatible with the devout Separatist community now established at Plymouth—and organized them for the next resupply voyage that would embark a couple months later.

Chapter 12

JOURNEY TO POKANOKET

New friendships rarely last if you do not maintain regular contact with one another. As one of Plymouth's leaders wrote:

> It seemed good to the company, for many considerations, to send some amongst them to Massasoit, the greatest commander amongst the savages bordering about us, partly to know where to find them, if occasion served, as also to see their strength, discover the country, prevent abuses in their disorderly coming unto us, make satisfaction for some conceived injuries to be done on our parts, and to continue the league of peace and friendship between them and us.

It was important to continue to pay respect to Massasoit, by visiting him and continuing their display of friendship and peace. The Pilgrims were also new to the area, and were eager to get out and explore. If their business was going to profit from trade, they needed to know where the Indian villages were, where the rivers went, which groups had what resources, and they needed to make social and business contacts with the natives that would further their profit prospects. The Pilgrims also realized they still had not paid their debts for the corn and beans they stole (or rather "borrowed") from the Nauset, or the items they removed from the Indian houses while exploring on Cape Cod—so it made good sense, to prevent any hard feelings from welling up and affecting future business, to make good on these debts.

The Plymouth colonists had yet another problem—one which they would have to address very carefully to prevent offense. Following the peace agreement with Massasoit, the "ordinary" Wampanoag felt no qualms with stopping by Plymouth for a visit—and expecting gifts and food as any friend and guest would be entitled to. But Plymouth was nearly out of food and supplies, they were just recovering from the horrific first winter where more than half the adults were decimated, their crops were not yet harvestable, . . . they simply could not afford to host so many uninvited guests on a continuing and regular basis. They needed to find a tactful way to ask Massasoit to have his people stop coming by so frequently, expecting food and entertainment as guests.

It was quite an important task, indeed, with lots of critical objectives—the ultimate success of the colony, and profitability for the company, depended on maintaining good relations with the Native Americans in the region. The Pilgrims selected two men for the job: Stephen Hopkins and Edward Winslow. Stephen Hopkins was selected because of his previous experience with the Indians in Virginia, and probably for his closeness with Squanto, who presumably was still residing in his house. And Edward Winslow was selected because he was the first Englishman to greet Massasoit and negotiate with him, and he had already spent the most time with the Wampanoag people of anyone, acting as the "hostage" by staying with the Indians across the brook during both Massasoit and Quadequinna's visits with Governor Carver.

Archaeologists generally believe the Wampanoag and their ancestors had been in the New England area for at least 10,000 to 12,000 years. They speak a language from the Algonquian language group and share many cultural similarities with other Algonquian peoples, including those found in Virginia around Jamestown. The staple crop was Indian corn, but beans and squash were also important. Other foods were obtained by hunting—deer, waterfowl, fish—and gathering—berries, nuts, roots, and shellfish.

Although the only primary source describing this expedition states that they departed Plymouth on 10 June 1621, it appears this is in error for several reasons. First, one of the objectives of the mission was to exchange corn seed; by June it would have been way too late in the season to plant corn. Second, Plymouth set out an expedition to Nauset on June 11, and it is unlikely they would have ever had two expeditions going simultaneously. Third, June 10 was a Sunday, and the Pilgrims would have never sent out an expedition on a Sunday. And fourth, the account of the expedition mentions that shad were then spawning—which happens in April, not June. More probably, the expedition set off on April 10, less than a week after the *Mayflower* had departed back to England.

Portrait of Edward Winslow made in 1651. Edward Winslow accompanied Stephen Hopkins on the voyage to visit Massasoit. He wrote several books and letters describing early Plymouth, and was governor on several occasions. Image reprinted from the Massachusetts Historical Society's 1912 edition of William Bradford's *History of Plymouth Plantation*. The original painting is on display at the Pilgrim Hall Museum, Plymouth, Massachusetts.

Hopkins and Winslow departed together, with Squanto as their guide, leaving about 9:00 AM for the nearest Indian village, Nemasket. The Pilgrims thought Nemasket was nearby, because they had so many frequent visitors from that village stop by Plymouth; but to their surprise, it turned out to be about fifteen miles away. Along the way, they met up with a group of twelve men, women and children from Nemasket returning from gathering lobster at a nearby bay; they "pestered" Hopkins and Winslow throughout most of the trip.

They arrived about 3:00 PM at Nemasket, and were entertained by the villagers. For a late lunch, they ate cornbread, "spawn of shad" (caviar, which Hopkins and Winslow "ate heartily"), and acorns. Hopkins and Winslow also demonstrated their guns to the curious Indians, who wanted them to shoot a crow that was eating their corn. Originally they had planned to spend the night here, but after arriving, Squanto decided they could make it to the next village—another eight miles away—before sunset, and suggested they might find better food and entertainment there as well. Hopkins and Winslow, willing to expedite their journey, agreed.

They arrived at their next stop right as the sun was beginning to set. They found some men from Nemasket there at a fishing weir, and traded some of their own food for some freshly caught bass, which they ate for their supper. The village was not a permanent settlement, but a spring and summer encampment, so there were no houses built—they slept that night in some open fields.

In the morning, as they looked around, they saw large areas of land that had been cleared, and farmed in previous years, by what they imagined were thousands of people. The fields were now abandoned. "[P]ity it was and is to see, so many goodly fields, and so well seated, without men to dress and manure the same." Winslow, Hopkins, and Squanto set off for Pokanoket early that morning, and were accompanied by six other Indians who decided to come along.

After walking about six miles along the banks of what is now called the Taunton River, they needed to cross over to the other side of the river bank. It was low tide, so Squanto and the other Indians indicated to Hopkins and Winslow that they needed to remove their breeches and wade across. As the group was just about to the other side of the river, two elderly men jumped out of the grass with bows and arrows drawn. It turned out these were the only two survivors from that area, and they had mistaken the group as enemy Narragansett. Winslow and Hopkins remembered these two elderly men as examples of "valor and courage," who with "shill voices and great courage . . .

charged upon us with bows . . . thinking to take advantage of us in the water." After they established they were friends and not enemies, they sat down and had a small meal together, and Hopkins and Winslow gave bead bracelets to the old men as a gift.

Stephen and Edward remembered the travel this day as very hot, but noted that the area was full of springs and rivers, so finding fresh water was not much of a problem. They also noted that the Indians who joined them in their travel were more than willing to help, by carrying clothing and supplies; Hopkins and Winslow even felt comfortable enough letting their native porters carry their guns. They would report back to Plymouth that the area was full of "much good timber, both oak, walnut tree, fir, beech, and exceeding great chestnut trees. The country in respect of the lying of it, is both champaign and hilly, like many places in England. In some places it is very rocky both above ground and in it: and though the country be wild and overgrown with woods, yet the trees stand not thick, but a man may well ride a horse amongst them."

A little further along in their journey, one of the Indians in the group spotted a man off in the distance. Unsure if it was a Narragansett, Hopkins and Winslow called for their guns, and relayed to Squanto they were not scared, their two guns would be good enough to defend them against twenty enemy. But after calling out to the man, they found it was just a local resident and two women. They shared a drink of water together, and continued on. Even further down the trail, they met another man with two women, with baskets full of roasted crab and dried shellfish, so they shared a meal together, and gave the women some strings of beads as gifts. Soon after, they arrived at a town not too far away from Pokanoket, and there they had a small meal of oysters and fish, before continuing on.

That afternoon they arrived at Pokanoket, only to find that Massasoit was not home. Luckily he was not too far away, so he was sent for and arrived a couple hours later. Hopkins and Winslow saluted him with a volley of shot—a demonstration of their weapons orchestrated by Squanto, perhaps in an early effort to intimidate his fellow natives into believing he had the power to control the English. Unfortunately, Squanto had failed to forewarn the women and children of the custom, so when Hopkins picked up his gun to prepare to shoot into the air to welcome Massasoit, the women and children panicked and screamed, thinking they were about to be attacked. They would not be pacified until Hopkins laid down his gun again—at which point Squanto was able to calm everyone down and explain the English custom of firing guns into the air to welcome a dignitary.

After the somewhat botched welcoming ceremony, they then went into Massasoit's house and sat down, and they presented him with various gifts, including a copper chain and a red cotton horseman's coat, and they delivered their messages, namely: their desire was to continue maintaining the peaceful relations they had established; that they wanted to trade for some corn seed; and that they wanted him to help them make contact to repay their debts for the corn and beans that were taken near the Pamet River when they had first come into the country. And they also expressed their situation: that they were just a small group of men that could not support so many Indian guests as were routinely visiting Plymouth, but that they welcomed anyone who came to trade, and that they would welcome any special guest that was sent by Massasoit. The copper chain was to be given to any special guest or messenger he wanted to send to Plymouth, and anyone with the chain would be treated as a special guest of Massasoit. But for everyone else, they could no longer afford to give of their meager food or supplies.

Massasoit responded very well to the entire message that Hopkins and Winslow had delivered to him. He answered that he was happy to continue their league of friendship. He replied that he would send a message to Pamet to find out who the corn had belonged to that had been taken by the Pilgrims, so that they could repay the Indians there for what was taken. He agreed to share some of his corn seed. And he told them that his men would stop pestering the colony.

Following his answers to Hopkins and Winslow, he then made a great speech to all the men that had gathered around him. Because Hopkins and Winslow could not understand the speech except for a few tidbits which Squanto translated, and because it was extraordinarily long, the two found it very tedious and boring. Massasoit went through a recitation of every town that reported to him, rhetorically asking each town, was he not the supreme leader of their community? And then instructing each town to bring skins and trade with Plymouth, and be at peace with them.

After that, Massasoit set down with Hopkins and Winslow, and had a more social conversation, while smoking a pipe together. Hopkins and Winslow described what England was like, and talked about King James, the greatest king of the English, . . . who did not have a wife. Massasoit could hardly believe it! One of the greatest kings in the world, and he does not have at least one wife? Massasoit had several wives.

Massasoit expressed his concern that the neighboring Narragansett were in league with the French—something that could potentially shift the balance of power, and probably another reason that Massasoit wanted ties with the English.

As evening grew on, Hopkins and Winslow were somewhat surprised that nobody offered them any supper—but Massasoit apparently did not have anything at the moment, because he had been away from his home for some time. When Hopkins and Winslow desired to go to sleep, Massasoit lodged them in his own bed, with himself and one of his wives too—so the four of them slept all together. The bed was simply some wooden planks set about a foot off the ground, with a thin mat covering on top. Later in the evening, two other men, "for want of room," pressed into the bed as well. The Indians "sang themselves to sleep," something the English were definitely not accustomed to, and Winslow and Hopkins were both pestered by fleas and lice all night—which was better than the mosquitoes outside, but still an annoyance. Winslow wrote they were just as tired from their lodging as they were from their journey.

The next day, things livened up a little. Many of the local sachems of the towns nearby received word that the Englishmen were at Pokanoket, and so they stopped by to visit. The men engaged themselves in gaming and gambling, with skins and knives as the reward for winning. Hopkins and Winslow challenged the Indians to shooting competitions, arrows vs. guns, and demonstrated hailshot by shooting into a target: everyone marveled at all the little holes it produced. Around noon, Massasoit brought in two large fish, which he shared with Hopkins and Winslow—and with forty other Indians—so they only got but a couple bites. Hopkins, desperate for additional sustenance, purchased a small partridge, which he shared with Winslow. It was the only food they had eaten in almost a day, so they were tired and ready to head home before they were too weak to make the journey.

On Friday, they made their departure in the very early morning. Massasoit assigned Squanto to visit some of the Indian villages to encourage them to come trade with Plymouth, and appointed another of his men, Tokamahamon, to guide Hopkins and Winslow back to Plymouth, whom they found "faithful before, and after upon all occasions."

Tokamahamon guided Hopkins and Winslow back to the fishing weir near modern-day Taunton, where they again received a string of dried shellfish, and a handful of parched corn, which was "very precious at that time of year." But there was not much food to be had; they gave the shellfish to the six Indians, including Tokamahamon, that were with them. They ate a spoonful of cornmeal whenever they sat and had a drink; and then smoked a tobacco pipe to help kill the hunger pains. Tokamahamon thought he knew of a house that would have more food, so they walked five miles off-track to reach the house, only to find nobody home and no food. That evening, they did manage to trade for half a muskrat and half of a fish called a shad, and somewhat later they did manage to catch a few fish themselves, which they roasted at night and ate for breakfast the next morning. There was a significant thunder and lightning storm that night, and it was so windy and rainy that Hopkins and Winslow were not able to keep a fire burning through the night. The storm continued into the next day, and for the remainder of their journey, save the last two miles. They arrived back at Plymouth that night, "wet, weary, and surbated."

Chapter 13

MRS. HOPKINS AND THE WOMEN OF PLYMOUTH

No doubt Elizabeth Hopkins and all the couple's children were relieved to see their father's safe return home from Pokanoket. On the other hand, Stephen must have been overjoyed that his wife had survived the *Mayflower's* voyage—pregnant no less—and survived the horrific first winter, so that she could be there to welcome him home from such a trip. There were eighteen adult women onboard the *Mayflower*—all married, and traveling with their husbands, and in some cases with their children as well. Only four were still alive: Eleanor Billington, Mary Brewster, Susanna White, and Elizabeth Hopkins.

Unlike the men who went ashore frequently and labored outdoors daily to construct buildings and houses, the women remained in their dirty, damp, dingy quarters on the *Mayflower* for months after arrival, coming ashore only to do laundry or to attend Sunday services. Those women who did get to spend any time ashore were likely working in the hospital house caring for the sick, exposing their bodies to even more pathogens.

William Bradford blamed the sickness and death the first winter on the hard conditions the explorers had to endure while seeking out a place to locate the colony—wading through water, sailing in sleet and snow, and lodging themselves in barricades with little protection from wind and rain. But in reality, it was the women, more than the men, who suffered the brunt of the first winter.

A couple of orphaned girls, Priscilla Mullins and Governor Carver's maidservant Dorothy, were nearing marriageable age, and there was a small group of young teenage girls, most about thirteen, who also helped out with some of the more traditionally female duties—Elizabeth Tilley, Desire Minter, Mary Chilton, and Constance Hopkins. All but Constance were orphaned—Desire had been orphaned prior to the *Mayflower's* voyage and came in the care of Governor Carver; Elizabeth Tilley and Mary Chilton both lost their fathers and mothers the first winter.

Most colonies that were funded by English investors did not bring women with them. These companies made money by labor: chopping wood, fishing, trading furs with the Indians, mining, constructing—the usefulness of women for such an enterprise was considered dubious at best. The laborers could cook, clean and care for themselves at a minimal level, and that was all that was necessary. If the companies were to bring women, they would have to be fed, clothed and housed at company expense, yet they would not provide hard labor, nor could they carry weapons or fight to help defend the colony. And women would be a distraction to men who were supposed to be concentrating on work: labor camps did not need women and girls.

But the Pilgrims' joint-stock company was different. It was organized by a church that wanted to relocate its congregation to America. They could not afford to do so by themselves, so they formed the joint-stock company for the purpose of gathering enough capital to undertake the move. Unlike Jamestown, Plymouth would be founded by families: men, women, and children: even toddlers like Damaris Hopkins and infants like Oceanus. The selling point for investors? There were several. First, the employees were honest, religiously-minded men, women, and children with strong moral fibers—they could be trusted to be honest and faithful, and as a result God would bless their business ventures. Second, they were family groups, so they would be long-term employees with a strong desire for the financial success of the company, which would bring financial success to their families. Third, having wives would make the men happier and more responsible and comfortable—meaning they would be healthier, more rested, and more productive employees. And lastly, the presence of women and children would make the colony seem less of a threat to the Native American groups, making trade and commerce easier.

Pilgrim wives took on numerous critical roles within the family, many of which are undervalued by today's society, but which were absolutely necessary to the success of the 17th century English household. Women were in charge of maintaining the household—the cooking of the family's meals, cleaning, doing laundry, gardening, and some farming and animal care. A lot more labor was involved with these tasks than it is today. With no running water, laundry and dishes started first with hauling buckets of water up from the nearest stream or lake—no small task. Cooking meant first milking the goat, gathering the eggs, grinding and pounding the corn into cornmeal, stripping the feathers off the goose, cleaning the fish, and getting a cooking fire just right. Laundry was done by manually soaking, scrubbing and wringing—over and over and over again. And men's clothes were not dirtied from a light day in the office! They were dirtied with one or more days of sweat from chopping and sawing wood, tilling the soil, baling hay, slaughtering a deer—or in Mrs. Hopkins' case, shipwrecking on Clark's Island after being attacked by Nauset and spending the day in sea-spray; or hiking thirty miles to visit Massasoit, crossing rivers and bays and sleeping in open fields and Indian houses. Men were extremely dirty creatures, but the women somehow managed to keep things halfway decent.

In the hierarchy that governed the Pilgrims' world, men ruled over women, but women were not at the bottom of the totem pole. In the household, the wife ruled over the servants (including manservants) and the children. She governed the household, and in the absence of her husband's authority, she was first in command.

Women in Plymouth did not normally own any personal property or real estate (unless they were widowed and inherited it); they had no vote in town meetings or other political venues; they were only entitled to a third of their husbands estate if he should die; divorce was not an option except in the most extreme circumstances; and in church, women had to sit separately from the men, and remain silent. Women were not without a voice, though: in the home, women could engage in political and religious discussions and try to influence their husband's decisions, as long as it was done with modesty and deference.

The Separatist church taught that women must be obedient and submissive to their husbands in all things. They were obligated to obey all their husband's "lawful commands" as if they had come from Christ Himself. Men, for their part, were taught that they must love and support their wives in the same way, and with the same passion, that Christ loves and supports his churches—leading her, guiding her, protecting her, and—when necessary—disciplining her.

The correct and appropriate way to discipline a wife was a hot topic in the seventeenth century. Discipline could take many forms, but misbehaving wives were subject to the same punishments that children could get, including corporal punishment. But despite its legality and general (if tenuous) social acceptability, the Separatist and Puritan churches did actually have misgivings about physically disciplining wives as an ordinary course of practice. The Bible says not to spare the rod for children, but makes no such statement with regard to women. Pastor John Robinson, the long time leader of the Pilgrims' congregation in Leiden, Holland, recommended alternative discipline for a wife, such as restricting her freedoms (think of that as the modern-day equivalent of a grounding), as did John Dod, one of the religious scholars whose interpretations of the Bible and religious discourses were widely read by the Pilgrims. For the most serious offenses, though, a beating may be necessary. Men received beatings too—the only difference is that women often received their punishment at home from their husband, whereas men usually received their whipping from the court system.

Child rearing was one of the main duties for a married English woman. Assuming a wife survived the childbirths, she could be expected to have a child every two to three years. The idea of using any form of birth control was completely counter to the Biblical command, "be fruitful and multiply," and large families were the norm. Large families were also beneficial in many ways—the more boys, the more laborers; the more girls, the more house-hands.

Stephen and Elizabeth Hopkins were married in 1617, and their first daughter Damaris came along in 1618. Their next child, Oceanus, was born during the *Mayflower's* voyage in 1620. The couple's next children came in rough succession: Caleb, born about 1622; Deborah, born about 1625; Damaris, born about 1628; Ruth, born about 1630; and Elizabeth, born about 1632. By the time of her namesake's birth, Mrs. Hopkins had had seven children, plus two step-children, and she was approaching her late 40s. Elizabeth would be the couple's last child.

Chapter 14

NAUSET, NEMASKET, AND MASSACHUSETT

The visit to Massasoit at Pokanoket in April 1621 was probably not Stephen's last expedition on behalf of the company. In early June, sixteen year old John Billington got himself lost in the woods and wandered "up and down for five days living on berries and what he could find." After about twenty miles, he stumbled into an Indian village at Manomet, and they shuffled him off to Nauset—the group of Indians that first accosted the Pilgrims shortly after their arrival at First Encounter Beach. The Pilgrims received word of where he was at, and on June 11, sent out an expedition of ten men, plus Tisquantum and Tokamahamon as guides, to go pick him up. The names of the men who went on the expedition were not recorded, but given Stephen's participation in most other Indian-related expeditions, he would seem to have been a likely candidate to have been among the ten who went. Others were likely Captain Myles Standish, Edward Winslow (who appears to have written the account of the expedition), and probably John Billington, father of the lost boy.

Stephen Hopkins, who had seen just about every maritime disaster and weather spectacle possible, was in for something new this time. The expedition shallop, on its way to Nauset, in the midst of a tremendous lightning and thunderstorm, encountered a funnel cloud that touched down in Cape Cod Bay not far away from them, forming a tornado known as a water spout.

The men pulled the shallop into Cummaquid, near modern-day Barnstable, where they spent the night. In the morning they made contact with some natives out catching lobster, and determined that young Billington was further up the Cape. They visited the local sachem, Iyanough, whom they reported was "a man not exceeding twenty six years of age, but very personable, gentle, courteous, and fair conditioned, indeed not like the savage, save for his attire; his entertainment was answerable to his parts, and his cheer plentiful and various." There they also met an elderly woman who came to see them because she had never seen English before. She wept and cried greatly, explaining that her three sons had been taken by Captain Hunt, and that she had been deprived of her children in her elderly years. The Pilgrims were "very grievous," but there was little they could do but condemn Hunt as a bad man, and give the old woman some "small trifles."

After lunch, they headed out for Nauset to find the wayward Billington boy. Arriving in the evening, the Nauset came out in large numbers to greet the shallop. But the ten Plymouth men were still leery of an ambush—these were, after all, the same men who had attacked them less than a year earlier. But the return party did make a key observation: "[I]ndeed it was no marvel they did so [attack the Pilgrims at First Encounter Beach], for howsoever, through snow or otherwise, we saw no houses, yet we were in the midst of them."

It was a very tense situation. The Pilgrims stood guard and allowed only a few to come close to the shallop—one of whom was the owner of the corn they had taken from Corn Hill. He was invited to Plymouth and promised full payment for what had been taken. They traded for a few token skins as well. When night began to fall, the local sachem, Aspinet, came with more than a hundred men, and young John, who was "behung with beads," was ceremoniously returned. A peace was agreed to, and some gifts were exchanged.

Just before departing, the men were told a rumor: it was believed the Narragansett had just attacked the Wampanoag and captured Massasoit. With half the men of Plymouth out on this expedition, that left the town rather defenseless; and had Massasoit been taken, Plymouth had an obligation to come to his aid. They tried to make a mad-dash back for home, but it was not to be—the winds were going the wrong way and they had run out of drinking water, so they returned instead to Iyanough at Cummaquid, where the entire village came out to greet them. Iyanough was not able to come up with much water for the thirsty expedition, but they did get some entertainment: "the women joined hand in hand, singing and dancing before the shallop, the men also showing all the kindness they could, Iyanough himself taking a bracelet from about his neck, and hanging it upon one of us."

First Encounter Beach, in modern-day Eastham, looking out into Cape Cod Bay. This is where the Pilgrim explorers were attacked in the morning by the Nauset. Back in the 17th century, this area was heavily wooded with juniper, pine, and oak, and not grassy as it is today.

They set off again that evening for home, but did not make it far. The next morning they were still within sight of Cummaquid, so Iyanough came to visit them once more, and they returned back to Cummaquid to get some water before heading back home.

Finally, that night, they made it back to Plymouth, where they learned that Massasoit had indeed been attacked and pushed out of his territory, and possibly taken by the Narragansett. Rumor had it that one of Massasoit's own petty sachems, Corbitant, was in close league with the Narragansett, and was plotting the overthrow of Massasoit, and that he was currently lodged at Nemasket—the town about fifteen miles from Plymouth that Hopkins and Winslow had previously stopped at. Tokamahamon was sent to Corbitant to see what the situation was, and Squanto and Hobomok, one of Massasoit's leading men, went in search of Massasoit himself to see what they could find. Hobomok and Squanto secretly lodged at Nemasket for a night, but were exposed, and Corbitant's guards surprised the men in their house and successfully took Squanto captive. Hobomok managed to escape, and fled back to Plymouth, assuming Squanto had been killed—Corbitant had been heard saying that if Squanto were dead, the English would lose their ability to communicate.

The news was taken very seriously at Plymouth. To have a rebellious sachem mutiny against Massasoit, and then turn around and kill their only interpreter—that was just unacceptable and had to be avenged. A show of force was needed. The Pilgrims appointed ten men (or fourteen by Bradford's account)—Stephen Hopkins and Edward Winslow amongst them—to avenge the killing of Squanto by killing Corbitant and taking captive another sachem, Nepeof, believed to be a co-conspirator.

Led by Captain Myles Standish, the gang of armed men set out for Nemasket with a well-planned surprise attack on Corbitant's house scheduled for midnight. When they got within a few miles of Nemasket, they went off the path a little distance to hide out until nightfall. Unfortunately, after nightfall, they got lost trying to find the trail again, and stumbled around in the rainy darkness for several hours, disheartening and frustrating everyone, until Stephen Hopkins—who had been there before—managed to pick up the trail again. Just outside the village, they all sat down, ate a midnight snack, said some prayers, and then marched quietly into town and surrounded Corbitant's house.

The surprise attack went off: some of the men entered the house, guns ablaze, demanding everybody freeze, and Corbitant identify himself. A few tried to flee the house, and were promptly assaulted for their attempt. Once everything calmed down after the sudden shock of the surprise attack, it was eventually communicated to the posse that their target, Corbitant, had left earlier that day and was not in the village. They were further told that Squanto had not been killed by Corbitant, but was still in the village, in another house, sleeping. The men commandeered the house for the night, and Hobomok rounded up Squanto and Tokamahamon to ensure they were Ok.

The following morning they marched into the middle of the town and had breakfast at Squanto's house at Nemasket, and then made a speech to the village: The Pilgrims were not afraid of Corbitant, and though he escaped this time, yet he could not hide from them forever—if he continued to threaten the Pilgrims and provoke others against them, it would not be tolerated. Further, if Massasoit was not safely returned, or if Corbitant ever attacked any of Plymouth's Indian guides and helpers, they would avenge it by killing him. They also apologized for the injuries that were sustained during the attack on Corbitant's house, and invited anyone who was injured to come back with them to Plymouth for medical treatment—an offer that two Indians, a man and a woman, took up.

Stephen Hopkins may have also been involved in another voyage to visit the Massachusett Indians a few months later in September 1621. The Massachusett Indians lived to the north of the Wampanoag in what is now Boston Harbor, and some were still technically subject to Massasoit. There had been rumors that some of the Massachusett were ill-disposed towards the English of Plymouth and were not in full agreement with Massasoit on the peace, so the colonists felt it was important to visit them, establish peace, and get themselves yet another trading partner to further their business.

Ten men were appointed for this expedition, but their names were not recorded—Captain Standish was one of them, and Edward Winslow appears to have been the chronicler of the expedition; presumably Hopkins went as well. Three Indians, including Tisquantum, and probably Hobomok and Tokamahamon, went and acted as guides and translators.

The expedition departed at midnight, because that is when the tide allowed for it. The Pilgrims thought the Massachusetts Bay would only be about six or eight hours away, but eighteen hours later they finally arrived, having significantly underestimated the distance. Captain Standish took four of his men, plus one of the Indian guides, to make contact with the Indians, leaving behind two sentinels to guard the hill, and three men to remain with the shallop. Along the way, Captain Standish and his four men met an Indian woman coming to gather her lobsters from the bayside, and she directed them where to find the others.

They there met with the sachem, Obbatinewat, who welcomed them. He explained he did not live in a settled place, for fear of his enemies, the Tarrantines, and a neighboring group led by the Squaw Sachem. After agreeing to peace with Plymouth, he went with the expedition so that they could sail across the bay to the other side and attempt to meet with the Squaw Sachem, Obbatinewat's enemy, to make peace with her as well. They anchored in the bay that night, and went ashore the following morning, leaving behind only two men to guard the shallop. Marching in arms, about four miles inland, they came to the house of the former sachem, Nanepeshemet, and his memorial. According to a later author, Thomas Morton, writing in 1637 (who despised the Plymouth Separatists) here they desecrated the memorial and tore it down. But this is not mentioned in the Pilgrims' own accounts.

After marching another mile, they finally encountered a group of women, but the men had all fled. Finally, they managed to get ahold of one man, who came trembling and shaking in fear. He told them that the Squaw Sachem was far away and was not available to be visited, and that everyone else had fled. Squanto recommended they just ransack the women and take what they had, because these Indians were "bad people," but Standish and the men wanted to set a good example, so they just watched the Indian entertainment of singing and dancing, boiled and ate some fish together, and departed without stealing anything.

The Indian women accompanied the expedition back to their shallop, and traded away all the skins they had—even the ones off their back. Edward Winslow noted that they did so with "great shamefacedness, for indeed they are more modest than some of our English women."

With a light moon in the sky, they set off in the early evening, returning home the following afternoon.

Chapter 15

THANKSGIVING

The situation at Plymouth was improving fast. The first winter had taken a severe toll, but since then only two people had died—Governor John Carver, of a sunstroke while working in his cornfield in mid-April, and his wife Katherine who died of a "broken heart" a little more than a month later. The new governor, William Bradford, oversaw continued peaceful relations with Massasoit, and successfully convinced numerous local sachems, from Aspinet at Nauset, Iyanough at Cummaquid, to Obbatinewat in the Massachusetts Bay, to also be at peace. He had come to the aid of Massasoit in the spat with the Narragansett, affirming his conviction to uphold the terms of the peace agreement. They had successfully explored their local area, learned the local paths and trails, followed rivers and streams inland, and even visited neighboring bays to the north and south of Cape Cod. They had established contacts and trading partners around the region. Eleven buildings had been constructed, seven of which were houses—each with their own small English gardens planted with lettuce, onions, and herbs, and they had planted twenty acres of Indian corn, and six acres of barley and peas.

Clearly, the colony had been blessed by God, so what could have been more appropriate than to set aside a special time for thanksgiving? After the harvest, probably in late September or early October (the exact date is not known), Governor Bradford sent out some men to hunt waterfowl and wild turkey, and others to fish for bass and cod, of which both parties brought back enough to feed the colony for an entire week. Massasoit and ninety of his men showed up for the party with five deer that were "bestowed upon our Governor, and upon the captain, and others." The "others" no doubt included Edward Winslow and Stephen Hopkins, whom Massasoit had been

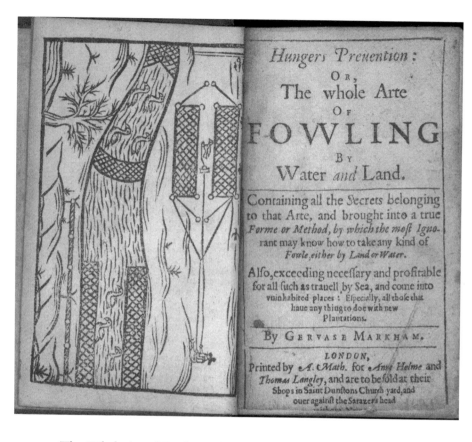

Hungers ℣*renention* :
OR,
The whole Arte
OF
FOWLING
BY
Water *and* Land.

Containing all the Secrets belonging
to that Arte, and brought into a true
Forme or Method, by which the most Igno-
rant may know how to take any kind of
Fowle ,either by Land or Water.

Alfo,exceeding neceffary and profitable
for all fuch as trauell by Sea, and come into
vninhabited places : Efpecially, all thofe that
haue any thing to doe with new
Plantations.

By GERVASE MARKHAM.

LONDON,
Printed by *A. Math.* for *Anne Helme* and
Thomas Langley, and are to be fold at their
Shops in Saint Dunftons Church yard,and
ouer againft the Sarazens head

The *Whole Art of Fowling*, a book by Gervase Markham, with a picture opposite the cover illustrating how to catch waterfowl using nets. Published in 1621, this book was dedicated to Sir Edwin Sandys, one of the men at the Virginia Company of London who was responsible for helping get the Pilgrims' voyage underway. It is quite possible that Markham wrote this book in response to the Pilgrims' voyage, and the need that he saw, that new and inexperienced settlers might want a book illustrating and describing the techniques for hunting waterfowl.

previously unable to provide for earlier that year when they had come to visit him. The Pilgrims and Wampanoag feasted and entertained each other for three days, where they "exercised their arms," and engaged in various sporting activities and recreations.

In a letter written back to England shortly after the Thanksgiving celebration, Edward Winslow wrote these comments about the Indians:

> We have found the Indians very faithful in their covenant of peace with us; very loving and ready to pleasure us: we often go to them, and they come to us; some of us have been fifty miles by land in the country with them; the occasions and relations whereof you shall understand by our general and more full declaration of such things as are worth the noting; yea, it hath pleased God so to possess the Indians with a fear of us, and love unto us, that not only the greatest king amongst them called Massasoit, but also all the princes and peoples round about us, have either made suit unto us, or been glad of any occasion to make peace with us, so that seven of them at once have sent their messengers to us to that end; . . . we entertain them familiarly in our houses, and they as friendly bestowing their venison on us . . . . They are . . . very trusty, quick of apprehension, ripe-witted, just.

All seemed to be going well. The small colony of about twenty-five men, four women, and twenty five children, had just enough corn preserved to comfortably last them through the winter. At least they did until November, when a ship suddenly and unexpectedly appeared on the horizon. It was the *Fortune*, the ship sent out by the company a few months after the *Mayflower's* return . . . the one that was full of laborers recruited from around London.

Onboard were more than thirty men and labor-aged boys, and only two women and one girl. Not onboard: food, provisions, tools, livestock, or anything of significant value to the colonists. The adult population of Plymouth nearly doubled in an instant—and with no additional food, everybody's winter rations were instantly cut in half. Governor Bradford wrote:

> [M]ost of them were lusty young men, and many of them wild enough, who little considered whether, or about what they went till they came into the harbor at Cape Cod, and there saw nothing but a naked and barren place; . . . So they were all landed, but there was not so much as biscuit cake or any other victual for them,

neither had they any bedding, but some sorry things they had in their cabins, nor pot, or pan to dress any meat in; nor over-many clothes, . . . the plantation was glad of this addition of strength, but could have wished, that many of them, had been of better condition; and all of them better furnished with provisions.

The day after landing, one of the two women who were onboard, Mrs. Martha Ford, gave birth. Though the ship consisted mostly of English laborers who had no significant ties to the Pilgrims or their church, there were a few familiar people onboard: Dutchman Moses Simmons and Frenchman Phillip de la Noye were both members of the Leiden church back in the Netherlands. De la Noye's name was "Anglicanized" to Delano; he was an ancestor of President Franklin Delano Roosevelt. There was Robert Cushman, with son Thomas, both of whom had been on the failed *Speedwell* voyage, and were among those who disembarked at that time. And there was Jonathan Brewster, the oldest son of Plymouth church Elder William Brewster.

Another passenger onboard was a nailer, William Palmer, and his son William. William Palmer the elder grew up with young Stephen Hopkins back in Upper Clatford, and as toddlers may well have been best friends—only a few months separated them in age. A letter from 1623 suggests that Hopkins and Palmer were somehow brother-in-laws,[20] but the exact relation has not yet been discovered. In any case, Palmer and Hopkins were reunited—William the father, and William the son, took up residence in the Hopkins household in Plymouth, and the two families appear to have lived together as a joint household at least through 1627, if not longer. William Palmer had left his wife Frances back in England, but she would make the voyage a couple years later.

Although the arrival of the *Fortune* was entirely unexpected, the planters at Plymouth had managed to build up a small store of beaver and otter skins they had received in trade (two hogsheads worth, according to Bradford), and had built up a supply of clapboard as well, so the ship was packed up with a modest cargo, which should have brought some satisfaction to the investors

---

[20]   R.G. Marsden, "A Letter of William Bradford and Isaac Allerton," *American Historical Review* 8(1903):294-301. William Palmer was the only recorded nailer in Plymouth, and the fact he lived in the Hopkins household, and was otherwise very closely associated with the Hopkins family, suggests he is the "nailer" referred to in the letter as being Hopkins' brother.

back in England who to date had received no return on their investment. The furs and clapboard could be sold and the cash obtained would buy a substantial amount of trade goods and trinkets to trade with the Indians for an even greater supply of furs. Everyone could see the profit rolling in!

Unfortunately, on its homeward voyage, the *Fortune* was intercepted by a French warship about twenty-four miles from the Isle d'Yeu, France. The warship was captained by Fontenau de Pennart, and he presented the *Fortune* and the thirteen crewmembers onboard to the governor of the Isle d'Yeu, Monsieur le Marquis de Cera. The *Fortune's* captain, Thomas Barton, was held prisoner in the castle on the island, while the couple passengers (including Robert Cushman) and the crew were held prisoner onboard the ship and "fed . . . with lights, livers, and entrails." The cargo and goods—valued at £500—were confiscated. The French even took away everyone's apparel, the ship's food and drink, ropes, rope lines, even the flags. The company's letters and relations were opened and read; the Marquis kept the ones he wanted.[21] Once they were stripped of everything, the Marquis forced them to sign papers stating he had taken nothing of value from them, and then they were allowed to sail their stripped-down ship back home to England. It was another substantial hit to the already financially-strapped company.

Thomas Weston, the organizer of the joint-stock company, decided it was a losing venture, and jumped ship. But that did not stop him from involving the Plymouth Colony in his future business ventures. He sent out a fishing ship called the *Sparrow* in May 1622, leaving seven more people at Plymouth (with no food or supplies—so the Plymouth joint-stock company had to feed them out if its own supply). In July 1622, two more ships sent out by Thomas Weston arrived, the *Charity* and the *Swan*, with sixty men for a brand new (and competing) colony that was to establish itself at Wessagussett, in the larger and lusher Massachusetts Bay. But the ships stopped at Plymouth, and unloaded their passengers. They lived at Plymouth for several weeks—again tapping Plymouth's business stores—before they headed off to start building their own colony. And when they finally did head out, they left their sick and injured at Plymouth to be cared for by the company's doctor, Samuel Fuller—again, at Plymouth's expense.

For Stephen Hopkins and the other investor-residents of Plymouth, the value of their shares in the company was dwindling fast. Morale was low. Many of the men had left their wives and children back in England, expecting the

---

[21] PRO, State Papers Colonial, Vol. 5, No. 112.

company to send them later—but without any profits to show, convincing additional investors to pay for sending over women and children seemed impossible. At least in this regard, Stephen was one of the lucky ones: of the sixty or so men then living at Plymouth, he was one of only five that actually had a wife already living with him.

What the colony wanted most—outside of trade goods and livestock—were women. Husbands wanted their wives. Widowers wanted new spouses. And young men wanted girls that they could marry. Somehow, as short of funds as they were, the company back in London and the Leiden church congregation back in Holland, managed to get a new voyage organized.

In the late summer of 1623, the colony's shipment of females arrived, via the ship *Anne*. Onboard was William Palmer's wife, Frances, adding another woman to the Hopkins' household. Also onboard: Elder William Brewster's two daughters, Patience and Fear; Francis Cooke's wife Hester, and two daughters Jane and Hester; Doctor Samuel Fuller's wife Bridget; Isaac Allerton's sister Sarah, and his nieces Sarah and Mary Priest; and Richard Warren's wife Elizabeth and five daughters Mary, Elizabeth, Anna, Sarah and Abigail. There were even some single women: Ellen Newton (who would marry *Fortune* passenger John Adams), Mary Buckett (who would marry *Mayflower* passenger George Soule), Christiana Penn (who would marry *Mayflower* passenger Francis Eaton), Alice Carpenter (who would marry Governor Bradford), and Barbara (who would marry Captain Standish). In all, there were at least 42 women and girls onboard. For a colony with only a few women, this was a huge change in the social dynamic.

Not to be lost, there were some men onboard the *Anne* as well, including Nicholas Snow. Nicholas was originally from the same region of London that Stephen and Elizabeth Hopkins had lived in from 1617 to 1620, and the two may have possibly known each other prior to meeting at Plymouth. Snow took up residence in the Hopkins and Palmer household, and within a couple of years he married Stephen's eldest surviving daughter, Constance.

Chapter 16

LAND, CATTLE, AND BUSINESS

Up until the *Anne's* arrival, the Plymouth colonists had worked and farmed collectively; all the crops were brought into a collective company storehouse and then rationed back out to everyone (the employees) in equal allotments. But Governor Bradford and the others soon realized this was not working out as well as had been intended—the productive individuals were getting allotted the same amount as the lazy do-nothings of the colony, and this was killing morale. Bradford's solution: allot everyone their own plots of land, for their own benefit and subsistence. Every person (man, woman and child) received an acre of land, which were logically combined together into larger family plots.

The Hopkins family received six acres: one for Stephen, one for Elizabeth, and one each for children Constance, Giles, Caleb, and Deborah. The family's six acres were located just south of Town Brook, upon what later became known as Watson's Hill—the hill that a couple years earlier, Massasoit had gazed down upon them. Perhaps it was not the best piece of farming ground, up on a hill where hauling water would be more laborious; but it had a great view at least. Hopkins' six acres were bordered by land that was allotted to, of all people, Hobomok and his family (including his multiple wives)—the only Indian to have ever been allotted acreage within the town's border. The next plot south after Hobomok's land was a four acre plot assigned out to John Howland's family.

Leiden Street, Plymouth. This is the street where the Pilgrims' original houses were located. Of course they have long since been replaced with more modern housing. Stephen's plot was located approximately where the shorter two-story building is, at the left-hand side of the image. The three story white house in the middle is sitting approximately on John Howland's plot, and the house in the immediate foreground is roughly sitting on Samuel Fuller's plot. From this angle, Plymouth Harbor is at the photographer's back, and Town Brook is at the photographer's left, past another row of houses on the other side of the street and then down a small hill.

The six acres were for farming, however: the Hopkins, Palmer, and Snow families continued to reside in their original house, built on the northeast corner of what is now Leyden and Main Street in Plymouth. Their next door neighbor to the east was the John and Elizabeth Howland, and the house beyond that was Doctor Fuller's. Across the highway to the west was Governor Bradford's household, and across the street to the south was Elder William Brewster's family. Kitty-corner was the rambunctious Billington family.

While life in Plymouth was indeed becoming more comfortable—there were now women and children, houses, and farmland—the business itself was sinking fast. Investors were frustrated at the continued lack of return; and they were frustrated that the Leiden church was insisting on sending women and children—whom they viewed as company liabilities because they consumed food and supplies without providing useful (i.e. profit-generating) labor. The company did have some valuable assets—a large territory of exclusive trading rights and large tracts of land—but it was failing to generate any further income; new competitors were moving in to the north at Wessagussett; and it was taking on more and more debt to fund its operations. Investors were jumping ship at an alarming rate, so something had to be done.

About this same time, Stephen had a minor financial dispute of his own with the treasurer of the joint-stock company, then John Peirce. Edward Doty and Edward Leister's contracts were up, and Stephen apparently wanted their two shares (£20 par value) cashed out. But the company was losing so much money, Stephen had to settle for just £6 cash out of the company's treasury. He would get the remainder, £14, in the form of goods from the company's assets in Plymouth, probably most of it in the form of corn. Peirce had originally asked Hopkins to take a £4 loss on his shares, but apparently Plymouth's leadership overruled that because Stephen's brother-in-law, William Palmer, had been providing them with a significant supply of nails.[22]

Following the initial financial difficulties, long-time Leiden church member and *Mayflower* passenger Isaac Allerton was appointed to return to England, to start negotiations with the London shareholders and other financial backers. In November 1626, an agreement was reached. The Plymouth colonist-shareholders would purchase the outstanding shares of the company from all the remaining English investors, for £1800 (to be

---

[22] R.G. Marsden, "A Letter of William Bradford and Isaac Allerton," *American Historical Review* 8(1903):294-301, and Charles Deane, "Records of the Council for New England," *Proceedings of the American Antiquarian Society* (Cambridge, 1867), pp. 93-94.

paid in £200 annual installments), and assume the colony's £600 of debt. The overall adventure was a substantial loss to the London investors—most only got back about a third of their original investment—but the forty-two remaining London shareholders were happy to get out with whatever they could, as most now expected they would eventually lose everything.

The Plymouth purchasers—who included Stephen Hopkins, son-in-law Nicholas Snow, and brother-in-law William Palmer, among fifty others—were in no position to afford their grand purchase, so to give themselves some level of financial credibility, four London investors—the most faithful shareholders of the original group, James Shirley, John Beauchamp, Timothy Hatherly and Richard Andrews—remained onboard to handle the company's business in England, such as receiving and selling off the furs and lumber sent back from Plymouth, and dispatching new supply ships. These moderately wealthy businessmen had also lent, and would continue to lend, the company money in the form of bonds, at favorable interest rates they could not have gotten on the open market.

Now that the Plymouth colonists fully owned the company, one of the first things they did was to divide up and assign out some of their landholdings—establishing true private property. For land, the residents now got official title to their house and house plot in Plymouth, as well as to the acreage they had received in the 1623 Division of Land. So now Stephen Hopkins owned six acres of Watson's Hill free and clear, as well as his house at the corner of the highway and street in the center of Plymouth.

The colonists also took the opportunity to divide up the company-owned livestock, which then consisted of about sixteen cattle and twenty-two goats. The livestock was grouped into twelve different lots, deemed to be roughly equal in value to one another. And the Plymouth households were likewise grouped into twelve groupings, and lots were drawn to see which family groups got possession of which livestock.

The Hopkins household at the time consisted of Stephen and Elizabeth and their children Giles, Caleb and Deborah, along with now-married daughter Constance Snow and her husband Nicholas; and Stephen's brother-in-law William Palmer, along with Palmer's wife Frances and son William. For the purpose of the Division, the Hopkins' kitty-corner neighbors, the Billingtons (consisting of John, his wife Ellen, and their youngest son Francis) were also grouped in with them. The lot they drew was for "a black weaning calf, to which was added the calf of this year to come of the black cow, which fell to John Shaw and his company, which proving a bull they were to keep it ungelt 5 years for common use and after to make their best of it." The lot also consisted of two female goats.

Kerry cattle, the ancient "black cow" breed most probably owned by Stephen Hopkins, and the other early Plymouth residents. They are now considered a rare historic breed. These cattle were photographed by Ruth Leslie on her croft in Ross-shire, Ireland.

The cow that belonged to John Shaw was the lesser of two black cows that had come on the *Anne* in 1623. Both black cattle in the Hopkins' lot (one apparently not yet born) were likely of the Kerry breed, an ancient dairy breed that still survives today. The Kerry cow is a long-lived dairy cow, capable of calving even at 15 years of age. It is described by the Kerry Cattle Society as being well ribbed with fine bone, slender white horns tipped with black, alert and light on her feet, equally suited to being one of a big herd or single house cows. The bull is usually docile and easily managed. They are extremely hardy and will out winter quite happily, growing a good coat of hair which keeps the cold out. The butterfat of the Kerry is easier to digest than most, with a typical cow producing two to three gallons of milk per day. [23] The two "she-goats" were also a valuable source of milk for the Hopkins'—especially since it would be a couple years before they would likely see any milk production from their "black weaning calf."

Cattle, it would turn out, would quickly become one of the most valuable commodities in early Plymouth, and the price for a cow would stay extraordinarily high for nearly a decade, until imports and local breeding would finally catch up with demand.

Poultry and swine were not formally divided up in the 1627 Division—they may have just been left "as is," with families keeping those that they already were maintaining. By 1628, a Dutch visitor to Plymouth, Isaac de Rasieres, would note there were about fifty pigs within the colony, so it is quite probable the Hopkins family had a number of swine as well. Peter Brown, a weaver by trade who lived across the street and down a house from the Hopkins', owned at least eight sheep and fourteen swine when he died in 1633. [24] That same year, Samuel Fuller, the town's doctor who lived in the second house to the west of Hopkins, owned thirty swine (14 of which were just little piglets), four sheep, six goats, and even an ass (the only one known in early Plymouth). [25]

---

[23]   http://www.kerrycattle.ie/

[24]   C.H. Simmons, ed., *Plymouth Colony Records, Volume 1: Wills and Inventories, 1633-1669*, pp. 21-23.

[25]   Ibid., pp. 51-54.

Chapter 17

PLYMOUTH GOVERNMENT

With the Plymouth colonists no longer beholden to their London shareholders, they began to focus more on their colony and its government. Within a few years, the Plymouth Colony was maintaining detailed court records, civil and vital records, and carefully recording property deeds. One of the very first records of the colony was a list of freemen, made in the winter of 1632/1633.[26] As would be expected, Stephen was recorded on the list, and undoubtedly had been a freeman from the very beginning.

Of perhaps more interest is the fact that Stephen is listed as one of seven men elected to the governor's council.[27] The governor's council handled civil disputes and cases that arose between the colony's quarterly court sessions. For example, on January 2, William Bennett sold Stephen Hopkins' former servant Edward Doty a flich of bacon for beaver skins that were supposed to have been worth three pounds sterling—but it turned out the beaver skins were really only worth half as much as claimed. The council decided to appoint Robert Hicks and Francis Eaton to arbitrate the dispute. Stephen also was present to hear the case of Thomas Brian, a servant of Samuel Eddy who had run away for five days before being returned by an Indian. Brian was sentenced to be "privately whipped before the governor and council." Other disputes were heard during the next three months, including a complaint by a servant whose master was not properly clothing him; a disputed doctor's bill between Francis Eaton and Samuel Fuller; acknowledgement of land transactions and

---

[26] PCR 1:3.
[27] PCR 1:5.

a cattle transaction; acknowledgement of labor agreements; and a request to establish a water work on Town Brook for grinding corn.[28]

Stephen Hopkins was also appointed to the tax assessment committee, which rated and taxed everyone at Plymouth based on their estates. Stephen himself was taxed £1, 7s. Of the nearly ninety people that were taxed, only five were taxed more than Stephen (Isaac Allerton, Edward Winslow, William Bradford, John Jenny, and Richard Church), indicating Stephen was among the more well-off in Plymouth. William Palmer was taxed for the same amount, and Nicholas Snow at a lesser 18 shillings.[29]

At the quarterly court sessions, the governor and council heard and ruled on criminal cases and made laws. For example, at the April 1633 session, the council heard a number of cases: John Holmes was sent to the stocks for two hours and fined twenty shillings for drunkenness; John and Joan Hewes were sentenced to the stocks for conceiving a child while they were engaged but not yet married; John and Alice Thorpe were dealt with more severely because their child was conceived prior to any engagement or marriage—so they both got the stocks, plus a forty shilling fine. And the bacon-for-beaver deal that went awry spawned a slander accusation: Edward Doty apparently called William Bennett a "rogue." Doty was fined fifty shillings—thirty to the victim and twenty as a punitive fine. The council also passed an act that required all households to supply one man sufficient for labor, at a time to be appointed by the governor, to repair the pathway that led to a nearby spring.[30]

At the July session of the court, Stephen Hopkins and the council agreed upon a new law, "That the person in whose house any were found or suffered to drink drunk to be left to the arbitrary fine and punishment of the governor and council, according to the nature and circumstance of the same.[31]" That law would eventually come back around to bite Stephen, but no doubt it seemed reasonable at the time.

As a part of the governor's council, Stephen Hopkins was also involved in assisting families with their probates—primarily by taking estate inventories. Stephen signed off on several estate inventories, including those of Godbert Godbertson, Doctor Samuel Fuller, and John Thorpe, who all had died in

---

[28] PCR 1:7-8.
[29] PCR 1:9-11.
[30] PCR 1:12-13.
[31] PCR 1:13.

1633 as an illness or disease of some kind spread through Plymouth and took a number of lives. Thorp, incidentally, owed Hopkins over £5 for "divers ptics" at the time of his death.[32] In 1634, he was one of the assessors for the estate of Stephen Deane.[33]

In 1634, Stephen was reelected to the governor's council—this time the governor was Thomas Prence. At that session, amongst many other issues, the court authorized a 2 pence bounty on wolves; and Stephen's former servant, Edward Doty, was back in court, this time fighting a complaint by a servant that he was not paying him.[34] Doty would be back at the March court session, this time charged with assaulting and drawing blood from Josias Cooke.[35]

Stephen was re-elected again in 1635, and again in 1636.[36] Aside from being a member of the governor's council, he also periodically took other one-time positions. He was on a couple of tax assessor committees; he was occasionally appointed to survey and divide up new tracts of land; and he was appointed to committees that investigated ways to further the colony's trade. At the March 1636 court session, Stephen was appointed to mow the ground between Thomas Clark and George Soule's property, as well as "up the river, as formerly.[37]"

---

[32] Simmons, PCR-WI 1:39.

[33] Ibid., 1:59.

[34] PCR 1:21,23.

[35] PCR 1:26.

[36] PCR 1:32, 36.

[37] PCR 1:41.

Chapter 18

BATTERY

Stephen Hopkins seemed to be on the up-and-up. As far as estate and wealth, he was in the top five percent of Plymouth residents. In politics, he had been a member of the Governor's council for at least five years, and probably had been on the council from the very first year. He had worked for three or four different governors—William Bradford, Edward Winslow, Thomas Prence, and probably John Carver. But just as things were coming together, Stephen had a sudden and entirely unexpected change of fortune. The Plymouth Colony court recorded the following, on 7 June 1636[38]:

> John Tisdale, yeoman, entereth an accusation of battery against Stephen Hopkins, assistant to the government, by whom the said John was dangerously wounded, as he affirmeth.

*   *   *

> At the same Court an action of battery was tried between John Tisdale, yeoman, plaintiff, and Stephen Hopkins, Assistant to the Government, def., wherein the def., Stephen Hopkins, was cast in five pounds sterling to our sov. Lord the King, whose peace he had broken, which he ought after a special manner to have kept, and also in forty shillings to the plaintiff, both which he was adjudged to pay.

---

[38]   PCR 1:41, 42.

The jury that served upon these trials were Capt. Myles Standish, John Howland, John Winslow, Edmund Chandler, John Dunham, Richard Church, John Cooke the younger, Thomas Cushman, Joseph Rogers, James Hurst, Kenelm Winslow, William Pontus.

Stephen Hopkins would never again be elected to any government position in Plymouth. This court record—the only historical record of this event—does not provide a significant amount of detail as to what happened. Clearly the two men had a physical altercation, and John was seriously injured as a result, but that is about all that can be said with any certainty.

John Tisdale was a young man, probably just twenty-one years of age, who had arrived at Plymouth not long before the June 1636 court session; he was later granted ten acres of land in October 1637, to the north of Plymouth on the path that led to modern-day Marshfield, and a year later also obtained additional lands in Duxbury. He married about 1640 and moved his family to Taunton, where he lived for more than thirty-five years, before being killed by Indians and having his house burned as a part of the hostilities that led up to King Philip's War in 1675 and 1676.

Why a fifty-five year old man, long time resident and governor's assistant, would pick a fight (and apparently beat up) a twenty-one year old newly-arrived young man, must pique one's curiosity. Hopkins had four unmarried daughters at the time, but the eldest was only about eleven, so the fight was probably not related to them. Hopkins seems to have taken on a lot of servants over his life, and many of those seemed to be troubled individuals—Edward Doty and Edward Leister, the servants that accompanied him on the *Mayflower*, a year after arrival got involved in a sword duel that had to be broken up. Leister, as soon as his term was up, took off for Virginia, while Doty continued to make appearances at court sessions throughout his life—in fact in October 1637, Stephen had actually sat as a juror on the assault trial of his former servant. Edward Doty was accused of assaulting his father-in-law George Clark. Stephen and the other eleven jurors found Doty guilty and sentenced him to a twelve pence fine—a relatively small fine, considering Clark was asking for £5 in damages.[39]

Whatever the case, Stephen was somewhat out of favor with the Plymouth leadership and freemen—at least out of favor enough to prevent him from any

---

[39]   PCR 7:7.

further leadership positions within the colony. He was, however, appointed in March 1637 as an advisor to the governor on matters of furthering the colony's trade, and was appointed to a minor survey group to check out hay ground from Plymouth to the Eel River.

At the June 1637 session of the Plymouth Court, Stephen was one of forty men that volunteered to fight for the English against the Pequot in Connecticut. The Pequot had attacked and killed a number of English settlers in Connecticut, and had attacked or were threatening to attack neighboring Indian groups, which included the Narragansett, Mohegan, and Wampanoag, all of whom were then allied with the English. Primarily a conflict involving the Connecticut governments and the Massachusetts Bay Colony, Plymouth had been asked to support their fellow Englishmen, and belatedly responded at the June 1637 court session by organizing volunteers. By the time Plymouth managed to get organized, the war was over and the Pequot had been almost completely and brutally obliterated—Stephen and the other Plymouth volunteers were never needed.

Perhaps as a result of losing his position as assistant governor, Stephen appears to have taken up a new profession beginning in late 1637—shopkeeper. It was what he and his first wife Mary had done back in Hursley many years ago. His business focus was apparently on "strong waters," as well as beer, wine, and spices—he appears to have had a tavern of sorts running out of his house. His first run-in with Plymouth authorities came at the October session of the 1637 court, when he was presented for "suffering men to drink in his house upon the Lord's day, before the meeting be ended, and also upon the Lord's day, both before and after the meeting, servants and others to drink more than for ordinary refreshing.[40]" The case was held over to the next court, so that testimony could be had from John Barnes.

He was presented with another offense at that same court, this time for "suffering servants and others to sit drinking in his house, contrary to the orders of this Court, and to play at shuffleboard, and such like misdemeanors." For this offense, he was fined forty shillings.[41]

At the next court session in January 1638, Stephen was again presented, this time for allowing his brother-in-law "Old man Palmer," as well as James Cole and William Reynolds, to get drunk at his house. Reynolds was fined and discharged; Old man Palmer died before the court session, and widow

---

[40]   PCR 1:68.

[41]   Ibid.

Frances Palmer testified on behalf of Hopkins, who was ultimately acquitted of the charge.[42]

At the June 1638 court session, Hopkins was back, this time defending the charge that he was selling beer for twice the value it was worth, according to witness Kenelm Winslow. He was also charged for selling wine at "excessive rates, to the oppressing and impoverishing of the colony." Kenelm and John Winslow were witnesses to that charge.[43]

At the September 1638 court session, Hopkins was back once more, this time charged with three more instances of "selling strong water, wine, beer, and nutmeg at excessive rates." For the five instances of price gouging (two at the previous court session, and three at this session), he was fined a total of £5, a fairly substantial fine.[44]

Stephen's overpricing of alcoholic beverages and nutmeg was but a minor issue at the September 1638 court, which spent most of its time dealing with a much more serious crime. Four men, Arthur Peach, Thomas Jackson, Richard Stinnings, and Daniel Cross, were indicted for murder. They had killed an Indian named Penowanyanquis, apparently to steal his wampum—the local Indian currency—and several coats that he had obtained earlier that day in trade. Daniel Cross had escaped custody and run away, but the remaining three men were found guilty by a jury of twelve Plymouth men and sentenced to death by hanging—a sentence that was executed that same day.[45]

Unbeknownst to Stephen at the time, one of the executed men—Arthur Peach—had impregnated one of his maidservants, Dorothy Temple. Indentures were essentially business agreements: Stephen had agreed to care for Dorothy until she turned twenty-one, paying her expenses such as food and clothing, in exchange for Dorothy working for the Hopkins family—helping prepare meals, wash clothes, perhaps even helping with the family business. Now Dorothy was pregnant, still had more than two years left on her contract, and the father of the baby had been executed. Instead of a fair exchange of food and clothing for household labor, the indenture deal had gone bad—the Hopkins family now had to feed, cloth, and support two people, neither of which would be very productive over the next two years!

---

[42] PCR 1:75.

[43] PCR 1:87.

[44] PCR 1:97.

[45] PCR 1:96-97.

Stephen was furious. He tossed the 19-year old girl out of his house and refused to support her—at which point the Plymouth Court stepped in. The Court ruled on 4 February 1639, that Stephen "shall keep her and her child" for the remainder of the term of the indenture, which was a little more than two years, and "if he refuse so to do, then the colony provide for her, and Mr. Hopkins to pay it."

Despite the Court's ruling, Stephen refused to have anything to do with Dorothy, not allowing her back in his house. He was arrested later that day and placed in jail "for his contempt to the Court, and so shall remain committed until he shall either receive his servant Dorothy Temple, or else provide for her elsewhere at his own charge during the term she hath yet to serve him.[46]"

Stephen sat in jail for four days, steadfastly refusing to take back his servant. He finally managed to make an agreement with John Holmes, whom he paid £3 to take custody of Dorothy and her baby, and assume control of the remaining two years of her indenture contract.

Stephen was back in court again in December of that year, charged with selling a looking glass for twice as much as what it could be purchased for in the Massachusetts Bay Colony. The court withheld sentence in the case, pending further information, and the matter appears to have been dropped.[47] He was also fined £3 for selling liquor without a license—it appears that Plymouth may have revoked his liquor license and put an end to the tavern business that had landed Stephen in court nearly every session since it had opened.[48]

There are some hints that Stephen may have been getting fed up with life in Plymouth. Starting in 1637, he began to sell off some of his lands situated in and around the town. He sold more than sixty acres of land near the Eel River to George Boare of Scituate, and later that year he also sold to Josias Cooke the six acres on Watson's Hill that he had obtained in the 1623 Division of Land.[49] In August 1638, Stephen requested and received permission to build a house at what is now Yarmouth—the first house in the area—and to cut hay there to winter his cattle, "provided that it be not to withdraw him from the town of Plymouth.[50]" Despite the caveat, it is quite

---

46   PCR 1:111-112.

47   PCR 1:137.

48   Ibid.

49   PCR 12:21, 39.

50   PCR 1:93.

probable Stephen did consider this a stepping stone to ultimately getting himself out of Plymouth.

In 1641, Stephen invested almost £13 in a 50 to 60 ton bark that was being built, making him a 1/16 owner of the vessel. The majority owners were William Paddy, William Hanbury, and John Barnes.[51] William Paddy simultaneously sought and received permission to establish a fishing stage at Sagaquash, one of the islands at the entrance of Plymouth Harbor, where presumably the new bark would be utilized. Stephen may have invested in another business venture of some kind as well, one that was altogether unsuccessful—he and a large number of other Plymouth residents ended up suing a man named James Luxford in December 1641; Stephen's claim against Luxford was for £12, 10s.[52] Exactly what the venture was is not clear from the surviving records, but whatever it was, it failed, and lots of people sued over the matter.

That same year, Stephen also took on another "difficult" servant, fifteen year old Jonathan Hatch. Jonathan had accused Nicholas Sympkins of sleeping with an Indian maidservant—an accusation that was apparently false, or at least the Plymouth court did not believe it. Rather than appear at the March 1641 court to receive punishment for slander, he took off. A year later, he was caught, returned to Plymouth, and whipped for misdemeanors, and for being a vagrant. In April 1642, the court assigned Stephen Hopkins to have "special care" of Jonathan.[53] Hopkins' influence on the troubled youth may well have been profound—Jonathan Hatch would only spend a couple years with Hopkins before moving on to Barnstable, marrying, and later helping to found the town of Falmouth.

51   PCR 2:31.

52   PCR 7:27.

53   PCR 2:36,38.

Chapter 19

STEPHEN'S LAST YEARS

Stephen turned sixty years old in 1641. By that time, his activities in Plymouth appear to have significantly subsided—there is little doubt he had entered his "golden years." He served on a couple of juries, but otherwise was not involved with the government, nor was he appointed to any committees. He very well could have been feeling his age.

The exact death date of his wife Elizabeth is not known, but her death occurred right around this time, somewhere apparently between 1639 and 1644. Stephen still had four unmarried daughters living at home, Deborah (about 19), Damaris (about 17), Ruth (about 15), and Elizabeth (about 13), and his nineteen year old son Caleb was likely at home as well.

Eldest daughter Constance had been married to Nicholas Snow for more than twelve years, and the family would move very soon to the newly-founded town of Eastham—where twenty five years earlier, the Nauset had attacked her father and the other Pilgrims at First Encounter Beach. By the time Stephen had turned sixty, Constance and Nicholas had already given him seven grandchildren, and five more were still yet to come.

Eldest son Giles moved into the house his father built in Yarmouth in 1638, and there in town met a young Yarmouth woman named Catherine Wheldon. The couple was married at Plymouth on 9 October 1639, and their first child, a daughter named Mary (whom Giles no doubt named after his mother), was born at Yarmouth thirteen months later, in November 1640. The couple would ultimately contribute an additional ten grandchildren.

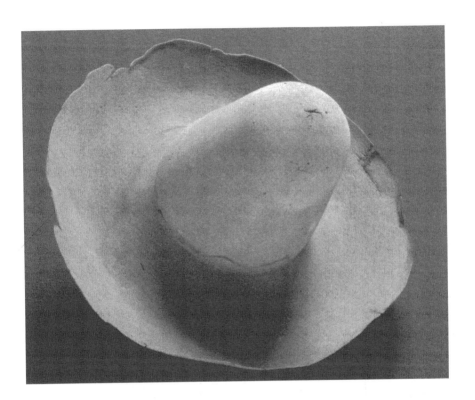

A steeple-crowned beaver felt hat thought to have originally belonged to Constance (Hopkins) Snow. The hat was probably made in England sometime between 1615 and 1640, and would likely have had a decorative band around it, now missing. Photo courtesy of the Pilgrim Hall Museum in Plymouth, Massachusetts, where the hat, and numerous other Pilgrim-related artifacts, are on display.

On 6 June 1644, Stephen Hopkins, "being weak yet in good and perfect memory, blessed by God," and apparently feeling the end was probably coming sooner rather than later, made out his last will and testament.[54] In his will, he requests that he "be buried as near as conveniently may be to my wife deceased." He specifies that his funeral expenses and debts be deducted from his estate, and then goes into how the remainder should be divided.

Quite unusually for other wills of the period, Stephen goes into great detail about his livestock, bequeathing specific animals to specific children. He gave his "great bull" that was currently in the possession of Mrs. Warren, to his son Giles. He gave his mare to his daughter Constance. To his daughter Deborah, he gave "the broad-horned black cow and her calf," and half of a cow named Motley. He gave to his daughter Damaris a cow whose ownership was probably not much in dispute, given that the cow's name was "Damaris' Heifer." Damaris also got the "white-faced calf," and the other half of Motley shared with her sister Deborah. Daughter Ruth received "the cow called Red Cole," along with half of Red Cole's calf, and also a bull that was currently in her brother Giles' possession at Yarmouth, and half of a cow called "Curled Cow." Youngest daughter Elizabeth got a cow named Symkins, along with Symkins' calf. She also got half of Curled Cow (sharing with her sister Ruth), and "a yearling heifer without a tail in the keeping of Gyles Hopkins at Yarmouth."

Stephen had a set of four silver spoons, which he also requested be given, one to each of his then-unmarried daughters—Deborah, Damaris, Ruth and Elizabeth. He bequeathed all other movable goods within the house (linen, beds, bedclothes, pots, kettles, pewter, etc.) to be equally divided between his four daughters still living at home with him.

Son Caleb was willed Stephen's house in Plymouth, as well as all his lands, in addition to a pair of oxen. He required that Caleb provide his four unmarried daughters "free recourse to my house in Plymouth upon any occasion there to abide and remain" for as long as they were single. Caleb was named executor of the estate, and Captain Myles Standish was appointed as a supervisor; Standish and Caleb Hopkins were also requested to "advise, devise, and dispose by the best ways and means they can" of his daughters in their future marriages. The will was witnessed by Captain Standish, as well as by Governor William Bradford.

---

54   PCR-WI 1:129-139. Stephen's will and estate inventory can be found reprinted in Appendix VII.

About a month later, Stephen died. Captain Standish, along with Thomas Willett and John Doane, made an inventory of his estate. The inventory included Motley cow, Damaris' heifer, Red cow, Curled cow, Symkins cow, Broad-horned's calf, White-faced calf, Coole's calf, and Symkins' calf, as well as the great bull, the mare, and the yearling heifer without a tail. The most valuable livestock was the yoke of oxen, valued at £15. Stephen also had two pigs and some poultry.

The Hopkins household contained a large number of movable goods—certainly more than most Plymouth residents owned. He had yellow and green rugs, checkered blankets, white caps, a gray cloak, shoes, ruffs, cotton stockings, several different coats, shirts and pants (breeches and drawers). There were four beds with bolsters and pillows, plus an old straw bed. There were table cloths, napkins, and even a diaper. In the kitchen there were pans, porringers, funnels, salt shakers, basins, dishes, earthen pots, brass pots, iron pots, skillets, trenchers (plates), kettles, spoons, graters, candles, and baking tubs. There were also cheese fats, a cheese rack, and a butter churn.

For the cooking fire, there was a pair of bellows, pothooks, a fire shovel and tongs, two spits, and a gridiron. There were chests, tubs, stools, and chairs. There were remnants of his shopkeeping business, including "scales and weights" and "wine measures." Even the "chamber pot" and a shoe horn made the inventory. Stephen also owned "divers books," although unfortunately the titles of the books were not given.

Following the taking of the estate inventory, the movable goods were equally divided up amongst the four daughters, as specified in the will. Each daughter's portion was actually recorded in the probate records, another unusual circumstance. Deborah, Damaris and Ruth each took their share.

Custody of daughter Elizabeth, still only sixteen years old, was given to Plymouth resident Richard Sparrow, who was to raise Elizabeth "as his own child until the time of her marriage or until she be nineteen years of age." Something was apparently wrong with Elizabeth, however; she may have been sick or disabled in some way. Richard Sparrow was given Elizabeth's share of Hopkins estate "in consideration of the weakness of the child and her inability to perform such service as may acquit their charges in bringing her up, and that she be not too much oppressed now in her childhood with hard labor." The record goes on to say "if it should please God to take away the said Elizabeth Hopkins by death, then her estate to return to Captain Standish and Caleb Hopkins to be disposed of amongst the rest of her sisters." The house that Richard Sparrow raised Elizabeth in is still standing in Plymouth today, where it is known simply as the Sparrow House.

The Richard Sparrow House, the oldest house in Plymouth, originally built about 1636. Following Stephen Hopkins' death in 1644, Richard Sparrow took custody of his daughter Elizabeth Hopkins, who apparently had a long-term illness, or was disabled in some way.

Chapter 20

EPILOGUE

The July 1644 death of Stephen Hopkins was a rather anticlimactic end indeed. Here was a man who had survived endless days of a hurricane onboard a sinking ship; was shipwrecked and marooned for nine months in Bermuda; lived for several years at Jamestown, witnessing everything from the greatest famine there to the marriage of Pocahontas; he had lived in Elizabethan and Jacobean England, walked on London Bridge, got his persona written into a Shakespearean play, and had invested in a bizarrely-organized joint-stock company founded by a bunch of religious Separatists that had fled to Holland. He sailed on the *Mayflower*, was attacked by Nauset, explored Cape Cod, and helped found and build Plymouth. He made missions to visit Massasoit, participated in the legendary Thanksgiving, lodged the famous Samoset and Squanto in his own house, was neighbors to Hobomok, and was a high-ranking member of the governor's council for many years. And when he died—he bequeathed his cows Motley, Curled, Sympkins, White-face, Broad-Horn, and Red, to his four daughters.

Stephen's youngest daughter, the weakly Elizabeth, never did marry. After being raised to adulthood by the Sparrow family, she disappeared sometime around 1659 and was never seen again. Her cattle and remaining estate was divided up in 1659 "incase Elizabeth Hopkins do come no more," and apparently she never did.

Next-youngest daughter Ruth also died unusually young, sometime within the decade following her father Stephen's death. She was never married either.

Deborah and Damaris, the eldest two daughters that were still living at home when Stephen died, both married in 1646. Damaris married Jacob

Cooke, the son of *Mayflower* passenger Francis Cooke, and the family remained living in Plymouth, giving Stephen six additional grandchildren. Deborah married Andrew Ring, son of William Ring, and they too remained in Plymouth, contributing nine additional grandchildren to Stephen's family tree. The Rings were among the original members of the Leiden congregation, and were amongst the *Speedwell* passengers who opted to disembark after the leaky adventures at sea, rather than continuing on with the *Mayflower*.

Caleb Hopkins, the administrator of Stephen's estate, became a seaman, and died at sea somewhere near Barbados. He died in his early twenties, having never married.

Eldest son Giles, who received nothing in his father's will (because he had already taken possession of Stephen's house and lands at Yarmouth and received full satisfaction as the eldest son) moved to Eastham shortly after his father's death, where he would live for many, many years, dying there sometime between 1689 and 1690. At the time of his death, he was one of the last surviving *Mayflower* passengers—outdone only Richard More, who died about 1694; John Cooke, who died in 1695; and Mary (Chilton) Winslow, who died in 1699.

Eldest daughter Constance, who had married Nicholas Snow even before the 1627 Division of Cattle took place, moved with her husband to Eastham about a year after Stephen's death, around the same time her brother Giles' family move there. The Snow family lived out their lives in Eastham, with Nicholas dying in November 1676, and Constance following him soon after in October 1677.

In all, Stephen had ten children: three by his first wife and seven by his second; and thirty-seven grandchildren. By the middle of the 18th century, Stephen had more than a thousand descendants living. Today, that number is probably in the tens of thousands, if not more—only five *Mayflower* passengers were more prosperous in this regard: John Alden, John Howland, Richard Warren, and Edward Doty.

Appendix I

THE TRUE ORIGIN OF
STEPHEN HOPKINS OF THE *MAYFLOWER*

By Caleb Johnson

This article is reproduced with the permission of *The American Genealogist*, where the article was originally published in volume 73 (July 1998), pp. 161-171.

Subscription information for *The American Genealogist* can be obtained from *http://www.americangenealogist.com*, or by writing to The American Genealogist, PO Box 398, Demorest GA 30535-0398.

Readers should take note that this article was published in 1998, and so does not include any of the discoveries made in 2004 by Ernie Christensen (see Appendix II for those additional findings).

THE TRUE ORIGIN OF
STEPHEN HOPKINS OF THE *MAYFLOWER*

With Evidence of His Earlier Presence in Virginia

By Caleb Johnson

It has been claimed for nearly seventy years that Stephen Hopkins, a passenger on the *Mayflower* in 1620, was born at Wortley, Wotton-under-Edge, Gloucestershire, England. Additionally, it has been claimed that his first wife was Constance Dudley, though this claim was made without any supporting evidence. This article will show that Stephen Hopkins was, in fact, from an entirely different part of England, and will disprove the long-standing Constance Dudley myth. Additionally, evidence will be presented supporting the conclusion that Stephen Hopkins of the *Mayflower* was indeed the same man as the Stephen Hopkins who sailed for Jamestown, Virginia, on the *Sea Venture* in 1609 and was wrecked in Bermuda, as has long been speculated.

Since the Wotton-under-Edge origin of Stephen Hopkins has been so widely accepted, it will be necessary to review how this theory came about. In 1929 Charles Edward Banks first published the suggestion that Stephen Hopkins might be from a Hopkins family he had located at Wortley, Wotton-under-Edge.[55] He based his suggestion on the fact that the name

---

[55] Charles Edward Banks, *The English Ancestry and Homes of the Pilgrim Fathers ...* (New York, 1929), 61-64, at 63-64; hereafter cited as Banks, *English Ancestry*.

Stephen occurred within the family, and presented his findings simply as possible clues. The much less careful George F. Willison in his popularized but frequently inaccurate book, *Saints and Strangers*, took Banks's few clues as absolute proof, and stated outright that Stephen Hopkins was from Wotton-under-Edge.[56]

Ralph D. Phillips furthered the theory in his "Hopkins Family of Wortley, Gloucestershire: Possible Ancestry of Stephen Hopkins" published in TAG for April 1963. He proposed that the unnamed child of a Stephen Hopkins baptized at Wotton-under-Edge on 29 October 1581 might have been named Stephen (since that was the father's name), and thus was possibly the *Mayflower* passenger. Two Stephen Hopkinses were then located in a 1608 Wortley "Men and Armour" list.[57] Phillips did not comment upon the fact that this Hopkins family carried the names of *Robert, Thomas, George, Edward, Gillian, Joan, Alice,* and *Agnes*—names which do not occur among the *Mayflower* passenger's children or grandchildren. Hence, the identification of Stephen Hopkins of the *Mayflower* with the Gloucestershire family depends entirely upon chronology and the name Stephen. Nonetheless, the theory became widely accepted.

In 1972 Margaret Hodges contributed greatly to its promotion by making the speculative Wooton-under-Edge origin the keystone to her biography, *Hopkins of the Mayflower: Portrait of a Dissenter*. She claims in her book that Stephen Hopkins was born [sic] on 29 October 1581 at Wortley, married Constance Dudley, was living in Wortley in 1608 (the "Men and Armour" list), and had children William and Stephen along with Constance and Giles.[58]

The alleged son William is based on Wotton-under-Edge records and does not need further comment since the Wortley origin will be disproven. The alleged son Stephen, however, should be mentioned. Hodges claims that Stephen, son of Stephen Hopkins, the *Mayflower* passenger, was baptized at St. Stephen's, Coleman Street, London, on 22 December 1609.[59] This baptism actually occurred on 3 December 1609 at St. Katherine Coleman, London (not 22 December at St. Stephen's, Coleman Street). This child was

---

[56]   George F. Willison, *Saints and Strangers* . . . (New York, 1945), 441.

[57]   Ralph D. Phillips, "Hopkins Family of Wortley, Gloucestershire: Possible Ancestry of Stephen Hopkins," TAG 39(1963):95-97.

[58]   Margaret Hodges, *Hopkins of the Mayflower: Portrait of a Dissenter* (New York, 1972), 7, 12-13, 66-67, 142; hereafter cited as Hodges, *Hopkins.*

[59]   Hodges, *Hopkins,* 142.

buried at St. Katherine Coleman on 19 February 1609/10, and John, son of Stephen Hopkins, was baptized there on 14 April 1611.[60] This second baptism eliminates the possibility that this is the correct family, for, as will be shown below, when the second child was conceived in 1610, the *Mayflower* passenger was in Virginia. The name Stephen Hopkins is fairly common, and I encountered no fewer than twelve individuals with this name living in England during the early 1600s, including four who were living in London.

The origin of the Constance Dudley myth is harder to explain, since there has never been any evidence to support it. It receives mention in Hodges's book, and even as recently as November 1997 an article in the *Mayflower Quarterly* accepts the Wortley origin as fact and adds that "it is the general consensus that she [Constance Dudley] was his wife," though "what seems to be in question is her relationship" to Robert Dudley, Earl of Leicester.[61] Even the Internet web pages of the Plimoth Plantation Museum (*http://www.plimoth.org/hopkins. htm*) have been tainted with this myth, claiming Stephen Hopkins was born [sic] at Wortley on 29 October 1581, and that his first wife "may have been named Constance." In the midst of all this, it is well to note that the best modern genealogy of this family, by John D. Austin, FASG, in the *Mayflower Families through Five Generations* series, mentions the claimed Gloucestershire origin as only a possibility and states that "no authority has been found for the oft-repeated identification of her [Stephen's first wife] as Constance Dudley."[62]

---

60 St. Katherine Coleman, London, parish register [Family History Library (FHL), Salt Lake City, film #560,022, item 1]. The mistake in the date of the 1609 baptism and in attributing it to St. Stephen's, Coleman Street, apparently originated in Banks, *English Ancestry*, 61.

61 Marian L. Worthen, "In Search of an Ancestor," *The Mayflower Quarterly* 63(1997):345-47, at 345; other recent articles accepting the Wotton origin include Jack Curry Redman, "Stephen Hopkins, Triple-Founder," *Mayflower Quart.* 51(1985):168-71; and Virginia W. Shaw, "A Visit to the Birthplace of Stephen Hopkins," *Mayflower Quart.* 51(1985):172.

62 *Mayflower Families Through Five Generations*, 15 vols. To date (Plymouth, 1975-), hereafter cited as *Mayflower Fams. 5Gs.*, 6: Stephen Hopkins, by John D. Austin, 2nd ed. (Plymouth 1995), 3-4, 7. Caution is also expressed in other careful works, including Mary Walton Ferris, *Dawes-Gates Ancestral Lines*, 2 vols. (n.p., 1931-43), 2:443 n.; Eugene Aubrey Stratton, *Plymouth Colony: Its History and People, 1620-1691* (Salt Lake City, 1986), 309; and Robert Charles Anderson, *The Great Migration Begins: Immigrants to New England, 1620-1633*, 3 vols. (Boston, 1995),

Now it is time to set the record straight and present documented evidence that Stephen Hopkins was not from Wortley, Wotton-under-Edge, Gloucestershire, but instead from Hursley, Hampshire, England. The parish registers of Hursley, searched and photocopied by Leslie Mahler at my request, contain the following baptismal entries, literally transcribed from the original Latin with my own translation appearing below:[63]

> [1604/5] decimo tercio die marti Elizabetha filia Stephani Hopkyns fuit baptizata [13th day of March, Elizabeth daughter of Stephen Hopkins was baptized][64]

> [1606] undecimo die Maij Constancia filia Steph Hopkyns fuit baptizata [11th day of May, Constance daughter of Steph[en] Hopkins was baptized]

> [1607/8] tricesima die Januarij Egidius filius Stephani Hopkyns fuit baptizatus [30th day of January, Giles[65] son of Stephen Hopkins was baptized]

The following burial record was also discovered, entered in English:

> [1613] Mary Hopkines the wife of Steeven Hopkines was buried the ix day of May

Governor William Bradford, in the *Mayflower* passenger list he wrote in the spring of 1651,[66] recorded the following:

2:988 (hereafter cited as Anderson, *Great Migration Begins*). See also Robert S. Wakefield, "Wrestling Brewster: An Old Hoax Resurfaces and Other Mayflower Family Fables," *The Mayflower Descendant* [MD] 43(1993):13-14, at 14; and Alicia Crane Williams, review of Hodges, *Hopkins of the Mayflower*, MD 43:88.

63   Hursley, Hampshire, parish register [FHL film #1,041,201].

64   This date and transcription has been corrected from the original article, where the date was incorrectly given as May 13, and incorrectly transcribed "Maij" rather than "Marti".

65   *Egidius* is the Latin form of the English name *Giles*.

66   George Ernest Bowman shows that it was written between 24 Feb. 1650[/1] and 24 March 1651, which Bowman shifts to New Style: 6 March 1651 and 3 April 1651 ("The Date of Governor Bradford's Passenger List," MD 1[1899]:161-163.

Mr. Steven Hopkins, and Elizabeth, his wife, and .2. children, caled Giles, and Constanta, a doughter, both by a former wife; and .2. more by this wife, caled Damaris and Oceanus; the last was borne at sea; and .2. servants, called Edward Doty and Edward Litster.[67]

And in his "decreasing and increasing," written about the same time, Bradford stated that:

Mr. Hopkins and his wife are now both dead, but they lived above .20. years in this place, and had one sone and .4. doughters borne here. Ther sone became a seaman, and dyed at Barbadoes; one daughter dyed here, and .2. are maried; one of them hath .2. children; and one is yet to mary. So their increase which still survive are .5. But his sone Giles is maried, and hath .4. children.

His doughter Constanta is also maried, and hath .12. children, all of them living, and one of them married.[68]

Bradford's comments accord exactly with these parish register records. Stephen and Mary Hopkins of Hursley, Hampshire, were the parents of Elizabeth, Constance, and Giles. It should also be noted that both Constance and Giles named their first daughter Mary.

At my request, the Hampshire Record Office undertook a search for Hopkins probate records, and uncovered only one at Hursley—an administration on the estate of Mary Hopkins in 1613. Her estate inventory was dated 10 May 1613, and administration was granted on 12 May 1613 to "Roberto Lyte [vir] gard de hursly" and "Thome Syms vir supra[vi]sor p[er] pauper'" during the minority of "Constance, Elize[beth] et Egidij" (in that order).[69] The inventory follows [*the lineation of the heading and of the Latin statement of the probate is indicated by slashes (/)*]:

---

[67] William Bradford, *History of Plymouth Plantation, 1620-1647*, ed. Worthington Chauncey Ford, 2 vols. (Boston, 1912), 2:400; hereafter cited as Bradford, *History of Plymouth.*

[68] Bradford, *History of Plymouth*, 2:406-7.

[69] Estate of Mary Hopkins 1613, Hampshire Records Office, Winchester, 1613AD/046.

An inventory of the goods and Chattells of / Mary Hopkins of Hursley in the Countie of / South[amp]ton widowe deceased taken [*interlined*: & prized] the tenth day / of May 1613 as followeth vizt.

Inprimis certen Beames in the garden & wood	
In the back side	ix^s
It[e]m the ymplem[en]ts in the Be[-]ehouse	vj^s
It[e]m certen things in the kitchin	iij^s
It[e]m in the hall one table, one Cupboorde	
& certen other things	vj^s
It[e]m in the buttry six small vessels & some	
other small things	vj^s
It[e]m brasse and pewter	xxij^s
It[e]m in the Chamber over the shop two beds	
One table & a forme wth some other	
small things	xxj^s
It[e]m in the Chamber over the hall one	
Featherbed & 3 Chests & one box	x^s
It[e]m Lynnen & wearing apparell	xij^s
It[e]m in the shop one shopborde & a plank	xij^d
It[e]m the Lease of the house wherin she	
Late dwelled	xij^{li}
It[e]m in ready mony & in debts by specialitie &	
wthout specialitie	xvij^{li}xij^s
S[umm]a total[is]	xxv^{li}xj^s

Gregory
His mark [*star*] horwood
William toot
Rychard Wolle

Commissa fuit Admi:° bonorum at Callorum' / Marie Hopkins nuper de Hursley vid' defunc[tae] / Roberto Lyte [vir] gard de hursly et / Thome Syms vir supra[vi]sor p[er] pauper' / [—][—] de par[—] duran' minor' / Constance, Elize[beth] et Egidij liberor' / d[i]c[t]i deft' duodecimo die maij / Anno Dni' 1613 de bene &c p[er]sonalir' iur' &c / salve iure cuiuscumq' salvaq' potestate &c'

There are several important observations to be made about this inventory. One is the reference to the shop and the "shopborde" (what we would call a counter),[70] which tells us that Mary and presumably her husband Stephen were shopkeepers. In addition, Mary is stated as having the lease on her dwelling at the time of her death, which may be a clue to her identity. Most striking, however, is that the estate inventory calls Mary Hopkins a widow, although her burial record calls her "wife," not widow. It would have been very unusual for an administration to have been granted on the estate of a woman whose husband was living (i.e. a feme covert), and Stephen was not dead, as he came on the *Mayflower* in 1620 with his children Constance and Giles. The solution to this odd puzzle is found in the facts that Stephen and Mary Hopkins stopped having children in 1608, and that there was a Stephen Hopkins aboard the *Sea Venture* which left for Virginia in 1609. If Mary's husband Stephen was in Virginia in 1613 and his condition was unknown, the court or the parish might well have found it expedient to assume he was dead in order to make the property available for his children's support. And that assumption was not an unlikely one: Mortality rates at Jamestown were extremely high.

Circumstantial evidence has always pointed to the likelihood that Stephen Hopkins of the *Mayflower* was the same man as the Stephen Hopkins of the *Sea Venture*,[71] and even as early as 1768 Thomas Hutchinson was speculating that the two men might be one and the same.[72] These parish register entries and probate records provide the first historical documentation to support this belief.

The voyage of the *Sea Venture* in 1609 would be one for the history books. Wrecked by a hurricane in the "Isle of Devils" (i.e. the Bermudas), the one hundred fifty castaways survived for ten months on the abundant sea turtles, flightless birds, shellfish, and wild hogs. After about six months, Stephen Hopkins began to challenge the authority of the governor, and went as far as to organize a mutiny.[73] What happened next, as Stephen was sentenced to death, is described by fellow *Sea Venture* passenger William Strachey [*emphasis added*]:

---

70 *Shop-board*: "A counter or table upon which a tradesman's business is transacted or upon which his goods are exposed to sale" (*Oxford English Dictionary*).

71 Rev. B. F. de Costa, "Stephen Hopkins of the *Mayflower*," The *New England Historical and Genealogical Register* [NEHGR] 33(1879):300-5. This identification is accepted in Virginia M. Meyer, and John Frederick Dorman, eds., *Adventurers of Purse and Person, Virginia, 1607-1624/5*, 3rd ed. (n.p., 1987), 374-75.

72 Thomas Hutchinson, *The History of the Colony and Province of Massachusetts-Bay*, ed. Lawrence Shaw Mayo, 3 vols. (Cambridge, Mass., 1936), 2:353.

73 William Thorndale points out that Strachey identifies Humfrey Reede and Samuel Sharpe as the two men to whom Hopkins broached the mutiny; given

... therein did one Stephen Hopkins commence the first act or overture [of mutiny]: A fellow who had much knowledge of Scriptures, and could reason well therein, whom our Minister therefore chose to be his Clarke, to reade the Psalmes, and Chapters upon Sondays ... it pleased the Governour to let this his factious offence to have a publique affront, and contestation by these two witnesses before the whole Company, who (at the toling of a Bell) assemble before a Corps du guard, where the Prisoner was brought forth in manacles, and both accused, and suffered to make at large, to every particular, his answere; which was onely full of sorrows and teares, pleading simplicity, and denial. But hee being onely found, at this time, both the Captaine, and the follower of this Mutinie, and generally held worthy to satisfie the punishment of his offence, with the sacrifice of his life, our Governour passed the sentence of a Martiall Court upon him, such as belongs to Mutinie and Rebellion. *But so penitent hee was, and made so much moane, alleadging the ruine of his Wife and Children in this his trespasse,* as it wrought in the hearts of all the better sorts of the Company, who therefore with humble intreaties, and earnest supplications, went unto our Governor, whom they besought ... and never left him until we had got his pardon.[74]

The castaways would eventually manage to work together to complete construction of two ships, which they used to sail to Jamestown, Virginia, the next year.[75] Strachey's account would shortly thereafter come into the hands of William Shakespeare, and it became partly responsible for inspiring his play *The Tempest*, which was first performed in November 1611. *The Tempest* relates the story of a shipwrecked group stranded on an enchanted island. A side plot includes a drunken and mutinous butler, whom Shakespeare named Stephano.

---

the tendency of "countrymen," as the word was used then, to associate with each other, we may have a clue to Reede's and Sharpe's origins.

[74] William Strachey, *A True Reporatory of the Wracke and Redemption of Sir Thomas Gates, Knight* ... in Samuel Purchas, *Hakluytus Posthumus or Purchas His Pilgrimes*, 4 vols., (London, 1625), 4:1744; repr. 20 vols. (Glasgow, 1905), 19:30-32. A modernized version can be found in Louis B. Wright, ed. *A Voyage to Virginia in 1609* (Charlottesville, Va., 1964).

[75] The basic story of the Sea Venture is related in Avery Kolb, "The Tempest," *American Heritage* 34 no. 3(1983):26-35.

There are a number of indications that Stephen Hopkins of the *Mayflower* had had previous contact with American Indians. *Mourt's Relation* (1622) tells us that Hopkins was a member of an exploring expedition on Cape Cod in November 1620. The group "came to a tree where a young sprit [i.e. sapling] was bowen down over a bow, and some acorns strewn underneath. Stephen Hopkins said it had been to catch some deer."[76] The same source says that in March 1620/1, the Pilgrims lodged the Indian Samoset with Hopkins,[77] and Bradford states that in July 1621, Edward Winslow and Stephen Hopkins were sent with Squanto to visit Massasoit.[78] Thereafter he undertook such missions frequently.[79] The English evidence, the presence of a Stephen Hopkins in Virginia, the indication that shortly after landing the *Mayflower* man was able to recognize an Indian deer trap, and his being made one of the colony's representatives to deal with the natives, all support the conclusion that the *Mayflower* passenger and the man who was earlier in Virginia were identical. And, while it does not prove the connection, the man we now know led a mutiny in Bermuda managed to get into trouble with the Plymouth authorities several times in the 1630s, despite his high social standing.[80] On one of these occasions, we learn the sort of retail business Hopkins may have had when he was in Hampshire: On 4 September 1638, "Mr Steephen Hopkins" was fined "for selling wine, beere, strong waters, and nutmegs at excessiue rates."[81]

Now that Stephen Hopkins's claimed origin in Gloucestershire has been disposed of, the Hursley records given above provide most of the information known about his immediate family in England. However, a letter written by William Bradford on 8 September 1623 and brought to my attention by John C. Brandon shows that Stephen Hopkins had a brother in England who provided nails to the Pilgrims [*emphasis added*]:

---

[76] Dwight B. Heath, ed., *A Journal of the Pilgrims at Plymouth: Mourt's Relation* (New York, 1963), 23 (hereafter cited as Heath, *Mourt's Relation*); Da Costa, "Stephen Hopkins," NEHGR 33:304.

[77] Heath, *Mourt's Relation*, 52.

[78] Bradford, *History of Plymouth*, 1:219.

[79] Anderson, *Great Migration Begins*, 2:989.

[80] Anderson, *Great Migration Begins* 2:989.

[81] Nathaniel B. Shurtleff and David Pulsifer, eds., *Records of the Colony of New Plymouth, in New England*, 12 vols. In 10 [Boston, 1855-61], 1:97; hereafter cited as Shurtleff and Pulsifer, *Plymouth Colony Records*.

About Hobkins and his men [Edward Doty and Edward
Leister] we are come to this isew. the men we retain in the generall
according to his resignation and equetie of the thinge. and about
that reckoning of .20. ode pounds, we have brought it to this pass,
he is to have .6.li payed by you ther, and the rest to be quite; it is
for nails and shuch other things as we have had of his brother here
for the companies use, and upon promise of payment by us, we
desire you will accordingly doe it.[82]

Paul C. Reed was brought in at this point to conduct a thorough search
of Hampshire records for information on Stephen Hopkins or his wife
Mary's ancestry. Unfortunately, the search failed to turn up any conclusive
proof on either count. The Hopkins families of Hampshire are found in
three main regions: Andover and surrounding parishes, Isle of Wight, and
Hursley-Winchester. The parish registers of Hursley, unfortunately, do not
begin until January 1599/1600, and there is no mention of Hopkinses in the
eleven wills surviving from the Peculiar Court of Hursley, 1566-1705; no wills
in this court survive between 1599 and 1682. Hursley wills in the Consistory
Court of Winchester and the Prerogative Court of Canterbury from this
period were also read without finding any mention of Hopkinses; there are
no Hursley wills in the indexes of the Archdeaconry Court of Winchester
from 1590 through 1613. Some significant clues were discovered, however,
and are briefly summarized below.

Hursley had one manor at the time, Merdon; and Stephen Hopkins is
mentioned in these records on "xx19" May 6 James I [1608] as one of the
men who were penalized or fined.[83] The records are not clear as to why he
was penalized. The name *Giles* was somewhat uncommon in the area. There
were three men of that name in the 1598 lay subsidy of Hursley: Giles Hobby,
Giles Kinge, and Giles Machilde;[84] no connections have yet been found to
Stephen Hopkins or his wife Mary.

---

[82] R.G. Marsden, "A Letter of William Bradford and Isaac Allerton," *American
      Historical Review* 8(1903):294-301. This portion of Bradford's letter is a
      response to a specific piece of business recorded in Charles Deane, "Records of
      the Council for New England," *Proceedings of the American Antiquarian Society*
      (Cambridge, Mass., 1867), 93-94.

[83] Merdon manorial court rolls [FHL film #1,471,826].

The name *Constance* was extremely rare in Hampshire, and only one occurrence of the name was found during the course of this research: the marriage of William Hopkins to Constance Marline at St. Swithin-over-Kingsgate, Winchester, Hampshire, on 16 April 1592.[85] The Soke of Winchester borders Hursley. The lay subsidies of Winchester list a John Hopkins in 1586, 1589, and 1590.[86] On 4 October 1593, administration on the estate of John Hopkyngs of Winchester was granted to the widow Elizabeth, Wm Hopkines posting bond; the inventory had been taken on the previous 10 September.[87] It seems probable that William Hopkins was the son of John Hopkins of Winchester and that he was the William who married Constance Marline. Stephen Hopkins of Hursley and Plymouth may also be a son of John, though no direct evidence for this relationship has been found. Listed in the lay subsidies in 1589 and 1590 is Rainold Marlin, who may have been the father of the Constance Marline who married William Hopkins.[88]

A Stephen Hopkins was named as a son in the 1636 will of Thomas Hopkins of Blashford in the parish of Ellingham on the Isle of Wight.[89] No records were found that could tie this Stephen Hopkins to the *Mayflower* pilgrim.

One additional clue deserves mention. On 20 September 1614, a letter was written to Sir Thomas Dale, Marshal of the Colony of Virginia, requesting that he "send home by the next ship Eliezer Hopkins."[90] It seems possible that Eliezer Hopkins of Jamestown in 1614 was related to Stephen.

This article has shown that Stephen Hopkins was actually from Hursley, Hampshire, England, and that his first wife was named Mary. The baptisms

---

84   Dougles F. Vick, *Central Hampshire Lay Subsidy Assessments, 1558-1603* (Farnham, Hants, n.d.); hereafter cited as Vick, *Central Hants. Subsidies*.

85   St. Swithin-over-Kingsgate, Winchester, Hampshire, parish register [FHL film #1,041,221]. [Note: The date has been corrected here from the original TAG article, where it was incorrectly given as 1591.]

86   Vick, *Central Hants. Subsidies*, 29-30.

87   Winchester administrations [FHL film #197,336]. [Note: See Ernie Christensen's article in Appendix II for newer information on this.]

88   Vick, *Central Hants. Subsidies*, 29-30. [Note: It is now known that Reynold Marlyn was the first husband of Constance Marlyn, not her father as suggested here.]

89   Archdeaconry Court of Winchester, original wills [FHL #186,925].

90   Alexander Brown, comp., *The Genesis of the United States: A Narrative of the Movements in England Which Resulted in the Plantation of North America by Englishmen . . .* , 2 vols. (Cambridge, Mass., 1890): 2:736.

of Constance and Giles have been revealed, and the additional child Elizabeth has been here identified for the first time. Evidence has been provided to document the long-standing belief that Stephen Hopkins of the *Mayflower* was the same man as Stephen Hopkins of the *Sea Venture*. And lastly the results of Paul C. Reed's search of Hampshire records has been presented, which provide some solid clues for future researchers.

SUMMARY

STEPHEN[1] HOPKINS was born probably in Hampshire, England, say 1578; the possibility that he was a son of John Hopkins of the city of Winchester merits further investigation. He died in Plymouth, now Massachusetts, between 6 June 1644, when he executed his will, and 17 July 1644, when the inventory of his estate was taken (see below). He married first, by 13 May 1604 (baptism of a child), MARY—, who was buried at Hursley, Hampshire, on 9 May 1613. He married secondly, at St. Mary Matfellon, Whitechapel, Middlesex, on 19 February 1617/8, ELIZABETH FISHER,[91] who died in Plymouth in the early 1640s, since Bradford stated that both Stephen Hopkins and his wife had "lived above .20. years in this place."[92] She was certainly dead when her husband executed his will.

"Steuen Hobkins" received six acres in the 1623 division of land, indicating five people in his household (since Stephen should have had an extra share).[93] In the Division of Cattle, 22 May 1627, the seventh lot "fell to Stephen Hopkins & his companie Joyned to him": wife Elizabeth Hopkins, Gyles

---

[91]   Banks, *English Ancestry*, 61. Given Bank's confusion between the London parishes of St. Stephen's, Coleman Street, and St. Katherine Coleman, and his providing an erroneous date (22 Dec. 1609 rather than 3 Dec.), it might be worthwhile to reconfirm this entry.

[92]   Bradford, *History of Plymouth*, 2:406. *Mayflower Fams. 5Gs.*, 6:7, states that she died after 4 February 1638/9. We have not been able to find a primary source that she was alive on this specific date. 4 Feb. 1638/9 is the date of the Plymouth court session that weighted the situation of Stephen Hopkins's pregnant servant, Dorothy Temple; Stephen's wife is not mentioned (Shurtleff and Pulsifer, *Plymouth Colony Records*, 1:111-13).

[93]   Shurtleff and Pulsifer, *Plymouth Colony Records*, 12:4; Robert S. Wakefield, "The 1623 Plymouth Land Division," *Mayflower Quart.* 40(1974):7-13, 55-59, at 10.

Hopkins, Caleb Hopkins, Debora Hopkins, Nickolas Snow, Constance Snow, Wil[l]iam Pallmer, Frances Pallmer, Wil[l]iam Pallmer Jr., John Billington Sr., Hellen Billington, and Francis Billington.[94]

Stephen Hopkins, "being weake," executed his will on 6 June 1644. He asked to be "buryed as neare as conveniently may be to my wyfe Deceased," and mentioned his son Giles; Giles's son Stephen; daughter Constanc[e] Snow, wife of Nicholas Snow; daughter Deborah Hopkins; daughter Damaris Hopkins; daughter Ruth; daughter Elizabeth; and Caleb Hopkins, "my sonn and heire apparent." The inventory was taken on 17 July 1644, and the will was proved on 20 August 1644. Verbatim transcripts of both the will and inventory are readily available.[95]

The portions of the estate for the daughters Deborah, Damaris, Ruth, and Elizabeth were divided "equally by Capt Myles Standish [and] Caleb Hopkins their brother" at a date not given, and an agreement was reached on 30 9th month [Nov.] 1644 between Capt. Myles Standish and Caleb Hopkins with Richard Sparrow that Sparrow would have "Elizabeth Hopkins as his owne child untill the tyme of her marryage or untill shee be nineteene years of age," noting "the weaknes of the Child and her inabillytie to p[e]rforme such service as may acquite their charge in bringing of her up and that shee bee not too much oppressed now in her childhood wth hard labour . . ." On 15 8th month [Oct.] 1644, Richard Sparrow acknowledged receiving "the half of a Cow from Capt Miles Standish wch is Ruth Hopkins," and on 19 May 1647, Myles Standish acknowledged to receiving "two young steers in full Satisfaction for halfe a Cow which was Ruth Hopkins which Richard Sparrow bought of me . . . ."[96]

The "Cattle that goeth under the Name of Elizabeth hopkinses" were valued on 29 7th month [Sept.] 1659, and an inventory of her estate was taken on 6 October 1659. On 5 October, the court ordered that, "incase Elizabeth Hopkins Doe Come Noe more," the cattle be awarded to Gyles Hopkins, and

---

94   Shurtleff and Pulsifer, *Plymouth Colony Records*, 12:11.

95   George Ernest Bowman, "The Will and Inventory of Stephen Hopkins," MD 2(1900):12–17; C.H. Simmons Jr., ed., *Plymouth Colony Records*, 1(Camden, Maine, 1996):129–33 (hereafter cited as Simmons, *Plymouth Colony Records*).

96   George Ernest Bowman, "The Portions of Stephen Hopkins' Daughters, and the Estate of Elizabeth[2] Hopkins," MD 4(1902):114–19, at 114–17; Simmons, *Plymouth Colony Records*, 1:137–39.

that he not "[d]emaund of; or molest . . . Andrew Ringe or Jacob Cooke in the peacable enjoyment of that which they have of the estate of Elizabeth hopkins."[97]

Children of Stephen[1] and Mary (—) Hopkins, all baptized at Hursley:[98]

i.   ELIZABETH[2] HOPKINS, bp. 13 March[99] 1604, living 1613 when she was mentioned in her mother's estate records; no further record found.

ii.   CONSTANCE HOPKINS, bp. 11 May 1606; m. NICHOLAS1 SNOW, by 22 May 1627, when they appeared in Stephen Hopkins's "companie" in the division of cattle.

iii. GILES HOPKINS, bp. 30 Jan. 1607/8; m. Plymouth, 9 Oct. 1639, CATHERINE[2] WHELDON (*Gabriel*[1]).[100]

Children of Stephen and Elizabeth (Fisher) Hopkins:

iv.   DAMARIS HOPKINS, b. say 1618, d. before 22 May 1627 (division of cattle). Either Damaris or Oceanus must have d. before the 1623 land division, which indicates, as Robert Wakefield has shown, that there were then five members in Stephen[1] Hopkins's family.[101]

v.   OCEANUS HOPKINS, b. on the *Mayflower* between 6 Sept. and 11 Nov. 1620 (Old Style), the dates that the ship was at sea, d. before 22 May 1627 (division of cattle) and possibly before the 1623 land division.

vi.   CALEB HOPKINS, b. say 1623, living Plymouth, 30 Nov. 1644, when he signed an agreement with Richard Sparrow to rear his sister

---

[97]   Bowman, ". . . Estate of Elizabeth[2] Hopkins," MD 4:118-19.

[98]   For further details on the children of both marriages, see *Mayflower Fams. 5Gs.*, 6:7-14, and Anderson, *Great Migration Begins*, 2:986-89; we have followed Anderson's "say" birth years, except for Caleb, whose birth year Anderson places as "say 1624." Researchers should also consult George Ernest Bowman's discussion of the Hopkins children ("The Mayflower Genealogies: Stephen Hopkins and His Descendants," MD 5[1903]:47-53).

[99]   This has been here corrected from "May" in the original TAG article.

[100] Shurtleff and Pulsifer, Plymouth Colony Records, 1:134. For the Wheldens, see Maclean W. McLean, "John and Mary (Folland) Whelden of Yarmouth, Mass.," TAG 48(1972):4-11,81-88; McLean accepts Catherine (Wheldon) Hopkins as a daughter of Gabrial[1] Wheldon of Yarmouth, Lynn, and Malden, Mass., but points out that explicit evidence for this relationship has not been found (TAG 48:4-5).

[101] Wakefield, "1623 Plymouth Land Division," *Mayflower Quart.* 40:8,10.

Elizabeth, d. Barbados, before spring 1651, when Bradford called him deceased.

vii.   DEBORAH HOPKINS, b. Plymouth, say 1626; m. Plymouth, 23 April 1646, ANDREW[2] RING (widow Mary[1]).[102]

viii.   DAMARIS HOPKINS (again), b. Plymouth, say 1628 (after 22 May 1627 [division of cattle]); m. shortly after 10 June 1646 (antenuptial agreement), JACOB[2] COOKE (*Francis[1]* of the *Mayflower*).[103]

ix.   RUTH HOPKINS, b. say 1630 (after 22 May 1627 [division of cattle]), d. unmarried after [30 Nov.?] 1644 (distribution of father's estate) and before spring 1651 (since Elizabeth must be the unmarried sister mentioned by Bradford).

x.   ELIZABETH HOPKINS (again), b. say 1632 (after 22 May 1627 [division of cattle]). She had left Plymouth by 29 7m [Sept.] 1659, when the process of settling her estate began; the records, however, are careful not to state that she was dead.

I would like to thank Leslie Mahler of San Jose, Calif., for searching and photocopying the Hopkins entries in the Hursley parish register and for assisting in locating Mary Hopkins's probate records; Paul C. Reed of Salt Lake City for extensive research in Hampshire records; John C. Brandon of Columbia, S.C., for providing significant bibliographical references; and Robert S. Wakfield, FASG, of Redwood City, Calif., John D. Austin Jr., FASG, of Queensbury, N.Y., Neil D. Thompson, FASG, of Salt Lake City, and William Thorndale of Salt Lake City for valuable comments.

---

[102] Shurtleff and Pulsifer, *Plymouth Colony Records*, 2:98. For the Rings, see John Insley Coddington, "The Widow Mary Ring, of Plymouth, Mass., and Her Children," TAG 42(1966):193-205; and Anderson, *Great Migration Begins*, 3:1586-88.

[103] "Plymouth Colony Deeds," MD 2(1900):27-28. For this Cooke family, see *Mayflower Families Through Five Generations*, 12: Francis Cooke, by Ralph Van Wood Jr. (Camden, Maine, 1996); and Anderson, *Great Migration Begins*, 1:467-71.

Appendix II

THE PROBABLE PARENTAGE OF STEPHEN[1] HOPKINS OF THE *MAYFLOWER*

By Ernest Martin Christensen

This article is reproduced with the permission of Ernest Christensen, and with the permission of *The American Genealogist*, where the article was originally published in volume 79 (October 2004), pp. 241-249.

Subscription information for *The American Genealogist* can be obtained from *http://www.americangenealogist.com*, or by writing to The American Genealogist, PO Box 398, Demorest GA 30535-0398.

THE PROBABLE PARENTAGE OF STEPHEN[1] HOPKINS OF THE *MAYFLOWER*

By Ernest Martin Christensen

In his seminal article, "The True Origin of Stephen[1] Hopkins of the *Mayflower*," Caleb Johnson proved that Hopkins came from Hursley, Hampshire, England, where the baptisms of his first three children are found.[104] In the same article, he mentioned a John Hopkins who is found in the lay subsidies of 1586, 1589, and 1590 for the cathedral city of Winchester, which is next to Hursley.[105] The administration on the estate of

---

[104] Caleb Johnson, "The True Origin of Stephen[1] Hopkins of the *Mayflower*, TAG 73(1998): 161-71.

[105] According to C. R. Davey, ed., *The Hampshire Lay Subsidy Rolls, 1586*, Hampshire Record Ser., 4(Winchester, 1981):1, "[t]he subsidy was a grant to the Crown, authorized by Act of Parliament, of a tax to support its necessary expenditures—including the payment of the forces and building of naval ships. It was 'lay' in that the clergy were subject to a separate clerical assessment (although they did appear in the lay subsidies in respect to their privately owned land), and separate arrangements were similarly made for peers . . . . The basic form of the tax from the 14th century to the early 17th century was the 'fifteenth and tenth'—an assessment based on a person's moveable goods (including crops), which was levied at a fifteenth of the valuation in rural areas, and at a tenth in cities and boroughs. By the early 16th century revenue had dropped . . . and the needs of the 16th century tended to require a different kind of supplement."

John Hopkins was granted on 4 October 1593 to his widow Elizabeth, with William Hopkins signing the bond.[106] William may have been the man who married Constance Marline at St. Swithin-over-Kingsgate, Winchester, on 16 April 1592.[107] Caleb Johnson suggested that this William Hopkins was John Hopkins's son, and added that "Stephen Hopkins of Hursley" and of the *Mayflower* "may also be a son of John, though no direct evidence for this has been found."[108] (William Hopkins could, of course, have been a different relation of John rather than his son; it would, for example, be quite possible for, say, a brother to have been appointed administrator if John's sons were still minors.)

To follow through on Caleb Johnson's hypothesis, I made a lengthy search for a family that included John Hopkins and wife Elizabeth, with at least two sons, William and Stephen—or perhaps some other combination of the final two names. The *Hopkins* surname is found frequently in Hampshire, but the name combination *Stephen Hopkins* is rare. In my search of some 137 parish records and other sources, I found the name *Stephen Hopkins* only in the parish registers of Upper Clatford and Hursley, and in the court records at Merdon Manor, which was included in the parish of Hursley.

Upper Clatford is a charming old English village with its river scenery; above it stands Bury Hill, fortified by prehistoric man and still wearing the natural diadem he placed about its brow. All Saints Church, located in a meadow watered by the River Anton, is approached by a delightful tunnel of lime trees leading to its eighteenth-century brick porch. It has walls with a mass clock carved on them, a blocked doorway built in the twelfth century, and a sixteenth-century tower.[109]

Passing motorists see little of the beauty of Upper Clatford; their main concern is to negotiate the twists and turns of the roadway.[110] It is located on the Andover Road, some ten miles from Winchester, which, as a trade center, attracted people from throughout the region. In that parish, we find not only

---

[106]   Winchester, Hampshire, Index to Administrations 1561-1616 (1593) [Family History Library (FHL), Salt Lake City, film #187,324].

[107]   Given incorrectly as 1591 in Johnson, "Stephen Hopkins," TAG 73(1998):168.

[108]   Johnson, "Stephen Hopkins," TAG 73(1998):168.

[109]   Arthur Mee, ed., *The King's England: Hampshire with the Isle of Wight* (London, 1939), 369.

[110]   *Where the Burdock Grows: A History of the Clatfords in Hampshire* (Andover: Upper Clatford and Goodworth Clatford Parish Councils, n.d.), no pagination.

the name *Stephen Hopkins* but also a family that provides a near match for Caleb Johnson's hypothesis.

The surname *Hopkins* is found in the village of Upper Clatford as early as 1553 [*emphasis added*]:

Pages 20-21 "Court Book 50, pp. 94-95 6 Feb. 1579
GATTENBYE v. TWYNE
The tithing of common fields"

THOMAS ASHRIDGE, miller, of Wonston 20 years, before of Upper Clatford 5 or 6 years, native of Chute, Wilts: "This deponent . . . came out of that parish (Upper Clatford) about 26 years past, and that time were in that parish but three common fields, which yearly were accustomed to be sown as is articulated, viz. one field with wheat, and another with barley and the third lay for a (summer) field."

EMMA ASHRIDGE, wife of the last deponent: "Whilst this deponent was in that parish [Upper Clatford], one Margaret Williams,[111] this deponent's mother, was a farmer of the parsonage there. And in those years *one Hopkyns* and one Guy, being farmers of the farm articulate called Normans Court Farm, did subtract from her certain tithe wheat and barley growing in the common fields belonging to that farm by a space of two years. Whereupon this deponent's mother sued them in the law for the said tithe and recovered it against them. And after that recovery, whilst this deponent dwelt in that parish, the said farmers and their successors in that farm did quietly and justly pay their tithe of all their corn grown in the common fields . . . ."[112]

This Hopkins family is found in the parish register covering the years 1571 to 1624 of All Saints Church, Upper Clatford, as follows:[113]

---

[111] Margaret Williams might be related to John Hopkins's second wife, Elizabeth Williams.

[112] Arthur J. Willis, ed., *Winchester Consistory Court Dispositions 1561-1602* (Winchester, 1960), 20-21.

[113] Upper Clatford, Parish Register, 1570-1624, Hampshire Record Office, Winchester, Volume/S 11M69/PR1.

"A Register of the Baptisms, Marriages and Buriales of Up-Clatforde"

Baptisms:
1575: "Wm the son of Jon Hopkins the 16th of June"
1577[/8]: "Alice the daughter of John Hopkins the 20th of March"
1581: "Stephen the son of John Hopkins the last of Aprill"
1584: "Susanna ye daughter of John Hopkins the 24 of June"
1601: "Edward the son of Edward Hopkins the 24th of May"

Marriages:
1574: "The 28th day of October Was married John Hopkns and Agnis
   Borrowe"
1579: "John Hopkines to Elizabeth Williames the 28th day [*interlined*:
   of] July"
1599: "Edwarde Hopkines to Alice Sweetaple the 12th of November"

In the burial section of the Upper Clatford register, there is no entry for Agnes (Borrowe) Hopkins. But it should be noted there were no burials recorded for the year 1579. It is possible that she was buried in one of the neighboring parishes or that burial entries were omitted for the year she died.

The parish register for Upper Clatford begins in 1570. The only entries for *Hopkins/Hopkines* are those for the families of John Hopkins and Edward Hopkins. All entries found appear above. No probate, administration, or inventories were found for any Edward Hopkins of Upper Clatford.[114]

It is highly probable that Stephen[1] Hopkins, the *Mayflower* passenger, is the child of that name who was baptized in the parish of Upper Clatford, Hampshire, England, "the last of April 1581," a son of John[A] Hopkins and

---

[114] "Mr." Edward Hopkins arrived in Boston in 1637 and soon after removed to Hartford, Conn., where he served for many years as Deputy Governor and Governor (Robert Charles Anderson, *The Great Migration Begins: Immigrants to New England 1620-1633*, 3 vols. [Boston 1995], 2:985 (hereafter cited as Anderson, *Great Migration Begins*). He was of considerably higher social rank than the Upper Clatford Hopkinses. Mary K. Talcott states that he was born in Shrewsbury, co. Salop, in 1600 ("The Original Proprietors," *The Memorial History of Hartford County, Connecticut*, ed. J. Hammond Trumbull, 2 vols. [Boston, 1886], 1:227-72, at 246; see also his sketch in *Dictionary of American Biography*).

his second wife Elizabeth (Williams) Hopkins. Note that the *Mayflower* passenger named his first-born child Elizabeth, probably after his mother. On that assumption, we have prepared the following genealogical summary:

JOHN[A] HOPKINS was born, probably in Hampshire, England, say 1550, probably related to "one Hopkins" of Upper Clatford, Hampshire, mentioned in the deposition above. He first appears in Upper Clatford when he was married in 1574. By 1586 he was living in Winchester, where his name is found in the lay subsidies for that year.[115] He died, probably in Winchester, before 4 October 1593, when the administration on his estate was granted to his widow Elizabeth, with her bond supported by William Hopkins; the inventory of goods for John Hopkins of Winchester appears in the appendix of this article. If the relationships suggested in this article are correct, this William Hopkins may have been John Hopkins's brother or other close relation; he could not have been the son William who was baptized in Upper Clatford in June 1575. The latter William would have been 18 in 1593 and could not legally have signed the bond; it is unlikely that he was the man of that name who married Constance Marline in April 1592, when he would have been younger than 17.

---

[115] Douglas F. Vick, ed., *Central Hampshire Lay Subsidy Assessments, 1558-1603* (Farnham, Surrey, 1987), 29-30 (hereafter cited as Vick). This same work includes the following later assessments for the Soke of Winchester and City of Winchester:

Soke of Winchester:
1589 The libertie John Hopkins G[oods] £4 (Vick, 29)
1590 The libertie John Hopkins G £4 (Vick, 30)

City of Winchester:
1563 St. Thomas Parish John Hopkins G £4 (Vick, 66)
1594 St. Thomas Parish Elizabeth Hopkins wid L[and] £1 (Vick, 66)
1594 The parishe of our Ladie of Calender John Hopkins G £3 (Vick, 64) [or the parishe of our Lady Kalender and Ladie Kalender]

It seems likely that the John Hopkinses listed in the Soke of Winchester and City of Winchester are two separate individuals. The Elizabeth Hopkins mentioned as a widow taxed for land in the Parish of St. Thomas is probably the widow of John Hopkins the assessor and the mother of Stephen Hopkins.

John[A] Hopkins married first in Upper Clatford on 28 October 1574, AGNES BORROWE. She died before 28 July 1579, when he married there, ELIZABETH WILLIAMS. She was probably living in Winchester in 1594.

Children of John[A] and Agnes (Borrowe) Hopkins, bp. Upper Clatford:

i   WILLIAM HOPKINS, bp. 16 June 1575.
ii   ALICE HOPKINS, bp. 20 March 1577[/8].

Children of John and Elizabeth (Williams) Hopkins, bp. Upper Clatford:

iii   STEPHEN[1] HOPKINS, bp. "last of Aprill" 1581. He was, we believe, the passenger on the *Mayflower* who d. Plymouth, now Mass., between 6 June 1644 (will) and 17 July 1644 (inventory). He m. (1) ca. 1603, MARY—, who was bur. Hursley, Hampshire, 9 May 1613; m. (2) ELIZABETH—. He has been considered the Stephen Hopkins who m. St. Mary Matfellon, Whitechapel, Middlesex, 19 Feb. 1617/8, ELIZABETH FISHER. Yet, other than similar names, no genealogical proof connecting the *Mayflower* Stephen Hopkins to the Stephen Hopkins who married at St. Mary Matfellon has surfaced. Only her first name is given in the early records of Plymouth.[116] A baptism at St. Mary Matfellon for Damaris Hopkins, the 1st child of Stephen's 2nd marriage, would clinch the identification, but a careful search of the parish register did not produce any such baptism.[117]
iv   SUSANNA HOPKINS, bp. 24 June 1584.

---

[116] *Editors' Note:* We know from *Mourt's Relation* (1622) that Stephen[1] Hopkins came from London. The basic discussion is in Banks, who says that this Whitechapel marriage "places Hopkins in the parish on the highroad entering London at Aldgate near which Bradford, Carver, Cushman and Southworth lived in or near Heneage House, Aldgate Ward" (Charles E. Banks, *The English Ancestry and Homes of the Pilgrim Fathers* [New York, 1929], 61). That this marriage belongs to the *Mayflower* passenger is accepted in John D. Austin, FASG, *Mayflower Families Though Five Generations*, 6: Stephen Hopkins, 2nd ed. (Plymouth, Mass., 1995), 4, 7, in Anderson, *Great Migration Begins*, 2:998, and in Robert Charles Anderson's recent revision of his *Great Migration* sketch of Stephen Hopkins (*The Pilgrim Migration* [Boston, 2004], 273).
[117] St. Mary Matfellon, Whitechapel, 1558-1875, parish register [FHL fiche #6,903,657]. St. Mary Matfellon, Whitechapel, was a chapel of ease for St.

SUMMARY

A Stephen Hopkins was baptized at All Saints Church, Upper Clatford, Hampshire, England, on "the last of Aprill" 1581 to John Hopkins and his second wife, Elizabeth Williams. It is probable that this Stephen Hopkins is the same man who joined the Mayflower Company and landed at Plymouth in 1620.

While the surname *Hopkins* appears in hundreds of parish records in Hampshire, when it is coupled with the Christian name *Stephen* only six instances were found in a seven-year search of over 137 parish registers and other available records from the sixteenth—and seventeenth-century time period:

1. Stephen Hopkins was baptized "last of Aprill" 1581 in Upper Clatford.
2. Three children were recorded as being baptized at Hursley, all explicitly as children of Stephen Hopkins:
   i.   ELIZABETHA, bp. 13 March 1604.[118]
   ii. CONSTANCIA, bp. 11 May 1606.
   iii. EGIDIUS [GILES], bp. 30 Jan. 1607[/8].
3. Stephen Hopkins was replaced as a tenant by the widow Kent on 6 May 1608 at Merdon Manor [the manor included the parish of Hursley].[119] Stephen Hopkins of the *Mayflower* would have been 27 years of age in 1608. Note that this was a year before Stephen Hopkins, minister's clerk, was the ringleader in a mutiny after the *Sea Venture* was shipwrecked on Bermuda; Caleb Johnson has presented strong circumstantial evidence that this man was later the *Mayflower* passenger.[120]
4. Mary, wife of Stephen Hopkins, was buried at Hursley, 9 May 1613.
5. Inventory of Mary Hopkins's estate was taken 10 May 1613, in which she was called, incorrectly, a "widow."
6. Administration of Mary's estate was granted on 12 May 1613, during the minority of her three children: Constancia, Elizabetha, and Egidius.

Dunstan's Parish until the 14th century, but a search of the parish records of St. Dunstan's did not reveal any baptism for a Damaris Hopkins (St. Dunstan's, Stepney, Middlesex, baptisms 1568-1656 [FHL film #595,417]).

[118] This has been corrected from the original article where the date was incorrectly given as 13 May 1604.

[119] Johnson, "Stephen Hopkins," TAG 73(1998):168.

[120] Johnson, "Stephen Hopkins," TAG 73(1998):165-67.

A John Hopkins died in 1593 at Winchester, Hampshire, and administration of his estate was given to widow Elizabeth, with William Hopkins signing the bond. The Stephen Hopkins baptized at Upper Clatford had a father named John, a mother named Elizabeth, and an older brother William. Although this William could not have been the man supporting Elizabeth's administration bond, the presence of all these names and the supporting chronology forge a strong probable link.

All of the evidence presented above occurs in a small geographical area. Upper Clatford is approximately ten to twelve miles from the City of Winchester and Hursley, which adjoins it.

APPENDIX

On 4 October 1593, administration on the estate of John Hopkyns of Winchester was granted to widow Elizabeth with William Hopkines posting bond.[121] Hursley historian S. C. Rawdon arranged to have the following transcription made by Mrs. Barbara Burbridge of Ampfield (near Romsey), Hampshire, which we have checked against a copy of the original:

[*In margin*] 1593
Joh[anne]s Hopkines de civitate Winton'
Ad[ministraci]o

4° october

[*Translation*: 1593 John Hopkines of the City of Winchester
Administration 4[th] October]

The 4th of septembe[r] 1593
a invy[n]tory taken of John Hopkings
goods late decesed by John Paye
& Henry Grene & Wyllyam Colsoune

in the hall i tabell bord w[i]t[h]   }
a frame i form & gyn stoles [*joined stools*] &   }   vj s viij d

---

[121]   Hampshire Record Office Ref: 1593 AD/42.

i chayre	}
ij cobards w[i]t[h] ij cobards clothes	xiij s iiij d
in the p[ar]lar i gyne [*joined*] bedsted	}
& i trokell [*truckle*] bedsted	} iij s
i fether bed & i fether bolstar i covarlet	}
& i flockbed w[i]t[h] a flockbolstar &	} xxx s
i ould covarlete	}
i squar[e] tabell w[i]t[h] a frame and i forme	iiij s
ij chests	ij s viij d
ix cosshyngs [*cushions*]	iij s iiij d
iiij payre of locrom chets [*sheets*]	} xlvj s
& iij payre of canvas shets	} vj
canvas tabell clouthes	xij s
ij diap[er] clothes	} xij s
w[i]t[h] a [—] twells [*towells*]	}
ij doz[en] of tabell napkyngs	viij s
v holon pellobars [*holland pillowberes*]	v s vj d
his waryn parell [*wearing apparel*] ij payre of	}
brechaers [*breeches*] ij pair of stockings i hat	} xxx s
ij doblats ij cols [*cowls*] i old goune	}
in the fore chambar i gyne [*joined*] bedsted	}
i trockell bedsted ij fether beds	}
& i covarlete i Ruge [*rug*] & i payre	} iij li x s
of blankats & ij fether bolstars	}
& i payr of cortens [*curtains*] & iij corten Rods	}
i tabell bord w[i]t[h] a frame and ij formes	viij s
in the second chamber i tabell	} iiij s
& i form & i syd [*side*] table & i chare	}
i gyn [*joined*] bedsted & i trokell bedsted	}
i fether bedsted & i fether bolstar	}
i payr of blankats i ould	} iij li
covar let of oryst [*arras, tapestry*] & i flock	}
bed and i fether bolstar i ould	}
covarlet	}
vij fether pelous [*pillows*] & iij quylts	xxj s
stayn clothes in [*interlined:* the] ij chambars	} x s

& in the parlar   }

in a letell chambar ij ould   }   v s
bedsted i old side tabele   }
in the chechan [*kitchen*] chambar   }
ij ould bedsted i flockbed   }   v s
i ould chest i vollon [*valence*] torn   }
i le[—] bolstar torn i han[d]baskat   }
i buo [*bow*] & i sheff of arous [*arrows*] i sored [*sword*]   }
i daggar i skoll i gries [*grieves*] & warbras   }   vj s

in the chechun ij tabel boards i   }   xx d
ould co[p]bard i ould stole [*stool*]   }
ij basens & i youar [*ewer*]   v s
viij platars & vj potengres vj sasars [*saucers*] }   xv s vj d
iij poryg [*porridge*] dishes iiij watar pots   }
iij saltsilars & **v** iij wt [*white metal*] can[dle]styks
   & ij [*interlined:* of] brase   }
iiij flour pots i drynkyng cope [*cup*]   }   ix s
ij pewtar pots   }
ij brase pots and i posnat   vj s
iij ceteles [*kettles*] two letel pans i skellat [*skillet*]   }
i chavyngdyshe [*chafing dish*] i brase mortar   }   xj s
i skemar [*skimmer*] i frying pann   }
ij broches ij andyres [*andirons*] ij dogs [*fire dogs*]   }
i frar [*frier*] panne i pare of tongs   }
i drypyng panne ij payr of   }
cottrell i payr of pothocks [*pothooks*]   }   xj s
i gyrdyar [*gridiron*] i old travat [*trivet*] i   }
ould boll [*bowl*]   }
i wellbokat [*well bucket*] & i chayn ij bokyng   }
tobes [*baking tubs?*] iij cevars [*kivers?*] a sope boll i   }   viij s
grensas [*grain?*] mortar i chopyng   }
bord   }
i c[or]d & d[midia] [*half*] of wod   xxx s
vj lode of haye   iij li xij s
i grot [*great*] cetele [*kettle*]   v s

Vaches & mangres [*vetches & mangels?*]   x s
Sum[ma]   xxxvij li ix s viijd

                    John Paye   Henry Grene
                    William Colson

Quarto die Octobris Anno d[o]m[ini]
1593 p[er] m[agist]rum William Say
vicar[ium] generalem etc. Commissa
fuit Admi[nistraci]o bonorum h[uius]mod[i]
def[unc]t[i] Elizabethe R[e]lic[t]e d[i]c[t]i
def[unc]t[i] de bene etc iruat
etc salvo iure cuiuscunque

Ips vid[ua] et W[illia]m
Hopkines
Translation: On the fourth day of October in the year of the lord 1593 by master
William Say vicar general etc. Administration was granted of all the goods of this
deceased to Elizabethe widow of the said deceased etc. to her being sworn etc. saving
whatsoever right.

The same widow and W[illia]m Hopkines

Particularly interesting items in John Hopkyng's inventory are his military
uniform and equipment kept in the kitchen: "1 bow & sheaf of arrows, 1
sword, 1 dagger, 1 skull [i.e., helmut], greave & warbrace [i.e., armor for
arms, hands and lower legs]." Most likely he was a yeoman archer serving in
the militia. From his military apparel, one can form a graphic picture of an
Elizabethan bowman fully dressed and ready for battle.

From the variety of beds included in all rooms of the house, we
can conclude that it was full with family members and perhaps some
servants. There were thirteen bed spaces: four in the parlor, two in the
fore chamber, four in the second chamber, three in the kitchen. While it
is impossible to determine if all beds were in use, the number certainly
indicates that the four rooms provided a large number of bed spaces and
this does not include two more in the little chamber, which was probably
used for storage.

Ernest M. Christensen is an 11th-generation descendant of Stephen[1] Hopkins through daughter Constance Hopkins who married Nicholas Snow. Now retired in Florida, he spent two decades working in higher education as a director, student affairs dean, professor, and another two decades in small business in the State of Maine.

Appendix III

WRECK AND REDEMPTION OF SIR THOMAS GATES, KNIGHT

A Letter by William Strachey,
Written in 1610, and First Published in:

Samuel Purchas,
Purchas His Pilgrimes (London, 1625).

A true reportory of the wreck, and redemption of Sir Thomas Gates Knight; upon, and from the islands of the Bermudas: his coming to Virginia, and the estate of that colony then, and after, under the government of the Lord La Warr, July 15, 1610, written by William Strachey, Esquire.

A most dreadful tempest (the manifold deaths whereof are here to the life described) their wreck on Bermuda, and the description of those islands

Excellent Lady,

Know that upon Friday late in the evening, we brake ground out of the sound of Plymouth, our whole fleet then consisting of seven good ships, and two pinnaces, all which from the said second of June, unto the twenty three of July, kept in friendly consort together, not a whole watch at any time losing the sight each of other. Our course when we came about the height of between 26 and 27 degrees, we declined to the northward, and according to our governor's instructions altered the trade and ordinary way used heretofore by Dominica, and Mevis, in the West Indies, and found the wind to this course indeed as friendly, as in the judgment of all seamen, it is upon a more direct line, and by Sir George Somers our admiral had been likewise in former time sailed, being a gentleman of approved assuredness, and ready knowledge in seafaring actions, having often carried command, and chief charge in many ships royal of Her Majesty's, and in sundry voyages made many defeats and attempts in the time of the Spaniard's quarreling with us upon the islands and Indies, etc. We had followed this course so long, as now we were within seven or eight days at the most, by Captain Newport's reckoning of making Cape Henry upon the coast of Virginia: when on St. James his day, July 24, being Monday (preparing for no less all the black night before) the clouds gathering thick upon us and the wind singing and whistling most unusually, which made us to cast off our pinnace towing the same until then astern, a dreadful storm and hideous began to blow from out the northeast, which swelling and roaring as it were by fits, some hours with more violence than others, at length did beat all light from Heaven; which like an hell of darkness turned black upon us, so much the more fuller of horror, as in such cases horror and fear use to overrun the troubled, and overmastered senses of all, which (taken up with amazement) the ears lay so sensible to the terrible cries, and murmurs of the winds and distraction of our company, as who was most armed and best prepared, was not a little shaken. For surely (Noble Lady) as death comes not so sudden nor apparent, so he comes not so elvish and painful (to men especially even then in health and perfect habitudes of body) as at sea; who comes at no time so welcome, but our frailty (so weak is the hold of hope in miserable demonstrations of danger) it makes guilty of many contrary changes and conflicts: for indeed death is accompanied at no time, nor place with circumstances every way so uncapable of particularities of goodness and inward comforts, as at sea. For it is most true, there ariseth commonly no such unmerciful tempest, compound of so many contrary and divers nations, but that it worketh upon the whole frame of the body, and most loathsomely affecteth all the powers thereof: and the manner of the sickness it lays upon the body, being so unsufferable, gives not the mind any free and quiet time to use her judgment and empire: which made the Poet say:

Hostium uxores, puerique caecos
Sentiant motus orientis Haedi, et
Aequoris nigri fremitum, et trementes
Verbere ripas.

For four and twenty hours the storm in a restless tumult, had blown so exceedingly, as we could not apprehend in our imaginations any possibility of greater violence, yet did we still find it, not only more terrible, but more constant, fury added to fury, and one storm urging a second more outrageous than the former; whether it so wrought upon our fears, or indeed met with new forces: sometimes strikes[122] in our ship amongst women, and passengers, not used to such hurly and discomforts, made us look one upon the other with troubled hearts, and panting bosoms: our clamors drowned in the winds, and the winds in thunder. Prayers might well be in the heart and lips, but drowned in the outcries of the officers: nothing heard that could give comfort, nothing seen that might encourage hope. It is impossible for me, had I the voice of Stentor, and expression of as many tongues, as his throat of voices, to express the outcries and miseries, not languishing, but wasting his spirits, and art constant to his own principles, but not prevailing. Our sails wound up lay without their use, and if at any time we bore but a hullock, or half forecourse, to guide her before the sea, six and sometimes eight men were not enough to hold the whipstaff in the steerage, and the tiller below in the gunner room, by which may be imagined the strength of the storm: in which, the sea swelled above the clouds, and gave battle unto Heaven. It could not be said to rain, the waters like whole rivers did flood in the air. And this I did still observe, that whereas upon the land, when a storm hath poured itself forth once in drifts of rain, the wind as beaten down, and vanquished therewith, not long after endureth: here the glut of water (as if throttling the wind ere while) was no sooner a little emptied and qualified, but instantly the winds (as having gotten their mouths now free, and at liberty) spake more loud and grew more tumultuous, and malignant. What shall I say? Winds and seas were as mad, as fury and rage could make them; for mine own part, I had been in some storms before, as well upon the coast of Barbary and Algiers, in the Levant, and once more distressful in the Adriatic gulf, in a bottom of Candy, so as I may well say: *Ego quid sit ater Adriae novi sinus, et quid albus Peccet Iapyx.* Yet all that I had ever suffered gathered together, might not hold comparison with this: there was not a moment in which the sudden splitting, or instant oversetting of the ship was not expected.

Howbeit this was not all; it pleased God to bring a greater affliction yet upon us; for in the beginning of the storm we had received likewise a mighty leak. And the ship in every joint almost, having spewed out her oakum, before we were aware (a casualty more desperate than any other that a voyage by sea draweth with it) was grown five foot suddenly deep with water above her ballast, and we almost drowned within, whilst we sat looking when to perish from above. This imparting no less terror than danger, ran through the whole ship with much fright and amazement, startled and turned the blood, and

---

[122] This is probably supposed to be "shrieks."

took down the braves of the most hardy mariner of them all, insomuch as he that before happily felt not the sorrow of others, now began to sorrow for himself, when he saw such a pond of water so suddenly broken in, and which he knew could not (without present avoiding) but instantly sink him. So as joining (only for his own sake, not yet worth the saving) in the public safety; there might be seen master, master's mate, boatswain, quartermaster, coopers, carpenters, and who not, with candles in their hands, creeping along the ribs viewing the sides, searching every corner and listening in every place, if they could hear the water run. Many a weeping leak was this way found, and hastily stopped, and at length one in the gunner room made up with I know not how many pieces of beef: but all was to no purpose, the leak (if it were but one) which drunk in our greatest seas, and took in our destruction fastest, could not then be found, nor ever was, by any labor, counsel, or search. The waters still increasing, and the pumps going, which at length choked with bringing up whole and continual biscuit (and indeed all we had, ten thousand weight) it was conceived, as most likely that the leak might be sprung in the bread-room, whereupon the carpenter went down, and ripped up all the room, but could not find it so.

I am not able to give unto Your Ladyship every man's thought in this perplexity, to which we were now brought; but to me, this leakage appeared as a wound given to men that were before dead. The Lord knoweth, I had as little hope, as desire of life in the storm, and in this, it went beyond my will; because beyond my reason, why we should labor to preserve life; yet we did, either because so dear are a few lingering hours of life in all mankind, or that our Christian knowledges taught us, how much we owed to the rites of nature, as bound, not to be false to ourselves, or to neglect the means of our own preservation; the most despairful things amongst men, being matters of no wonder nor moment with Him, who is the rich fountain and admirable essence of all mercy.

Our governor, upon the Tuesday morning (at what time, by such who had been below in the hold, the leak was first discovered) had caused the whole company, about one hundred forty, besides women, to be equally divided into three parts, and opening the ship in three places (under the forecastle, in the waist, and hard by the binnacle) appointed each man where to attend; and thereunto every man came duly upon his watch, took the bucket, or pump for one hour, and rested another. Then men might be seen to labor, I may well say, for life, and the better sort, even our governor, and admiral themselves, not refusing their turn, and to spell each the other, to give example to other. The common sort stripped naked, as men in galleys, the easier both to hold out and to shrink from under the salt water, which continually leapt in among them, kept their eyes waking, and their thoughts and hands working, with tired bodies and wasted spirits, three days and four nights destitute of outward comfort, and desperate of any deliverance, testifying how mutually willing they were, yet by labor to keep each other from drowning, albeit each one drowned whilst he labored.

Once so huge a sea brake upon the poop and quarter, upon us, as it covered our ship from stern to stem, like a garment or a vast cloud, it filled her brim full for a while within, from the hatches up to the spar deck. The source or confluence of water was so violent as it rushed and carried the helmsman from the helm, and wrested the whipstaff out of his hand, which so flew from side to side, that when he would have seized the same again, it so tossed him from starboard to larboard, as it was God's mercy it had not split him; it so beat him from his hold, and so bruised him, as a fresh man hazarding in by chance fell fair with it, and by main strength, bearing somewhat up, made good his place, and with much clamor encouraged and called upon others, who gave her now up, rent in pieces and absolutely lost. Our governor was at this time below at the capstan, both by his speech and authority heartening every man unto his labor. It struck him from the place where he sat, and groveled him, and all us about him on our faces, beating together with our breaths all thoughts from our bosoms, else, than that we were now sinking. For my part, I thought her already in the bottom of the sea; and I have heard him say, wading out of the flood thereof, all his ambition was but to climb up above-hatches to die in *aperto coelo*, and in the company of his old friends. It so stunned the ship in her full pace, that she stirred no more, than if she had been caught in a net, or then, as if the fabulous remora had stuck to her forecastle. Yet without bearing one inch of sail, even then she was making her way nine or ten leagues in a watch. One thing, it is not without his wonder (whether it were the fear of death in so great a storm, or that it pleased God to be gracious unto us) there was not a passenger, gentleman, or other, after he began to stir and labor, but was able to relieve his fellow, and make good his course: and it is most true, such as in all their lifetimes had never done hour's work before (their minds now helping their bodies) were able twice forty-eight hours together to toil with the best.

During all this time, the heavens looked so black upon us, that it was not possible the elevation of the Pole might be observed: nor a star by night, nor sunbeam by day was to be seen. Only upon the Thursday night Sir George Somers being upon the watch, had an apparition of a little round light, like a faint star, trembling, and streaming along with a sparkling blaze, half the height upon the main mast, and shooting sometimes from shroud to shroud, 'tempting to settle as it were upon any of the four shrouds: and for three or four hours together, or rather more, half the night it kept with us; running sometimes along the main yard to the very end, and then returning. At which, Sir George Somers called divers about him, and showed them the same, who observed it with much wonder and carefulness: but upon a sudden, toward the morning watch, they lost the sight of it, and knew not what way it made. The superstitious seamen make many constructions of this sea fire, which nevertheless is usual in storms: the same (it may be) which the Grecians were wont in the Mediterranean to call Castor and Pollux, of which, if one only appeared without the other, they took it for an evil sign of great tempest. The Italians, and such who lie open to the Adriatic and Tyrrhenian Sea, call it (a sacred body) *Corpo sancto*; the Spaniards call it St. Elmo, and have an authentic and miraculous legend for it. Be it what it will, we laid other foundations of safety or ruin, than in the rising or falling of it, could it have served us now miraculously to have taken our height by, it might have strucken amazement, and a reverence in our devotions, according to the due of a miracle. But it did not light us any whit the more to our known way, who ran now (as do hoodwinked men) at all adventures, sometimes north, and northeast, then north and by west, and in an instant again varying two or three points, and sometimes half the compass. East and by south we steered away as much as we could to bear upright, which was no small carefulness nor pain to do, albeit we much unrigged our ship, threw overboard much luggage, many a trunk and chest (in which I suffered no mean loss) and staved many a butt of beer, hogsheads of oil, cider, wine, and vinegar, and heaved away all our ordnance on the starboard side, and had now purposed to have cut down the main mast, the more to lighten her, for we were much spent, and our men so weary as their strengths together failed them, with their hearts, having travailed now from Tuesday till Friday morning, day and night, without either sleep or food; for the leakage taking up all the hold, we could neither come by beer nor fresh water; fire we could keep none in the cook room to dress any meat, and carefulness, grief, and our turn at the pump or bucket were sufficient to hold sleep from our eyes.

And surely Madam, it is most true, there was not any hour (a matter of admiration) all these days, in which we freed not twelve hundred barricos of water, the least whereof contained six gallons, and some eight, besides three deep pumps continually going, two beneath at the capstan and the other above in the half deck, and at each pump four thousand strokes at the least in a watch; so as I may well say, every four hours, we quitted one hundred tons of water: and from Tuesday noon till Friday noon, we bailed and pumped two thousand ton, and yet do what we could, when our ship held least in her (after Tuesday night second watch) she bore ten foot deep, at which stay our extreme working kept her one eight glasses, forbearance whereof had instantly sunk us, and it being now Friday, the fourth morning, it wanted little, but that there had been a general determination, to have shut up hatches, and commending our sinful souls to God, committed the ship to the mercy of the sea: surely, that night we must have done it, and that night had we then perished: but see the goodness and sweet introduction of better hope, by our merciful God given unto us. Sir George Somers, when no man dreamed of such happiness, had discovered, and cried land. Indeed the morning now three quarters spent, had won a little clearness from the days before, and it being better surveyed, the very trees were seen to move with the wind upon the shore side: whereupon our governor commanded the helm-man to bear up, the boatswain sounding at the first, found it thirteen fathom, and when we stood a little in seven fathom; and presently heaving his lead the third time, had ground at four fathom, and by this, we had got her within a mile under the southeast point of the land, where we had somewhat smooth water. But having no hope to save her by coming to an anchor in the same, we were enforced to run her ashore, as near the land as we could, which brought us within three quarters of a mile of shore, and by the mercy of God unto us, making out our boats, we had ere night brought all our men, women, and children, about the number of one hundred and fifty, safe into the island.

We found it to be the dangerous and dreaded island, or rather islands, of the Bermuda: whereof let me give Your Ladyship a brief description, before I proceed to my narration. And that the rather, because they be so terrible to all that ever touched on them, and such tempests, thunders, and other fearful objects are seen and heard about them, that they be called commonly, the Devil's Islands, and are feared and avoided of all sea travelers alive, above any other place in the world. Yet it pleased our merciful God, to make even this hideous and hated place, both the place of our safety, and means of our deliverance.

And hereby also, I hope to deliver the world from a foul and general error: it being counted of most, that they can be no habitation for men, but rather given over to devils and wicked spirits; whereas indeed we find them now by experience to be as habitable and commodious as most countries of the same climate and situation: insomuch as if the entrance into them were as easy as the place itself is contenting, it had long ere this been inhabited, as well as other islands. Thus shall we make it appear, that Truth is the daughter of Time, and that men ought not to deny everything which is not subject to their own sense.

The Bermudas be broken islands, five hundred of them in manner of an archipelago (at least if you may call them all islands that lie, how little so ever into the sea, and by themselves) of small compass, some larger yet than other, as time and the sea hath won from them and eaten his passage through, and all now lying in the figure of a croissant, within the circuit of six or seven leagues at the most, albeit at first it is said of them that they were thirteen or fourteen leagues; and more in longitude as I have heard. For no greater distance is it from the northwest point to Gates' Bay, as by this map Your Ladyship may see, in which Sir George Somers, who coasted in his boat about them all, took great care to express the same exactly and full, and made his draft perfect for all good occasions and the benefit of such, who either in distress might be brought upon them, or make sail this way.

It should seem by the testimony of Gonzalus Ferdinandus Oviedus, in his book entitled, *The Summary or Abridgment of His General History of the West Indies*, written to the Emperor Charles the Fifth, that they have been indeed of greater compass (and I easily believe it) than they are now; who thus saith: In the year 1515, when I came first to inform Your Majesty of the state of the things in India, and was the year following in Flanders, in the time of your most fortunate success in these your kingdoms of Aragon and Castile, whereas at that voyage I sailed above the island Bermudas, otherwise called Gorza, being the farthest of all the island that are yet found at this day in the world, and arriving there at the depth of eight yards of water, and distant from the land as far as the shot of a piece of ordnance, I determined to send some of the ship to land, as well to make search of such things as were there, as also to leave in the island certain hogs for increase, but the time not serving my purpose, by reason of contrary wind I could bring my ships no nearer: the island being twelve leagues in length, and sixteen in breadth, and about thirty in circuit, lying in the thirty-three degrees of the north side. Thus far he.

True it is, the main island, or greatest of them now, may be some sixteen miles in length east-northeast and west-southwest, the longest part of it standing in thirty-two degrees and twenty minutes, in which is a great bay on the north side, in the northwest end, and many broken islands in that sound or bay, and a little round island at the southwest end. As occasions were offered, so we gave titles and names to certain places.

These islands are often afflicted and rent with tempests, great strokes of thunder, lightning and rain in the extremity of violence: which (and it may well be) hath so sundered and torn down the rocks and whirred whole quarters of islands into the main sea (some six, some seven leagues, and is like in time to swallow them all), so as even in that distance from the shore there is no small danger of them, and with them of the storms continually raging from them, which once in the full and change commonly of every moon (winter or summer) keep their unchangeable round, and rather thunder than blow from every corner about them, sometimes forty-eight hours together: especially if the circle, which the philosophers call halo were (in our being there) seen about the moon at any season, which bow indeed appeared there often and would be of a mighty compass and breadth. I have not observed it anywhere one quarter so great, especially about the twentieth of March, I saw the greatest when followed upon the eve's Eve of the Annunciation of Our Lady, the mightiest blast of lightning and most terrible rap of thunder that ever astonished mortal men, I think. In August, September, and until the end of October, we had very hot and pleasant weather only (as I say) thunder, lightning, and many scattering showers of rain (which would pass swiftly over, and yet fall with such force and darkness for the time as if it would never be clear again) we wanted not any; and of rain more in summer than in winter, and in the beginning of December we had great store of hail (the sharp winds blowing northerly) but it continued not, and to say truth, it is wintry or summer weather there according as those north and northwest winds blow. Much taste of this kind of winter we had; for those cold winds would suddenly alter the air: but when there was no breath of wind to bring the moist air out of the seas from the north and northwest, we were rather weary of the heat, than pinched with extremity of cold. Yet the three winter months, December, January, and February, the winds kept in those cold corners, and indeed then it was heavy and melancholy being there, nor were the winds more rough in March than in the foresaid months, and yet even then would the birds breed. I think they bred there, most months in the year, in September, and at Christmas I saw young birds, and in February, at which time the mornings are there (as in May in England) fresh and sharp.

Well may the Spaniards, and these Biscayan pilots, with all their traders into the Indies, pass by these islands as afraid (either bound out or homewards) of their very meridian, and leave the fishing for the pearl (which some say, and I believe well is as good there, as in any of their other Indian islands, and whereof we had some trial) to such as will adventure for them. The seas about them are so full of breaches, as with those dangers, they may well be said to be the strongest situate in the world. I have often heard Sir George Somers and Captain Newport say, how they have not been by any chance or discovery upon their like. It is impossible without great and perfect knowledge, and search first made of them to bring in a bauble boat, so much as of ten ton without apparent ruin, albeit within there are many fair harbors for the greatest English ship: yea, the argosies of Venice may ride there with water enough, and safe landlocked. There is one only side that admits so much as hope of safety by many a league, on which (as before described), it pleased God to bring us, we had not come one man of us else ashore, as the weather was: they have been ever therefore left desolate and not inhabited.

The soil of the whole island is one and the same, the mold dark, red, sandy, dry, and uncapable I believe of any of our commodities or fruits. Sir George Somers in the beginning of August, squared out a garden by the quarter, the quarter being set down before a goodly bay, upon which our governor did first leap ashore and therefore called it (as aforesaid), Gates his Bay, which opened into the east, and into which the sea did ebb and flow according to their tides, and sowed muskmelons, peas, onions, radish, lettuce, and many English seeds and kitchen herbs. All which in some ten days did appear above ground, but whether by the small birds, of which there be many kinds, or by flies (worms I never saw any, nor any venomous thing, as toad, or snake, or any creeping beast hurtful, only some spiders, which as many affirm, are signs of great store of gold: but they were long and slender leg spiders, and whether venomous or no I know not; I believe not, since we should still find them amongst our linen in our chests, and drinking cans; but we never received any danger from them: a kind of melantha or black beetle there was, which bruised, gave a savor like many sweet and strong gums punned together) whether, I say, hindered by these, or by the condition or vice of the soil they came to no proof, nor thrived. It is like enough that the commodities of the other western islands would prosper there, as vines, lemons, oranges, and sugar canes: our governor made trial of the latter, and buried some two or three in the garden mold, which were reserved in the wreck amongst many which we carried to plant here in Virginia, and they began to grow, but the hogs breaking in, both rooted them up and ate them: there is not through the whole islands, either champaign ground, valleys, or fresh rivers. They are full of shaws of goodly cedar, fairer than ours here of Virginia: the berries, whereof our men seething, straining, and letting stand some three or four days, made a kind of pleasant drink: these berries are of the same bigness, and color of Corinths, full of little stones, and very restringent or hard-building. Peter Martyr saith, that at Alexandria in Egypt there is a kind of cedar, which the Jews dwelling there, affirm to be the cedars of Libanus, which bear old fruit and new all the year, being a kind of apple which taste like prunes: but then, neither those there in the Bermudas, nor ours here in Virginia are of that happy kind.

Likewise there grow great store of palm trees, not the right Indian palms such as in San Juan, Puerto Rico, are called cocos, and are there full of small fruits like almonds (of the bigness of the grains in pomegranates) nor of those kind of palms which bears dates, but a kind of simerons or wild palms in growth, fashion, leaves, and branches, resembling those true palms, for the tree is high, and straight, sappy and spongious, unfirm for any use, no branches but in the uppermost part thereof, and in the top grow leaves about the head of it (the most inmost part whereof they call palmetto, and it is the heart and pith of the same trunk, so white and thin, as it will peel off into pleats as smooth and delicate as white satin into twenty folds, in which a man may write as in paper) where they spread and fall downward about the tree like an overblown rose, or saffron flower not early gathered; so broad are the leaves, as an Italian umbrella, a man may well defend his whole body under one of them, from the greatest storm rain that falls. For they being stiff and smooth, as if so many flags were knit together, the rain easily slideth off. We oftentimes found growing to these leaves, many silkworms involved therein, like those small worms which Acosta writeth of, which grew in the leaves of the tunall tree, of which being dried, the Indians make their cochinile so precious and merchantable. With these leaves we thatched our cabins, and roasting the palmetto or soft top thereof, they had a taste like fried melons, and being sod they eat like cabbages, but not so offensively thankful to the stomach. Many an ancient burgher was therefore heaved at, and fell not for his place, but for his head: for our common people, whose bellies never had ears, made no breach of charity in their hot bloods and tall stomachs to murder thousands of them. They bear a kind of berry, black and round, as big as a damson, which about December were ripe and luscious: being scalded (whilst they are green) they eat like bullaces. These trees shed their leaves in the winter months, as withered or burnt with the cold blasts of the north wind, especially those that grow to the seaward, and in March, there burgeon new in their room fresh and tender.

Other kinds of high and sweet-smelling woods there be, and divers colors, black, yellow, and red, and one which bears a round blue berry, much eaten by our own people, of a styptic quality and rough taste on the tongue like a slow to stay or bind the flux, which the often eating of the luscious palm berry would bring them into, for the nature of sweet things is to cleanse and dissolve. A kind of pea of the bigness and shape of a Catherine pear, we found growing upon the rocks full of many sharp subtle pricks (as a thistle) which we therefore called, the prickle pear, the outside green, but being opened, of a deep murrey, full of juice like a mulberry, and just of the same substance and taste, we both ate them raw and baked.

Sure it is that there are no rivers nor running springs of fresh water to be found upon any of them: when we came first we digged and found certain gushings and soft bubblings, which being either in bottoms, or on the side of hanging ground, were only fed with rain water, which nevertheless soon sinketh into the earth and vanisheth away, or emptieth itself out of sight into the sea, without any channel above or upon the superficies of the earth: for according as their rains fell, we had our wells and pits (which we digged) either half full, or absolute exhausted and dry, howbeit some low bottoms (which the continual descent from the hills filled full, and in those flats could have no passage away) we found to continue as fishing ponds, or standing pools, continually summer and winter full of fresh water.

The shore and bays round about, when we landed first afforded great store of fish, and that of divers kinds, and good, but it should seem that our fires, which we maintained on the shore's side drove them from us, so as we were in some want, until we had made a flat-bottom gondola of cedar with which we put off farther into the sea, and then daily hooked great store of many kinds, as excellent angelfish, salmon peal, bonitos, stingray, cabally, snappers, hogfish, sharks, dogfish, pilchards, mullets, and rockfish, of which be divers kinds: and of these our governor dried and salted, and barreling them up, brought to sea five hundred, for he had procured salt to be made with some brine, which happily was preserved, and once having made a little quantity, he kept three or four pots boiling, and two or three men attending nothing else in an house (some little distance from his bay) set up on purpose for the same work.

Likewise in Frobisher's building bay we had a large seine, or trammel net, which our governor caused to be made of the deer toils, which we were to carry to Virginia, by drawing the masts more straight and narrow with rope yarn, and which reached from one side of the dock to the other: with which (I may boldly say) we have taken five thousand of small and great fish at one hale. As pilchards, breams, mullets, rockfish, etc., and other kinds for which we have no names. We have taken also from under the broken rocks crevices oftentimes greater than any of our best English lobsters; and likewise abundance of crabs, oysters, and whelks. True it is, for fish in every cove and creek we found snails, and skulls in that abundance, as (I think) no island in the world may have greater store or better fish. For they sucking of the very water which descendeth from the high hills mingled with juice and verdure of the palms, cedars, and other sweet woods (which likewise make the herbs, roots, and weeds sweet which grow about the banks) become thereby both fat and wholesome. As must those fish needs be gross, slimy, and corrupt the blood, which feed in fens, marshes, ditches, muddy pools, and near unto places where much filth is daily cast forth. Unscaled fishes, such as Junius calleth *mollis pisces*, as tenches, eel, or lampreys, and such feculent and dangerous snakes we never saw any, nor may any river be envenomed with them (I pray God) where I come. I forbear to speak what a sort of whales we have seen hard aboard the shore followed sometime by the swordfish and the thresher, the sport whereof was not unpleasant. The swordfish, with his sharp and needle fin pricking him into the belly, when he would sink and fall into the sea; and when he startled upward from his wounds, the thresher with his large fins (like flails) beating him above water. The examples whereof gives us (saith Oviedus) to understand, that in the selfsame peril and danger do men live in this mortal life, wherein is no certain security neither in high estate nor low.

Fowl there is great store, small birds, sparrows fat and plump like a bunting, bigger than ours, robins of divers colors green and yellow, ordinary and familiar in our cabins, and other of less sort. White and gray heron-shaws, bitterns, teal, snipes, crows, and hawks, of which in March we found divers aeries, goshawks and tassels, oxen-birds, cormorants, bald coots, moor hens, owls, and bats in great store. And upon New Year's Day in the morning, our governor being walked forth with another gentleman Master James Swift, each of them with their pieces killed a wild swan, in a great seawater bay or pond in our island. A kind of web-footed fowl there is, of the bigness of an English green plover, or sea mew, which all the summer we saw not, and in the darkest nights of November and December (for in the night they only feed) they would come forth, but not fly far from home, and hovering in the air and over the sea, made a strange hollow and harsh howling. Their color is inclining to russet, with white bellies, (as are likewise the long feathers of their wings russet and white) these gather themselves together and breed in those islands, which are high, and so far alone into the sea, that the wild hogs cannot swim over them, and there in the ground they have their burrows, like conies in a warren, and so wrought in the loose mold, though not so deep: which birds with a light bough in a dark night (as in our lowbelling) we caught. I have been at the taking of three hundred in an hour, and we might have laden our boats. Our men found a pretty way to take them, which was by standing on the rocks or sands by the seaside, and hollowing, laughing, and making the strangest outcry that possibly they could: with the noise whereof the birds would come flocking to that place and settle upon the very arms and head of him that so cried, and still creep nearer and nearer, answering the noise themselves: by which our men would weigh them with their hand, and which weighed heaviest they took for the best and let the others alone, and so our men would take twenty dozen in two hours of the chiefest of them; and they were a good and well-relished fowl, fat and full as a partridge. In January we had great store of their eggs, which are as great as an hen's egg and so fashioned and white shelled, and have no difference in yolk nor white from an hen's egg. There are thousands of these birds, and two or three islands full of their burrows, whither at any time (in two hours warning) we could send our cockboat, and bring home as many as would serve the whole company: which birds for their blindness (for they see weakly in the day) and for their cry and hooting, we called the sea owl: they will bite cruelly with their crooked bills.

We had knowledge that there were wild hogs upon the island, at first by our own swine preserved from the wreck and brought to shore: for they straying into the woods, an huge wild boar followed down to our quarter, which at night was watched and taken in this sort. One of Sir George Somers' men went and lay among the swine, when the boar being come and groveled by the sows, he put over his hand and rubbed the side gently of the boar, which then lay still, by which means he fastened a rope with a sliding knot to the hinder leg and so took him, and after him in this sort two or three more. But in the end (a little business over) our people would go a-hunting with our ship dog and sometimes bring home thirty, sometimes fifty boars, sows and pigs in a week alive: for the dog would fasten on them and hold, whilst the huntsmen made in: and there be thousands of them in the islands, and at that time of the year, in August, September, October, and November, they were well fed with berries that dropped from the cedars and the palms, and in our quarter we made sties for them, and gathering of these berries served them twice a day, by which means we kept them in good plight: and when there was any fret of weather (for upon every increase of wind the billow would be so great, as it was no putting out with our gondola or canoe) that we could not fish nor take tortoises, then we killed our hogs. But in February when the palm berries began to be scant or dry, and the cedar berries failed two months sooner; true it is the hogs grew poor, and being taken so, we could not raise them to be better, for besides those berries we had nothing wherewith to frank them: but even then the tortoises came in again, of which we daily both turned up great store, finding them on land, as also sculling after them in our boat struck them with an iron goad, and sod, baked, and roasted them. The tortoise is reasonable toothsome (some say) wholesome meat. I am sure our company liked the meat of them very well, and one tortoise would go further amongst them, than three hogs. One turtle (for so we called them) feasted well a dozen messes, appointing six to every mess. It is such a kind of meat, as a man can neither absolutely call fish nor flesh, keeping most what in the water and feeding upon sea grass like a heifer, in the bottom of the coves and bays, and laying their eggs (of which we should find five hundred at a time in the opening of a she turtle) in the sand by the shore side, and so covering them close, leave them to the hatching of the sun, like the manatee at Saint Dominique, which made the Spanish friars (at their first arrival) make some scruple to eat them on a Friday, because in color and taste the flesh is like to morsels of veal. Concerning the laying of their eggs and hatching their young, Peter Martyr writeth thus in his *Decades* of the Ocean: at such time as the heat of nature moveth them to generation, they come forth of the sea, and making a deep pit in the sand, they lay three or four hundred eggs therein: when they have thus emptied their bag of conception, they put as much of the same again into the pit as may satisfy to cover the eggs, and so resort again unto the sea, nothing careful of their succession. At the day appointed of nature to the procreation of these creatures, there creepeth out a multitude of tortoises, as it were pismires out of an anthill, and this only by the heat of the sun, without any help of their parents: their eggs are as big as geese eggs and themselves, grown to perfection, bigger than great round targets.

II.

Actions and occurrents while they continued in the islands: Ravens sent for Virginia; divers mutinies; Paine executed; two pinnaces built

So soon as we were a little settled after our landing, with all the conveniency we might, and as the place and our many wants would give us leave, we made up our longboat (as Your Ladyship hath heard) in fashion of a pinnace, fitting her with a little deck, made of the hatches of our ruined ship, so close that no water could go in her, gave her sails and oars, and entreating with our master's mate Henry Ravens (who was supposed a sufficient pilot) we found him easily won to make over therewith, as a bark of aviso for Virginia, which being in the height of thirty-seven degrees, five degrees from the island which we were, might be some one hundred and forty leagues from us, or thereabouts (reckoning to every degree that lies northeast, and westerly twenty-eight English leagues) who the twenty-eight of August being Monday, with six sailors, and our cape merchant Thomas Whittingham departed from us out of Gates his Bay: but to our much wonder returned again upon the Wednesday night after, having attempted to have got clear of the island from the north-northeast to the southwest, but could not, as little water as she drew, (which might not be above twenty inches) for shoals and breaches, so as he was fain to go out from Somers' Creeks, and the same way we came in on the south-southeast of the islands, and from thence he made to sea the Friday after the first of September, promising if he lived and arrived safe there to return unto us the next new moon with the pinnace belonging to the colony there: according unto which instructions were directed unto the new lieutenant governor, and council from our governor here, for which the islands were appointed carefully to be watched, and fires prepared as beacons to have directed and wafted him in, but two moons were wasted upon the promontory before mentioned, and gave many a long and wished look round about the horizon, from the northeast to the southwest, but in vain, discovering nothing all the while, which way so ever we turned our eye, but air and sea.

You may please, excellent Lady, to know the reason which moved our governor to dispatch this longboat, was the care which he took for the estate of the colony in this his enforced absence: for by a long-practiced experience, foreseeing and fearing what innovation and tumult might happily arise, amongst the younger and ambitious spirits of the new companies to arrive in Virginia, now coming with him along in this same fleet, he framed his letters to the colony, and by a particular commission confirmed Captain Peter Wynne his lieutenant governor, with an assistance of six councilors, writing withal to divers and such gentlemen of quality and knowledge of virtue, and to such lovers of goodness in this cause whom he knew, entreating them by giving examples in themselves of duty and obedience, to assist likewise the said lieutenant governor, against such as should attempt the innovating of the person (now named by him) or form of government, which in some articles he did likewise prescribe unto them: and had fair hopes all should go well, if these his letters might arrive there, until such time as either some ship there (which he fairly believed) might be moved presently to adventure for him: or that it should please the Right Honorable, the Lords and the rest of His Majesty's Council in England, to address thither the Right Honorable the Lord La Warr (one of more eminency and worthiness) as the project was before his coming forth, whilst by their honorable favors a charitable consideration in like manner might be taken of our estates to redeem us from hence. For which purpose likewise our governor directed a particular letter to the Council in England, and sent it to the foresaid Captain Peter Wynne (his now-to-be-chosen lieutenant governor) by him to be dispatched (which is the first) from thence into England.

In his absence, Sir George Somers coasted the islands, and drew the former plat of them, and daily fished and hunted for our whole company, until the seven-and-twentieth of November, when then well perceiving that we were not likely to hear from Virginia, and conceiving how the pinnace which Richard Frobisher was a-building would not be of burden sufficient to transport all our men from thence into Virginia (especially considering the season of the year wherein we were likely to put off) he consulted with our governor, that if he might have two carpenters (for we had four, such as they were) and twenty men, over with him into the main island, he would quickly frame up another little bark, to second ours, for the better fitting and conveyance of our people. Our governor, with many thanks (as the cause required) cherishing this so careful and religious consideration in him (and whose experience likewise was somewhat in these affairs) granted him all things suitable to his desire and to the furthering of the work: who therefore had made ready for him all such tools and instruments, as our own use required not: and for him, were drawn forth twenty of the ablest and stoutest of the company, and the best of our men to hew and square timber, when himself then, with daily pains and labor, wrought upon a small vessel, which was soon ready as ours: at which we leave him a while busied and return to ourselves. In the mean space did one Frobisher, born at Gravesend, and at his coming forth now dwelling at Limehouse (a painful and well-experienced shipwright and skillful workman) labor the building of a little pinnace: for the furtherance of which, the governor dispensed with no travail of his body, nor forbear any care or study of mind, persuading (as much and more an ill-qualified parcel of people by his own performance than, by authority) thereby to hold them at their work, namely to fell, carry, and saw cedar fit for the carpenter's purpose (for what was so mean, whereto he would not himself set his hand, being therefore up early and down late?) yet nevertheless were they hardly drawn to it, as the tortoise to the enchantment, as the proverb is, but his own presence and hand being set to every mean labor, and employed so readily to every office, made our people at length more diligent, and willing to be called thereunto, where, they should see him before they came. In which, we may observe how much example prevails above precepts, and how readier men are to be led by eyes, than ears.

And sure it was happy for us, who had now run this fortune and were fallen into the bottom of this misery, that we both had our governor with us, and one so solicitous and careful, whose both example (as I said) and authority could lay shame and command upon our people: else, I am persuaded, we had most of us finished our days there, so willing were the major part of the common sort (especially when they found such a plenty of victuals) to settle a foundation of ever inhabiting there; as well appeared by many practices of theirs (and perhaps of some of the better sort). Lo, what are our affections and passions, if not rightly squared? How irreligious, and irregular they express us? Not perhaps so ill as we would be, but yet as we are; some dangerous and secret discontents nourished amongst us, had like to have been the parents of bloody issues and mischiefs; they began first in the seamen, who in time had fastened unto them (by false baits) many of our landmen likewise, and some of whom (for opinion of their religion) was carried an extraordinary and good respect. The angles wherewith chiefly they thus hooked in these disquieted pools, were, how that in Virginia, nothing but wretchedness and labor must be expected, with many wants and a churlish entreaty, there being neither that fish, flesh, nor fowl, which here (without wasting on the one part, or watching on theirs, or any threatening, and are of authority) at ease, and pleasure might be enjoyed: and since both in the one, and the other place, they were (for the time) to lose the fruition both of their friends and country, as good, and better were it for them to repose and seat them where they should have the least outward wants the while. This, thus preached, and published each to other, though by such who never had been more onward toward Virginia than (before this voyage) a sculler could happily row him (and what hath a more adamantine power to draw unto it the consent and attraction of the idle, untoward, and wretched number of the many, than liberty, and fullness of sensuality?) begat such a murmur and such a discontent, and disunion of hearts and hands from this labor and forwarding the means of redeeming us from hence, as each one wrought with his mate how to divorce him from the same.

And first (and it was the first of September) a conspiracy was discovered of which six were found principals, who had promised each unto the other not to set their hands to any travail or endeavor which might expedite or forward this pinnace: and each of these had severally (according to appointment) sought his opportunity to draw the smith, and one of our carpenters, Nicholas Bennett, who made much profession of Scripture, a mutinous and dissembling impostor; the captain, and one of the chief persuaders of others, who afterward brake from the society of the colony, and like outlaws retired into the woods to make a settlement and habitation there, on their party, with whom they purposed to leave our quarter, and possess another island by themselves: but this happily found out, they were condemned to the same punishment which they would have chosen (but without smith or carpenter) and to an island far by itself, they were carried, and there left. Their names were John Want, the chief of them, an Essex man of Newport by Saffron Walden, both seditious and a sectary in points of religion, in his own prayers much devout and frequent, but hardly drawn to the public, insomuch as being suspected by our minister for a Brownist, he was often compelled to the common liturgy and form of prayer. The rest of the confederates were Christopher Carter, Francis Pearepoint, William Brian, William Martin, Richard Knowles: but soon they missed comfort (who were far removed from our store) besides, the society of their acquaintance had wrought in some of them, if not a loathsomeness of their offense, yet a sorrow that their complement was not more full, and therefore a weariness of their being thus untimely prescribed; insomuch, as many humble petitions were sent unto our governor, fraught full of their seeming sorrow and repentance and earnest vows to redeem the former trespass, with example of duties in them all to the common cause and general business; upon which our governor (not easy to admit any accusation and hard to remit an offense, but at all times sorry in the punishment of him in whom may appear either shame or contrition) was easily content to reacknowledge them again.

Yet could not this be any warning to others, who more subtly began to shake the foundation of our quiet safety, and therein did one Stephen Hopkins commence the first act or overture: a fellow who had much knowledge in the Scriptures, and could reason well therein, whom our minister therefore chose to be his clerk, to read the psalms, and chapters upon Sundays, at the assembly of the congregation under him: who in January the twenty-four, brake with one Samuel Sharpe and Humfrey Reede (who presently discovered it to the governor) and alleged substantial arguments, both civil and divine (the Scripture falsely quoted) that it was no breach of honesty, conscience, nor religion to decline from the obedience of the governor, or refuse to go any further led by his authority (except it so pleased themselves) since the authority ceased when the wreck was committed, and with it, they were all then freed from the government of any man; and for a matter of conscience, it was not unknown to the meanest, how much we were therein bound each one to provide for himself, and his own family: for which were two apparent reasons to stay them even in this place; first, abundance by God's Providence of all manner of good food: next, some hope in reasonable time, when they

might grow weary of the place, to build a small bark, with the skill and help
of the aforesaid Nicholas Bennett, whom they insinuated to them, albeit he
was now absent from his quarter, and working in the main island with Sir
George Somers upon his pinnace, to be of the conspiracy, that so might get
clear from hence at their own pleasures: when in Virginia, the first would be
assuredly wanting, and they might well fear to be detained in that country by
the authority of the commander thereof, and their whole life to serve the turns
of the adventurers with their travails and labors. This being thus laid, and by
such a one who had gotten an opinion (as I before remembered) of religion;
when it was declared by those two accusers, not knowing what further ground
it had or complices, it pleased the governor to let this his factious offense to
have a public affront, and contestation by these two witnesses before the whole
company, who (at the tolling of a bell) assemble before a *corps de garde*, where
the prisoner was brought forth in manacles, and both accused, and suffered
to make at large, to every particular, his answer; which was only full of sorrow
and tears, pleading simplicity, and denial. But he being only found, at this
time, both the captain and the follower of this mutiny, and generally held
worthy to satisfy the punishment of his offense with the sacrifice of his life,
our governor passed the sentence of a martial court upon him, such as belongs
to mutiny and rebellion. But so penitent he was, and made so much moan,
alleging the ruin of his wife and children in this his trespass, as it wrought in
the hearts of all the better sort of the company, who therefore with humble
entreaties, and earnest supplications, went unto our governor, whom they
besought (as likewise did Captain Newport, and myself) and never left him
until we had got his pardon.

In these dangers and devilish disquiets (whilst the Almighty God wrought
for us, and sent us miraculously delivered from the calamities of the sea, all
blessings upon the shore to content and bind us to gratefulness) thus enraged
amongst ourselves, to the destruction each of other, into what a mischief and
misery had we been given up, had we not had a governor with his authority
to have suppressed the same? Yet was there a worse practice, faction and
conjuration afoot, deadly and bloody, in which the life of our governor, with
many others, were threatened, and could not but miscarry in his fall. But such
is ever the will of God (who in the execution of His judgments breaketh the
firebrands upon the head of him who first kindleth them) there were, who
conceived that our governor indeed neither durst, nor had authority to put in
execution, or pass the act of justice upon anyone, how treacherous or impious
so ever; their own opinions so much deceiving them for the unlawfulness of
any act, which they would execute: daring to justify among themselves, that

if they should be apprehended, before the performance, they should happily suffer as martyrs. They persevered therefore not only to draw unto them such a number, and associates as they could work into the abandoning of our governor, and to the inhabiting of this island. They had now purposed to have made a surprise of the storehouse, and to have forced from thence, what was therein either of meal, cloth, cables, arms, sails, oars, or what else it pleased God that we had recovered from the wreck, and was to serve our general necessity and use, either for the relief of us while we stayed here, or for the carrying of us from this place again, when our pinnace should have been furnished.

But as all giddy and lawless attempts, have always something of imperfection, and that as well by the property of the action, which holdeth of disobedience and rebellion (both full of fear) as through the ignorance of the devisers themselves; so in this (besides those defects) there were some of the association, who not strong enough fortified in their own conceits, brake from the plot itself, and (before the time was ripe for the execution thereof) discovered the whole order, and every agent, and actor thereof, who nevertheless were not suddenly apprehended, by reason the confederates were divided and separated in place, some with us, and the chief with Sir George Somers in his island (and indeed all his whole company) but good watch passed upon them, every man from thenceforth commanded to wear his weapon, without which before we freely walked from quarter to quarter, and conversed among ourselves, and every man advised to stand upon his guard, his own life not being in safety whilst his next neighbor was not to be trusted. The sentinels and night-warders doubled, the passages of both the quarters were carefully observed, by which means nothing was further attempted; until a gentleman amongst them, one Henry Paine, the thirteenth of March, full of mischief, and every hour preparing something or other, stealing swords, addices, axes, hatchets, saws, augers, planes, mallets, etc., to make good his own bad end, his watch night coming about, and being called by the captain of the same to be upon the guard, did not only give his said commander evil language but struck at him, doubled his blows, and when he was not suffered to close with him, went off the guard, scoffing at the double diligence and attendance of the watch appointed by the governor for much purpose, as he said: upon which, the watch telling him, if the governor should understand of this his insolency, it might turn him to much blame, and happily be as much as his life were worth. The said Paine replied with a settled and bitter violence, and in such unreverent terms, as I should offend the modest ear too much to express it in his own phrase; but the contents were, how that the governor had no authority of that quality, to justify upon anyone (how mean so ever in the colony) an action of that nature, and therefore let the governor (said he) kiss, etc. Which words, being with the omitted additions, brought the next day unto every common and public discourse, at length they were delivered over to the governor, who examining well the fact (the transgression so much the more exemplary and odious as being in a dangerous time, in a confederate, and the success of the same wishedly listened after, with a doubtful conceit, what might be the issue of so notorious a boldness and impudency) calling the said Paine before him and the whole company, where (being soon convinced both by the witness, of the commander, and many which were upon the watch with him) our governor, who had now the eyes of the whole colony fixed upon him, condemned him to be instantly hanged; and the ladder being ready, after he had made many confessions, he earnestly desired, being a gentleman, that he might be shot to death, and towards the evening he had his desire, the sun and his life setting together.

But for the other which were with Sir George, upon the Sunday following (the bark being now in good forwardness) and ready to launch in short time, from that place (as we supposed) to meet ours at a pond of fresh water, where they were both to be moored, until such time as being fully tackled, the wind should serve fair, (for our putting to sea together) being the eighteenth of March, hearing of Paine's death, and fearing he had appeached them, and discovered the attempt (who poor gentleman therein, in so bad a cause, was too secret and constant to his own faith engaged unto them, and as little needed, as urged thereunto, though somewhat was voluntarily delivered by him) by a mutual consent forsook their labor, and Sir George Somers, and like outlaws betook them to the wild woods: whether mere rage, and greediness after some little pearl (as it was thought) wherewith they conceived they should forever enrich themselves, and saw how to obtain the same easily in this place, or whether, the desire forever to inhabit here, or what other secret else moved them thereunto, true it is, they sent an audacious and formal petition to our governor, subscribed with all their names and seals, not only entreating him, that they might stay here, but (with great art) importuned him, that he would perform other conditions with them, and not waive, nor evade from some of his own promises, as namely to furnish each of them with two suits of apparel and contribute meal ratably for one whole year, so much among them as they had weekly now, which was one pound and an half a week (for such had been our proportion for nine months). Our governor answered this their petition, writing to Sir George Somers to this effect.

That true it was, at their first arrival upon this island, when it was feared how our means would not extend to the making of a vessel, capable and large enough, to transport all our countrymen at once, indeed out of his Christian consideration (mourning for such his countrymen, who coming under his command, he foresaw that for a while he was like enough to leave here behind, compelled by tyranny of necessity) his purpose was not yet to forsake them so, as given up like savages, but to leave them all things fitting to defend them from want and wretchedness, as much at least as lay in his power to spare from the present use (and perhaps necessity of others, whose fortunes should be to be transported with him) for one whole year or more (if so long by any casualty, the ships which he would send unto them might be stayed before their arrival, so many hazards accompanying the sea) but withal entreated Sir George to remember unto his company (if by any means he could learn where they were) how he had vowed unto him that if either his own means, his authority in Virginia, or love with his friends in England, could dispatch for them sooner, how far it was from him, to let them remain abandoned, and neglected without their redemption so long: and then proceeded, requesting Sir George Somers again, to signify unto them, since now our own pinnace did arise to that burden, and that it would sufficiently transport them all, beside the necessity of any other bark: and yet, that since his bark was now ready too, that those consultations, howsoever charitable and most passionate in themselves, might determine, as taken away thereby, and therefore, that he should now be pleased to advise them well, how unanswerable this grant or consent of his should be: first, to His Majesty for so many of his subjects; next to the adventurers, and lastly, what an imputation and infamy it might be to both their own proper reputations, and honors, having each of them authority in their places, to compel the adversant and irregular multitude, at any time, to what should be obedient and honest, which if they should not execute, the blame would not lie upon the people (at all times wavering and insolent) but upon themselves so weak and unworthy in their command. And moreover entreated him by any secret practice to apprehend them, since that the obstinate and precipitate many, were no more in such a condition and state to be favored, than the murmuring and mutiny of such rebellious and turbulent humorists, who had not conscience nor knowledge, to draw in the yoke of goodness, and in the business for which they were sent out of England: for which likewise, at the expense and charge of the adventurers, they were to him committed, and that the meanest in the whole fleet stood the company in no less than twenty pounds for his own personal transportation, and things necessary to accompany him. And therefore lovingly conjured Sir

George, by the worthiness of his (heretofore) well-maintained reputation, and by the powers of his own judgment, and by the virtue of that ancient love and friendship, which had these many years been settled between them, to do his best to give this revolted company (if he could send unto them) the consideration of these particulars, and so work with them (if he might) that by fair means (the mutiny reconciled) they would at length survey their own errors, which he would be as ready, upon their rendering and coming into pardon, as he did now pity them; assuring them in general and particular, that whatsoever they had sinisterly committed, or practiced hitherto against the laws of duty and honesty, should not in any sort be imputed against them.

In which good office Sir George Somers did so nobly work, and heartily labor, as he brought most of them in, and indeed all but Christopher Carter, and Robert Waters, who (by no means) would any more come amongst Sir George's men, hearing that Sir George had commanded his men (since they would not be entreated by fair means) to surprise them (if they could) by any device or force. From which time they grew so cautious and wary for their own ill, as at our coming away, we were fain to leave them behind. That Waters was a sailor, who at his first landing upon the island (as after you shall hear) killed another fellow sailor of his, the body of the murdered and murderer so dwelling, as prescribed now together.

During our time of abode upon these islands, we had daily every Sunday two sermons preached by our minister, besides every morning and evening at the ringing of a bell, we repaired all to public prayer, at what time the names of our whole company were called by bill, and such as were wanting, were duly punished.

The contents (for the most part) of all our preacher's sermons, were especially of thankfulness and unity, etc.

It pleased God also to give us opportunity, to perform all the other offices, and rites of our Christian profession in this island: as marriage, for the six and twentieth of November, we had one of Sir George Somers his men, his cook, named Thomas Powell, who married a maidservant of one Mistress Horton, whose name was Elizabeth Persons: and upon Christmas Eve, as also once before, the first of October, our minister preached a godly sermon, which being ended, he celebrated a Communion, at the partaking whereof our governor was, and the greatest part of our company: and the eleventh of February, we had the child of one John Rolfe christened, a daughter, to which Captain Newport and myself were witnesses, and the aforesaid Mistress Horton and we named it Bermuda, as also, the five and twentieth of March, the wife of one Edward Eason, being delivered the week before of a boy, had him then christened, to which Captain Newport and myself and Master James Swift were godfathers, and we named it Bermudas.

Likewise, we buried five of our company: Jeffery Briars, Richard Lewis, William Hitchman, and my goddaughter Bermuda Rolfe, and one untimely Edward Samuel a sailor, being villainously killed by the foresaid Robert Waters, (a sailor likewise) with a shovel, who struck him therewith under the lift of the ear, for which he was apprehended and appointed to be hanged the next day, (the fact being done in the twilight) but being bound fast to a tree all night, with many ropes, and a guard of five or six to attend him, his fellow sailors (watching the advantage of the sentinels' sleeping) in despite and disdain that justice should be showed upon a sailor, and that one of their crew should be an example to others, not taking into consideration the unmanliness of the murder, nor the horror of the sin, they cut his bonds and conveyed him into the woods, where they fed him nightly, and closely, who afterward by the mediation of Sir George Somers, upon many conditions, had his trial respited by our governor.

We had brought our pinnace so forward by this time, as the eight and twentieth of August we having laid her keel. The six and twentieth of February, we now began to caulk: old cables we had preserved unto us, which afforded oakum enough; and one barrel of pitch, and another of tar, we likewise saved, which served our use some little way upon the bilge, we breamed her otherwise with lime made of whelk shells, and an hard white stone which we burned in a kiln, slaked with fresh water, and tempered with tortoises' oil. The thirtieth of March being Friday, we towed her out in the morning spring tide, from the wharf where she was built, buoying her with four casks in her run only: which opened into the northwest and into which when the breeze stood north and by west with any stiff gale, and upon the spring tides, the sea would increase with that violence, especially twice it did so, as at the first time (before our governor had caused a solid causeway of an hundred load of stone to be brought from the hills and neighbor rocks, and round about her ribs from stem to stern, where it made a pointed balk, and thereby brake the violence of the flow and billow) it endangered her overthrow and ruin, being green as it were upon the stocks. With much difficulty, diligence, and labor, we saved her at the first, all her bases, shores, and piles which underset her, being almost carried from her, which was the second of January, when her knees were not set to, nor one joint firm: we launched her unrigged, to carry her to a little round island, lying west-northwest, and close aboard to the back side of our island, both nearer the ponds and wells of some fresh water, as also from thence to make our way to the sea the better: the channel being there sufficient and deep enough to lead her forth, when her masts, sails, and all her trim should be about her. She was forty foot by the keel, and nineteen foot broad at the beam, six foot floor, her rake forward was fourteen foot, her rake aft from the top of her post (which was twelve foot long) was three foot; she was eight foot deep under her beam, between her decks she was four foot and an half, with a rising of half a foot more under her forecastle, of purpose to scour the deck with small shot, if at any time we should be boarded by the enemy. She had a fall of eighteen inches aft to make her steerage and her great cabin the more large: her steerage was five foot long, and six foot high, with a close gallery right aft, with a window on each side, and two right aft. The most part of her timber was cedar, which we found to be bad for shipping, for that it is wondrous false inward, and besides it is so spault or brickle, that it will make no good planks, her beams were all oak of our ruined ship, and some planks in her bow of oak, and the rest as is aforesaid. When she began to swim (upon her launching) our governor called her the *Deliverance*, and she might be some eighty tons of burden.

Before we quitted our old quarter and dislodged to the fresh water with our pinnace, our governor set up in Sir George Somers' garden a fair mnemosynon in figure of a cross, made of some of the timber of our ruined ship, which was screwed in with strong and great trunnels to a mighty cedar, which grew in the midst of the said garden and whose top and upper branches he caused to be lopped, that the violence of the wind and weather might have the less power over her.

In the midst of the cross, our governor fastened the picture of His Majesty in a piece of silver of twelve pence, and on each side of the cross he set an inscription graven in copper, in the Latin and English to this purpose:

In memory of our great deliverance, both from a mighty storm and leak: we have set up this to the honor of God. It is the spoil of an English ship (of three hundred ton) called the *Sea Venture*, bound with seven ships more (from which the storm divided us) to Virginia, or Nova Britannia, in America. In it were two knights, Sir Thomas Gates Knight, Governor of the English forces and colony there: and Sir George Somers Knight, Admiral of the Seas. Her captain was Christopher Newport, passengers and mariners she had beside (which came all safe to land) one hundred and fifty. We were forced to run her ashore (by reason of her leak) under a point that bore southeast from the northern point of the island, which we discovered first the eight and twentieth of July 1609.

About the last of April, Sir George Somers launched his pinnace, and brought her from his building bay, in the main island, into the channel where ours did ride; and she was by the keel nine and twenty foot: at the beam fifteen foot and an half: at the loof fourteen, at the transom nine, and she was eight foot deep, and drew six foot water, and he called her the *Patience*.

III.

Their departure from Bermuda and arrival in Virginia: miseries there, departure and return upon the Lord La Warr's arriving; Jamestown described

From this time we only awaited a favorable westerly wind to carry us forth, which longer than usual now kept at the east and southeast, the way which we were to go. The tenth of May early, Sir George Somers and Captain Newport went off with their longboats, and with two canoes buoyed the channel, which we were to lead it out in, and which was no broader from shoals on the one side and rocks on the other, than about three times the length of our pinnace. About ten of the clock, that day being Thursday, we set sail an easy gale, the wind at south, and by reason no more wind blew, we were fain to tow her with our longboat; yet neither with the help of that, were we able to fit our buoys, but even when we came just upon them, we struck a rock on the starboard side, over which the buoy rid, and had it not been a soft rock, by which means she bore it before her and crushed it to pieces, God knows we might have been like enough, to have returned anew, and dwelt there, after ten months of carefulness and great labor a longer time: but God was more merciful unto us. When she struck upon the rock, the coxswain one Walsingham being in the boat with a quick spirit (when we were all amazed and our hearts failed) and so by God's goodness we led it out at three fathom and three fathom and an half water. The wind served us easily all that day and the next, when (God be ever praised for it) to the no little joy of us all, we got clear of the islands. After which holding a southerly course, for seven days we had the wind sometimes fair, and sometimes scarce and contrary: in which time we lost Sir George Somers twice, albeit we still spared him our main topsail, and sometimes our forecourse too.

The seventeenth of May we saw change of water and had much rubbish swim by our ship side, whereby we knew we were not far from land. The eighteenth about midnight we sounded, with the dipsey lead, and found thirty-seven fathom. The nineteenth in the morning we sounded, and had nineteen and an half fathom, stony, and sandy ground. The twentieth about midnight, we had a marvelous sweet smell from the shore (as from the coast of Spain, short of the Straits) strong and pleasant, which did not a little glad us. In the morning by daybreak (so soon as one might well see from the foretop) one of the sailors descried land about an hour after, I went up and might discover two hummocks to the southward, from which (northward all along) lay the land which we were to coast to Cape Henry. About seven of the clock we cast forth an anchor, because the tide (by reason of the freshet that set into the bay) made a strong ebb there, and the wind was but easy, so as not being able to stem the tide, we purposed to lie at an anchor until the next flood; but the wind coming southwest a loom gale about eleven, we set sail again, and having got over the bar, bore in for the Cape.

This is the famous Chesapeake Bay, which we have called (in honor of our young Prince) Cape Henry over against which within the Bay lieth another headland, which we called, in honor of our princely Duke of York Cape Charles; and these lie northeast and by east, and southwest and by west, and they may be distant each from the other in breadth seven leagues, between which the sea runs in as broad as between Queenborough and Leigh. Indeed it is a goodly bay and a fairer, not easily to be found.

The one-and-twentieth, being Monday in the morning, we came up within two miles of Point Comfort, when the captain of the fort discharged a warning piece at us, whereupon we came to an anchor, and sent off our longboat to the fort, to certify who we were; by reason of the shoals which lie on the south side, this fort easily commands the mouth of the river, albeit it is as broad as between Greenwich, and the Isle of Dogs.

True it is, such who talked with our men from the shore, delivered how safely all our ships the last year (excepting only the admiral, and the little pinnace in which one Michael Philes commanded, of some twenty ton, which we towed astern till the storm blew) arrived, and how our people (well increased) had therefore builded this fort; only we could not learn anything of our longboat, sent from the Bermudas, but what we gathered by the Indians themselves, especially from Powhatan, who would tell our men of such a boat landed in one of his rivers, and would describe the people, and make much scoffing sport thereat: by which we have gathered that it is most likely, how it arrived upon our coast, and not meeting with our river were taken at some time or other, at some advantage by the savages, and so cut off. When our skiff came up again, the good news of our ships', and men's arrival the last year, did not a little glad our governor: who went soon ashore and as soon (contrary to all our fair hopes) had new unexpected, uncomfortable, and heavy news of a worse condition of our people above at Jamestown.

Upon Point Comfort our men did the last year (as you have heard) raise a little fortification, which since hath been better perfected and is likely to prove a strong fort, and is now kept by Captain James Davies with forty men, and hath to name Algernon Fort, so called by Captain George Percy, whom we found at our arrival president of the colony and at this time likewise in the fort. When we got into the Point, which was the one and twentieth of May, being Monday about noon; where riding before an Indian town called Kecoughtan, a mighty storm of thunder, lightning, and rain gave us a shrewd and fearful welcome.

From hence in two days (only by the help of tides, no wind stirring) we plied it sadly up the river, and the three and twentieth of May we cast anchor before Jamestown, where we landed, and our much grieved governor first visiting the church caused the bell to be rung, at which (all such as were able to come forth of their houses) repaired to church where our minister Master Buck made a zealous and sorrowful prayer, finding all things so contrary to our expectations, so full of misery and misgovernment. After service our governor caused me to read his commission, and Captain Percy (then president) delivered up unto him his commission, the old patent and the council seal. Viewing the fort, we found the palisades torn down, the ports open, the gates from off the hinges, and empty houses (which owners' death had taken from them) rent up and burned, rather than the dwellers would step into the woods a stone's cast off from them, to fetch other firewood: and it is true the Indian killed as fast without, if our men stirred but beyond the bounds of their blockhouse, as famine and pestilence did within; with many more particularities of their sufferances (brought upon them by their own disorders the last year) than I have heart to express. In this desolation and misery our governor found the condition and state of the colony, and (which added more to his grief) no hope how to amend it or save his own company, and those yet remaining alive, from falling into the like necessities. For we had brought from the Bermudas no greater store of provision (fearing no such accidents possible to befall the colony here) than might well serve one hundred and fifty for a sea voyage: and it was not possible, at this time of the year to amend it, by any help from the Indian. For besides that they (at their best) have little more, than from hand to mouth, it was now likewise but their seed time, and all their corn scarce put into the ground: nor was there at the fort, (as they whom we found related unto us) any means to take fish, neither sufficient seine, nor other convenient net, and yet if there had, there was not one eye of sturgeon yet come into the river. All which considered, it pleased our governor to make a speech unto the company, giving them to understand, that what provision he had, they should equally share with him, and if he should find it not possible, and easy to supply them with something from the country, by the endeavors of his able men, he would make ready and transport them all into their native country (accommodating them the best that he could) at which there was a general acclamation, and shout of joy on both sides, for even our own men began to be disheartened and faint, when they saw this misery amongst the others, and no less threatened unto themselves. In the meanwhile, our governor published certain orders and instructions, which he enjoined them strictly to observe, the time that he should stay amongst them, which being written out fair, were set up upon a post in the church for everyone to take notice of.

If I should be examined from whence, and by what occasion, all these disasters, and afflictions descended upon our people, I can only refer you (honored Lady) to the book, which the adventurers have sent hither entitled, *Advertisements unto the Colony in Virginia*: wherein the ground and causes are favorably abridged, from whence these miserable effects have been produced, not excusing likewise the form of government of some error, which was not powerful enough among so heady a multitude, especially, as those who arrived here in the supply sent the last year with us: with whom the better authority and government now changed into an absolute command, came along and had been as happily established, had it pleased God, that we with them had reached our wished harbor.

Unto such calamity can sloth, riot, and vanity, bring the most settled and plentiful estate. Indeed (right noble Lady) no story can remember unto us, more woes and anguishes, than these people, thus governed, have both suffered and pulled upon their own heads. And yet true it is, some of them, whose voices and command might not be heard, may easily be absolved from the guilt hereof as standing untouched, and upright in their innocencies; whilst the privy factionaries shall never find time nor darkness, to wipe away or cover their ignoble and irreligious practices, who, it may be, lay all the discredits and imputations the while upon the country. But under pardon, let me speak freely to them: let them remember that if riot and sloth should both meet in any one of their best families, in a country most stored with abundance and plenty in England, continual wasting, no husbandry, the old store still spent on, no order for new provisions, what better could befall unto the inhabitants, landlords, and tenants of that corner, than necessarily following cleanness of teeth, famine, and death? Is it not the sentence and doom of the wise man?

Yet a little sleep, a little slumber, and a little folding of the hands to sleep: so thy poverty cometh, as one that traveleth by the way, and thy necessity like an armed man. And with this idleness, when something was in store, all wasteful courses exercised to the height, and the headless multitude, (some neither of quality nor religion) not employed to the end for which they were sent hither, no not compelled (since in themselves unwilling) to sow corn for their own bellies, nor to put a root, herb, etc., for their own particular good in their gardens or elsewhere: I say in this neglect and sensual surfeit, all things suffered to run on, to lie sick and languish, must it be expected, that health, plenty, and all the goodness of a well ordered state, of necessity for all this, to flow in this country? You have a right and noble heart (worthy Lady) be judge of the truth herein. Then suffer it not be concluded unto you, nor believe, I beseech you, that the wants and wretchedness which they have endured, ascend out of the poverty and vileness of the country, whether be respected the land or rivers: the one, and the other having not only promised, but poured enough in their veins, to convince them in such calumnies, and to quit those common calamities, which (as the shadow accompanies the body) the precedent neglects touched at, if truly followed, and wrought upon. What England may boast of, having the fair hand of husbandry to manure and dress it, God and nature have favorably bestowed upon this country, and as it hath given unto it, both by situation, height, and soil, all those (past hopes) assurances which follow our well planted native country, and others lying under the same influence: if, as ours, the country and soil might be improved, and drawn forth: so hath it endowed it, as is most certain, with many more, which England fetcheth far unto her from elsewhere. For first we have experience, and even our eyes witness (how young so ever we are to the country) that no country yieldeth goodlier corn, nor more manifold increase: large fields we have, as prospects of the same, and not far from our palisade. Besides, we have thousands of goodly vines in every hedge, and bosk running along the ground, which yield a plentiful grape in their kind. Let me appeal then to knowledge, if these natural vines were planted, dressed, and ordered by skillful vintners, whether we might not make a perfect grape, and fruitful vintage in short time? And we have made trial of our own English seeds, kitchen herbs, and roots, and find them to prosper as speedily as in England.

Only let me truly acknowledge, they are not a hundred or two of deboist hands, dropped forth by year after year, with penury, and leisure, ill provided for before they come, and worse to be governed when they are here, men of such distempered bodies, and infected minds, whom no examples daily before their eyes, either of goodness or punishment, can deter from their habitual impieties, or terrify from a shameful death, that must be the carpenters, and workmen in this so glorious a building.

Then let no rumor of the poverty of the country (as if in the womb thereof there lay not those elemental seeds, which could produce as many fair births of plenty, and increase, and better hopes, than any land under the heaven, to which the sun is no nearer a neighbor) I say, let no imposture rumor, nor any fame of some one, or a few more changeable actions, interposing by the way, or at home, waive any man's fair purposes hitherward, or wrest them to a declining and falling off from the business.

I will acknowledge, dear Lady, I have seen much propenseness already toward the unity, and general endeavors: how contentedly do such as labor with us go forth, when men of rank and quality, assist, and set on their labors? I have seen it, and I protest it, I have heard the inferior people, with alacrity of spirit profess, that they should never refuse to do their best in the practice of their sciences and knowledges, when such worthy, and noble gentlemen go in and out before them, and not only so, but as the occasion shall be offered, no less help them with their hand, than defend them with the sword. And it is to be understood, that such as labor, are not yet so taxed, but that easily they perform the same, and ever by ten of the clock have done their morning's work: at what time, they have their allowances set out ready for them, and until it be three of the clock again, they take their own pleasure, and afterward with the sunset, their day's labor is finished. In all which courses, if the business be continued, I doubt nothing, with God's favor toward us, but to see it in time, a country, an haven, and a staple, fitted for such a trade, as shall advance assureder increase, both to the adventurers and free burghers thereof, than any trade in Christendom, or than that (even in her early days, when Michael Cavacco, the Greek, did first discover it to our English factor in Poland) which extends itself now from Calpe and Abila, to the bottom of Sidon, and so wide as Alexandria, and all the ports and havens north and south through the arches to Cio, Smyrna, Troy, the Hellespont, and up to Pompey's Pillar, which as a pharos, or watchtower, stands upon the wondrous opening into the Euxine Sea.

From the three and twentieth of May, unto the seventh of June, our governor attempted, and made trial of all the ways, that both his own judgment could prompt him in, and the advice of Captain George Percy, and those gentlemen whom he found of the council, when he came in, as of others; whom he caused to deliver their knowledges, concerning the state and condition of the country: but after much debating, it could not appear how possibly they might preserve themselves (reserving that little which we brought from the Bermudas in our ships and was upon all occasions to stand good by us) ten days from starving. For besides that the Indians were of themselves poor, they were forbidden likewise (by their subtle King Powhatan) at all to trade with us; and not only so, but to endanger and assault any boat upon the river or straggler out of the fort by land, by which (not long before our arrival) our people had a large boat cut off and divers of our men killed, even within command of our blockhouse; as likewise, they shot two of our people to death, after we had been four and five days come in: and yet would they dare then to enter our ports, and truck with us (as they counterfeited underhand) when indeed, they came but as spies to discover our strength, trucking with us upon such hard conditions that our governor might very well see their subtlety, and therefore neither could well endure, nor would continue it. And I may truly say beside, so had our men abased, and to such a contempt, had they brought the value of our copper, that a piece which would have bought a bushel of their corn in former time, would not now buy a little cade or basket of a pottle. And for this misgovernment, chiefly our colony is much bound to the mariners, who never yet in any voyage hither, but have made a prey of our poor people in want; insomuch, as unless they might advance four or five for one (how assured so ever of the payments of their bills of exchange) they would not spare them a dust of corn, nor a pint of beer, to give unto them the least comfort or relief, although that beer purloined, and stolen perhaps, either from some particular supply, or from the general store: so uncharitable a parcel of people they be, and ill conditioned. I myself have heard the master of a ship say (even upon the arrival of this fleet, with the lord governor and captain general, when the said master was treated with for such commodities as he brought to sell) that unless he might have an East Indian increase, four for one, all charges cleared, he would not part with a can of beer. Besides, to do us more villainy and mischief, they would send of their longboats still by night, and (well guarded) make out to the neighbor villages, and towns, and there (contrary to the articles of the fort, which now pronounce death for a trespass of that quality) truck with the Indians, giving for their trifles otter skins, beavers, raccoon furs, bears' skins, etc., so large a quantity, and measure of copper, as when the truck master for the colony, in the daytime offered trade, the Indians would laugh and scorn the same, telling what bargains they met withal by night from our *mangot quintons* (so calling our great ships) by which means the market with them forestalled thus by these dishonest men, I may boldly say, they have been a consequent cause (this last year) to the death and starving of many a worthy spirit; but I hope to see a true amendment and reformation, as well of those as of divers other intolerable abuses, thrust upon the colony by these shameless people; as also, for the transportation of such provisions and supplies as are sent hither, and come under the charge of pursers (a parcel, fragment, and odd ends of fellows' dependencies to the others) a better course thought upon: of which supplies, never yet came into the store, or to the parties, unto whom such supplies were sent, by relation hitherto, a moiety or third part; for the speedy redress of this, being so sovereign a point, I understand how the lord governor and captain general, hath advised unto the council, that there may be no more provisions at all delivered unto pursers, but hath entreated to have the provision thus ordered. He would have a commissary general of the victuals to be appointed, who (receiving the store for the colony, by indenture from the treasurer, and victualers in England) may keep a just account, what the gross amounteth unto, and what is transported every voyage, in several kinds, as of bread, meat, beer, wine, etc., which said commissary shall deliver over the same to the master of every ship, and take an indenture from the said master of what he hath in charge, and what he is to deliver to the treasurer of the store in Virginia: of which, if any be wanting, he, the said master shall make it good out of his own entertainment, otherwise the pursers, stewards, coopers, and quartermasters, will be sure still, not only to give themselves and their friends double allowances, but think it all well gotten that they can purloin and steal away.

Besides that the Indian thus evil entreated us, the river (which were wont before this time of the year to be plentiful of sturgeon) had not now a fish to be seen in it, and albeit we labored, and hauled our net twenty times day and night, yet we took not so much as would content half the fishermen. Our governor therefore sent away his longboat to coast the river downward, as far as Point Comfort, and from thence to Cape Henry, and Cape Charles, and all within the Bay: which after a seven night's trial and travail, returned without any fruits of their labors, scarce getting so much fish as served their own company.

And to take anything from the Indian by force, we never used, nor willingly ever will: and though they had well deserved it, yet it was not now time, for they did (as I said before) but then set their corn, and at their best, they had but from hand to mouth; so as what now remained? Such as we found in the fort, had we stayed but four days, had doubtless been the most part of them starved, for their best relief was only mushrooms, and some herbs, which sod together, made but a thin and unsavory broth, and swelled them much. The pity hereof moved our governor to draw forth such provision as he had brought, proportioning a measure equally to everyone alike. But then our governor began to examine how long this his store would hold out, and found it (husbanded to the best advantage) not possible to serve longer than sixteen days: after which nothing was to be possibly supposed out of the country (as before remembered) nor remained there then any means to transport him elsewhere. Whereupon he then entered into the consultation with Sir George Somers, and Captain Newport, calling unto the same the gentlemen and council of the former government, entreating both the one and the other to advise with him what was best to be done. The provision which they both had aboard himself and Sir George Somers, was examined, and delivered, how it, being racked to the uttermost, extended not above, as I said, sixteen days, after two cakes a day. The gentlemen of the town, who knew better of the country, could not give him any hope, or ways, how to improve it from the Indian. It soon then appeared most fit, by a general approbation, that to preserve and save all from starving, there could be no readier course thought on, than to abandon the country, and accommodating themselves the best that they might, in the present pinnaces then in the road, namely in the *Discovery* and the *Virginia*, and in the two, brought from, and builded at the Bermudas, the *Deliverance* and the *Patience*, with all speed convenient to make for the Newfoundland, where (being the fishing time) they might meet with many English ships into which happily they might disperse most of the company.

This consultation taking effect, our governor having caused to be carried aboard all the arms, and all the best things in the store, which might to the adventurers make some commodity upon the sale thereof at home, and burying our ordnances before the fort gate, which looked into the river. The seventh of June, having appointed to every pinnace likewise his complement and number, also delivered thereunto a proportionable rate of provision, he commanded every man at the beating of the drum to repair aboard. And because he would preserve the town (albeit now to be quitted) unburned, which some intemperate and malicious people threatened, his own company he caused to be left ashore, and was himself the last of them, when about noon giving a farewell, with a peal of small shot, we set sail, and that night, with the tide, fell down to an island in the river, which our people have called Hog Island; and the morning tide brought us to another island, which we have called Mulberry Island; where lying at an anchor, in the afternoon, stemming the tide, we discovered a longboat making toward us from Point Comfort: much descant we made thereof, about an hour it came up; by which, to our no little joys, we had intelligence of the Honorable my Lord La Warr's arrival before Algernon Fort the sixth of June, at what time, true it is, His Lordship having understood of our governor's resolution to depart the country, with all expedition caused his skiff to be manned, and in it dispatched his letters by Captain Edward Brewster (who commandeth His Lordship's company) to our governor, which preventing us before the aforesaid Mulberry Island (the eighth of June aforesaid) upon the receipt of His Honor's letters, our governor bore up the helm, with the wind coming easterly, and that night (the wind so favorable) relanded all his men at the fort again: before which (the tenth of June, being Sunday) His Lordship had likewise brought his ships, and in the afternoon, came ashore with Sir Ferdinando Weinman and all His Lordship's followers.

Here (worthy Lady) let me have a little your pardon, for having now a better heart, than when I first landed, I will briefly describe unto you the situation and form of our fort. When Captain Newport in his first voyage, did not like to inhabit upon so open a road as Cape Henry, nor Point Comfort he plied it up to the river, still looking out for the most apt and securest place, as well for his company to set down in, as which might give the least cause of offense, or distaste, in his judgment, to the inhabitants. At length, after much and weary search (with their barge coasting still before, as Virgil writeth Aeneas did, arriving in the region of Italy called Latium, upon the banks of the river Tiber) in the country of a werowance called Wowinchapuncke (a ditionary to Powhatan) within this fair river of Paspahegh, which we have called the King's River, a country least inhabited by the Indian, as they all the way observed, and threescore miles and better up the fresh channel, from Cape Henry, they had sight of an extended plain and spot of earth which thrust out into the depth and midst of the channel, making a kind of chersonese or peninsula, for it was fastened only to the land with a slender neck no broader than a man may well quaite a tile shard, and no inhabitants by seven or six miles near it. The trumpets sounding, the admiral struck sail, and before the same the rest of the fleet came to an anchor, and here (as the best yet offered unto their view, supposed so much the more convenient by how much, with their small company, they were like enough the better to assure it), to lose no further time, the colony disembarked, and every man brought his particular store and furniture, together with the general provision ashore: for the safety of which, as likewise for their own security, ease, and better accommodating, a certain canton and quantity of that little half island of ground, was measured, which they began to fortify and thereon in the name of God, to raise a fortress, with the ablest and speediest means they could: which fort, growing since to more perfection, is now at this present in this manner.

A low level of ground about half an acre (or so much as Queen Dido might buy of King Hyarbas, which she compassed about with the thongs cut out of one bull hide, and therein built her castle of Byrza) on the north side of the river, is cast almost into the form of a triangle, and so palisaded. The south side next the river (howbeit extended in a line, or curtain six score foot more in length, than the other two, by reason the advantage of the ground doth so require) contains one hundred and forty yards: the west and east sides a hundred only. At every angle or corner, where the lines meet, a bulwark or watchtower is raised, and in each bulwark, a piece of ordnance or two well mounted. To every side, a proportioned distance from the palisade, is a settled street of houses, that runs along, so as each line of the angle hath his street. In the midst is a market place, a storehouse, and a *corps du garde*, as likewise a pretty chapel, though (at this time when we came in) as ruined and unfrequented: but the lord governor, and captain general, hath given order for the repairing of it, and at this instant, many hands are about it. It is in length three score foot, in breadth twenty four, and shall have a chancel in it of cedar, and a communion table of the black walnut, and all the pews of cedar, with fair broad windows, to shut and open, as the weather shall occasion, of the same wood, a pulpit of the same, with a font hewn hollow, like a canoe, with two bells at the west end. It is so cast as it be very light within, and the lord governor and captain general doth cause it to be kept passing sweet, and trimmed up with divers flowers, with a sexton belonging to it, and in it every Sunday we have sermons twice a day, and every Thursday a sermon, having true preachers which take their weekly turns, and every morning at the ringing of a bell, about ten of the clock, each man addresseth himself to prayers, and so at four of the clock before supper. Every Sunday, when the lord governor, and captain general goeth to church, he is accompanied with all the councilors, captains, other officers, and all the gentlemen, and with a guard of halberdiers in His Lordship's livery, fair red cloaks, to the number of fifty, both on each side, and behind him: and being in the church, His Lordship hath his seat in the choir, in a green velvet chair, with a cloth, with a velvet cushion spread on a table before him, on which he kneeleth, and on each side sit the council, captains, and officers, each in their place, and when he returneth home again, he is waited on to his house in the same manner.

And thus enclosed, as I said, round with a palisade of planks and strong posts, four foot deep in the ground, of young oaks, walnuts, etc. The fort is called in honor of His Majesty's name, Jamestown; the principal gate from the town, through the palisade, opens to the river, as at each bulwark there is a gate likewise to go forth, and at every gate a demi-culverin, and so in the market place. The houses first raised, were all burnt by a casualty of fire the beginning of the second year of their seat, and in the second voyage of Captain Newport, which since have been better rebuilded, though as yet in no great uniformity, either for the fashion or beauty of the street. A delicate wrought fine kind of mat the Indians make, with which (as they can be trucked for or snatched up) our people do dress their chambers and inward rooms, which make their houses so much the more handsome. The houses have wide and large country chimneys, in the which is to be supposed (in such plenty of wood) what fires are maintained; and they have found the way to cover their houses: now (as the Indians) with barks of trees, as durable, and as good proof against storms, and winter weather, as the best tile defending likewise the piercing sunbeams of summer, and keeping the inner lodgings cool enough, which before in sultry weather would be like stoves, whilst they were, as at first, pargeted and plastered with bitumen or tough clay: and thus armed for the injury of changing times, and seasons of the year, we hold ourselves well apaid, though wanting arras hangings, tapestry, and gilded Venetian cordovan, or more spruce household garniture and wanton city ornaments, remembering the old epigraph:

> We dwell not here to build us bowers,
> And halls for pleasure and good cheer:
> But halls we build for us and ours,
> To dwell in them whilst we live here.

True it is, I may not excuse this our fort, or Jamestown, as yet seated in somewhat an unwholesome and sickly air, by reason it is in a marsh ground, low, flat to the river, and hath no freshwater springs serving the town, but what we drew from a well six or seven fathom deep, fed by the brackish river oozing into it, from whence I verily believe, the chief causes have proceeded of many diseases and sicknesses which have happened to our people, who are indeed strangely afflicted with fluxes and agues; and every particular season (by the relation of the old inhabitants) hath his particular infirmity too, all which (if it had been our fortunes, to have seated upon some hill, accommodated with fresh springs and clear air, as do the natives of the country) we might have, I believe, well escaped: and some experience we have to persuade ourselves that it may be so, for of some hundred and odd men which were seated at the

Falls, the last year when the fleet came in with fresh and young able spirits, under the government of Captain Francis West, and of one hundred to the seawards (on the south side of our river) in the country of the Nansemonds, under the charge of Captain John Martin, there did not so much as one man miscarry, and but very few or none, fall sick, whereas at Jamestown, the same time, and the same months, one hundred sickened, and half the number died: howbeit, as we condemn not Kent in England, for a small town called Plumstead, continually assaulting the dwellers there (especially newcomers) with agues and fevers; no more let us lay scandal, and imputation upon the country of Virginia, because the little quarter wherein we are set down (unadvisedly so choosed) appears to be unwholesome, and subject to many ill airs, which accompany the like marsh places.

IV

The Lord La Warr's beginnings and proceedings in Jamestown. Sir Thomas Gates sent into England; his and the Company's testimony of Virginia, and cause of the late miseries.

Upon His Lordship's landing at the south gate of the palisade (which looks into the river) our governor caused his company in arms to stand in order, and make a guard: it pleased him, that I should bear his colors for that time: his Lordship landing, fell upon his knees and before us all made a long and silent prayer to himself, and after, marched up into the town, where at the gate, I bowed with the colors, and let them fall at His Lordship's feet, who passed on into the chapel, where he heard a sermon by Master Buck our governor's preacher; and after that caused a gentleman, one of his own followers, Master Anthony Scot his ancient to read his commission, which entitled him lord governor, and captain general during his life, of the colony and plantation in Virginia (Sir Thomas Gates, our governor hitherto, being now styled therein lieutenant general).

After the reading of His Lordship's commission, Sir Thomas Gates rendered up unto His Lordship his own commission, both patents, and the council seal: after which, the lord governor and captain general, delivered some few words unto the company, laying many blames upon them for many vanities, and their idleness, earnestly wishing, that he might no more find it so, lest he should be compelled to draw the sword of justice, to cut off such delinquents, which he had much rather, he protested, draw in their defense, to protect them from injuries; heartening them with the knowledge of what store of provisions he had brought for them, viz. sufficient to serve four hundred men for one whole year.

The twelfth of June, being Tuesday, the lord governor and captain general, did constitute, and give places of office and charge to divers captains and gentlemen, and elected unto him a council, unto whom he did administer an oath, mixed with the Oath of Allegiance, and Supremacy to His Majesty: which oath likewise he caused to be administered the next day after to every particular member of the colony, of faith, assistance, and secrecy. The council which he elected were: Sir Thomas Gates, Knight, lieutenant general. Sir George Somers, Knight, admiral. Captain George Percy Esquire and in the fort captain of fifty. Sir Ferdinando Weinman Knight, master of the ordnance. Captain Christopher Newport, vice-admiral. William Strachey Esquire, secretary, and recorder.

As likewise the lord governor and captain general nominated Captain John Martin, master of the battery works for steel and iron: and Captain George Webb sergeant major of the fort: and especial captains over companies, were these appointed; Captain Edward Brewster, who hath the command of His Honor's own company. Captain Thomas Lawson. Captain Thomas Holecroft. Captain Samuel Argall. Captain George Yeardley, who commandeth the lieutenant general's company. Divers other officers were likewise made, as Master Ralph Hamor and Master Browne, clerks of the council, and Master Daniel Tucker and Master Robert Wilde, clerks of the store, etc.

The first business which the lord governor and captain general (after the settling of these officers) thought upon, was to advise with his council, for the obtaining of such provisions of victuals for store, and quality, as the country afforded. It did not appear that any kind of flesh, deer, or what else of that kind could be recovered from the Indian, or to be sought in the country by the travail or search of his people, and the old dwellers in the fort (together with the Indians not to friend) who had the last winter, destroyed and killed up all the hogs, insomuch, as of five or six hundred (as it is supposed) there was not one left alive; nor an hen, nor chick in the fort; and our horses and mares, they had eaten with the first, and the provision which the lord governor and captain general had brought, concerning any kind of flesh, was little or nothing; in respect it was not dreamt of by the adventurers in England, that the swine were destroyed.

In council therefore the thirteenth of June, it pleased Sir George Somers, Knight, admiral, to propose a voyage, which for the better relief and good of the colony, he would perform into the Bermudas, from whence he would fetch six months provision of flesh and fish, and some live hogs to store our colony again: and had a commission given unto him the fifteenth of June, 1610, who in his own Bermuda pinnace, the *Patience*, consorted with Captain Samuel Argall in the *Discovery* (whom the lord governor, and captain general, made of the council before his departure), the nineteenth of June, fell with the tide from before our town, and the twenty two left the bay, or Cape Henry astern.

And likewise, because at the lord governor, and captain general's first coming, there was found in our own river no store of fish; after many trials, the lord governor, and captain general, dispatched in the *Virginia*, with instructions, the seventeenth of June 1610, Robert Tyndall, master of the *De La Warr*, to fish unto, all along, and between Cape Henry, and Cape Charles, within the bay; who the last of the said month returned to us again, but as ill speeding as the former, whom our governor (now lieutenant general) had addressed thither before for the same purpose. Nor was the lord governor, and captain general in the meanwhile idle at the fort, but every day and night he caused the nets to be hauled, sometimes a dozen times one after another. But it pleased not God so to bless our labors, that we did at any time take one quarter so much, as would give unto our people one pound at a meal apiece, by which we might have better husbanded our peas and oatmeal, notwithstanding the great store we now saw daily in our river: but let the blame of this lie where it is, both upon our nets, and the unskillfulness of our men to lay them.

The sixth of July, Sir Thomas Gates, lieutenant general, coming down to Point Comfort, the north wind (blowing rough) he found had forced the longboat belonging to Algernon Fort, to the other shore upon Nansemond side, somewhat short of Weroscoick: which to recover again, one of the lieutenant general's men Humphrey Blunt, in an old canoe, made over, but the wind driving him upon the strand, certain Indians (watching the occasion) seized the poor fellow, and led him up into the woods, and sacrificed him. It did not a little trouble the lieutenant governor, who since his first landing in the country (how justly so ever provoked) would not by any means be wrought to a violent proceeding against them, for all the practices of villainy, with which they daily endangered our men, thinking it possible, by a more tractable course, to win them to a better condition: but now being startled by this, he well perceived, how little a fair and noble entreaty works upon a barbarous disposition, and therefore in some measure purposed to be revenged.

The ninth of July, he prepared his forces, and early in the morning set upon a town of theirs, some four miles from Algernon Fort, called Kecoughtan, and had soon taken it, without loss or hurt of any of his men. The governor and his women fled (the young King Powhatan's son not being there) but left his poor baggage, and treasure to the spoil of our soldiers, which was only a few baskets of old wheat, and some other of peas and beans, a little tobacco, and some few women's girdles of silk, of the grass silk, not without art, and much neatness finely wrought; of which I have sent divers into England, (being at the taking of the town) and would have sent Your Ladyship some of them, had they been a present so worthy.

We purposed to set a Frenchman here a work to plant vines, which grew naturally in great plenty. Some few cornfields it hath, and the corn in good forwardness, and we despair not but to be able (if our men stand in health) to make it good against the Indian.

The continual practices of the subtle King Powhatan, doth not meanly awaken all the powers and workings of virtue and knowledge, in our lord governor and captain general, how to prevent not only his mischiefs, but to draw him upon some better terms, and acknowledgment of our forces and spirits, both able and daring to quit him in any valiant and martial course whatsoever, he shall dare to run with us, which he doth yet scarcely believe. For this therefore, since first, and that so lately, he hath set on his people to attempt us with private conspiracies and actual violence, into the one drawing his neighbor confederates and underprinces, and by the other working the loss and death of divers of our men, and by such their loss, seizing their arms, swords, pieces, etc., of which he hath gathered into his store a great quantity and number by intelligence above two hundred swords, besides axes, and poleaxes, chisels, hoes, to pare and cleanse their ground, with an infinite treasure of copper, our lord governor and captain general sent two gentlemen with an embassy unto him, letting him to understand of his practices and outrage, hitherto used toward our people, not only abroad but at our fort also: yet flattering him withal how the lord governor and captain general did not suppose that these mischiefs were contrived by him, or with his knowledge, but conceived them rather to be the acts of his worst and unruly people, His Lordship therefore now complaining unto him required, that he (being so great and wise a king) would give an universal order to his subjects, that it might be no more so, lest the lord governor and captain general should be compelled (by defending him and his) to offend him, which he would be loath to do: withal he willed the messengers to demand of him the said Powhatan, that he would either punish or send unto His Lordship such of his people whom Powhatan knew well not long before, had assaulted our men at the blockhouse, and but newly killed four of them, as also to demand of

Powhatan, willing him to return unto the English fort, both such men as he detained of ours, and such arms as he had of theirs in his possession, and those conditions performed, he willed them to assure unto Powhatan that then their great werowance, the lord governor and captain general would hold fair quarter and enter friendship with him, as a friend to King James and his subjects. But refusing to submit to these demands, the lord governor and captain general gave in charge to the messengers, so sent to signify unto Powhatan that His Lordship would by all means public and private, seek to recover from him such of the English as he had, being subjects to his king and master, unto whom even Powhatan himself had formerly vowed not only friendship but homage, receiving from His Majesty therefore many gifts, and upon his knees a crown and scepter with other ornaments, the symbols of civil state and Christian sovereignty, thereby obliging himself to offices of duty to His Majesty. Unto all which Powhatan returned no other answer, but that either we should depart his country, or confine ourselves to Jamestown only, without searching further up into his land, or rivers, or otherwise, he would give in command to his people to kill us, and do unto us all the mischief, which they at their pleasure could and we feared: withal forewarning the said messengers not to return any more unto him, unless they brought him a coach and three horses, for he had understood by the Indians which were in England, how such was the state of great werowances, and lords in England, to ride and visit other great men.

After this divers times, and daily he sent sometimes two, sometimes three, unto our fort, to understand our strength and to observe our watch and guard, and how our people stood in health, and what numbers were arrived with this new werowance: which being soon perceived our lord governor and captain general forewarned such his spies, upon their own peril, to resort no more unto our fort. Howbeit, they would daily press into our blockhouse and come up to our palisade gates, supposing the government as well now, as fantastical and negligent in the former times, the whilst, some quarter of a mile short of the blockhouse, the greatest number of them would make assault and lie in ambush about our glasshouse, whither, divers times indeed our men would make out either to gather strawberries or to fetch fresh water; any one of which so straggled, if they could with conveniency, they would assault and charge with their bows and arrows, in which manner they killed many of our men: two of which being Paspaheans, who were ever our deadliest enemies, and not to be reconciled; at length being apprehended (and one of them a notable villain, who had attempted upon many in our fort) the lord governor caused them to be manacled, and convented before him and his council, where it was determined that he that had done so much mischief, should have his right hand struck off, sending him away withal, with a message to Powhatan, that unless he would yet return such Englishmen as he detained, together with all such their arms (as before spoken of) that not only the other (now prisoner) should die, but all such of his savages (as the lord governor and captain general could by any means surprise) should run the same course: as likewise the lord governor and captain general would fire all his neighbor cornfields, towns, and villages, and that suddenly, if Powhatan sent not to contract with him the sooner.

What this will work with him, we know not as yet, for this was but the day before our ships were now falling to Point Comfort, and so to set sail for England: which ships riding before Weroscoick to take in their freight of cedar, clapboard, black walnut, and iron ore, took prisoners likewise the chief king of Weroscoick, called Sasenticum, with his son, Kainta, and one of his chief men. And the fifteenth day of July, in the *Blessing* Captain Adams brought them to Point Comfort, where at that time (as well to take his leave of the lieutenant general, Sir Thomas Gates, now bound for England, as to dispatch the ships) the lord governor and captain general had pitched his tent in Algernon Fort.

The king's son Kainta the lord governor and captain general, hath sent now into England, until the ships arrive here again the next spring, dismissing the old werowance and the other with all terms of kindness, and friendship, promising further designs to be effected by him, to which he hath bound himself, by divers savage ceremonies, and admirations.

And thus (right noble Lady), once more this famous business, as recreated and dipped anew into life and spirit, hath raised it (I hope) from infamy, and shall redeem the stains and losses under which she hath suffered, since her first conception: your graces still accompany the least appearance of her, and vouchsafe her to be limned out, with the beauty which we will beg, and borrow from the fair lips: nor fear you, that she will return blushes to your cheeks for praising her, since (more than most excellent Lady) like yourself (were all tongues dumb and envious) she will praise herself in her most silence: may she once be but seen, or but her shadow lively by a skillful workman set out indeed, which here (bungerly as I am) I have presumed (though defacing it) in these papers to present unto your Ladyship.

Appendix IV

SILVESTER JOURDAINE'S DESCRIPTION OF THE *SEA VENTURE'S* WRECK IN BERMUDA AND THEIR ESCAPE TO JAMESTOWN.

Taken from
A Plain Description of Bermudas
(London, 1613)

A DISCOVERY
OF THE BERMUDAS,
NOW CALLED
THE SOMER
Islands.

Being in ship called the *Sea Venture*, with Sir Thomas Gates our Governor, Sir George Somers, and Captain Newport, three most worthy honored Gentlemen, (whose valor and fortitude the world must needs take notice of, and that in most Honorable designs) bound for Virginia, in the height of thirty degrees of northerly latitude, or thereabouts: we were taken with a most sharp and cruel storm upon the five and twentieth day of July, Anno. 1609, which did not only separate us from the residue of our fleet, (which were eight in number) but with the violent working of the Seas our ship became so shaken, torn, and leaked, that she received so much water as covered two tire of hogsheads above the ballast; that our men stood up to the middles, with buckets, baricos, and kettles, to bail out the water, and continuously pumped for three days and three nights together, without any intermission; and yet the water seemed rather to increase, than to diminish: in so much that all our men, being utterly spent, tired, and disabled for longer labor, were even resolved, without any hope of their lives, to shut up the hatches, and to have committed themselves to the mercy of the sea, (which is said to be merciless) or rather to the mercy of their mighty God and Redeemer, (whose mercies exceed all his works) seeing no help, nor hope, in the apprehension of man's reason, that any mother's child could escape that inevitable danger, which every man had proposed and digested to himself of present sinking.

So that some of the having some good and comfortable waters in the ship, fetched them, and drunk one to the other, taking their last leave one of the other, until their more joyful and happy meeting in a more blessed world; when it pleased God out of his most gracious and mercifull providence so to direct and guide our ship, (being left to the mercy of the sea) for her most advantage; that Sir George Somers sitting upon the poop of the ship, (where he sat three days and three nights together, without meals, meat, and little or no sleep) couning the ship to keep her as upright as he could (for otherwise she must needs instantly have foundered) most wishedly and happily descried land; whereupon he most comfortably encouraged the company to follow their pumping, and by no means to cease bailing out of the water, with their buckets, baricos, and kettles; whereby they were so over-wearied, and their spirits so spent with long fasting, and continuance of their labor, that for the most part they were fallen asleep in corners, and wheresoever they chanced first to sit or lie: but hearing news of land, wherewith they grew to be somewhat revived, being carried with will and desire beyond their strength, every man bustled up, and gathered his strength and feeble spirits together, to perform as much as their weak force would permit them: through which weak means, it pleased God to work so strongly as the water was staid for that little time, (which as we all much feared, was the last period of our breathing) and the ship kept from present sinking, when it pleased God to send her within half an English mile of that land that Sir George Somers had not long before descried: which were the islands of the Bermudas. And there neither did our ship sink, but more fortunately in so great a misfortune fell in-between two rocks, where she was fast lodged and locked, for further budging: whereby we gained not only sufficient time, with the present help of our boat, and skiff, safely to set and convey our men ashore, (which were one hundred and fifty in number) but afterwards had time and leisure to save some good part of our goods and provision, which the water had not spoiled, with all the tackling of the ship, and much of the iron about her, which were necessaries not a little available for the building and furnishing of a new ship and pinnace, which we made there, for the transporting and carrying of us to Virginia. But our delivery was not more strange in falling so opportunely and happily upon the land, as our feeding and preservation was beyond our hopes, and all men's expectations, most admirable.

For the islands of the Bermudas, as every man knoweth that hath heard or read of them, were never inhabited by any Christian or heathen people, but ever esteemed, and reputed, a most prodigious and enchanted place, affording nothing but gusts, storms, and foul weather; which made every navigator and mariner to avoid them, as Scylla and Charibdis; or as they would . the Devil himself; and no man was ever heard to make for the place, but . against their wills, they have by storms and dangerousness of the rocks, lying seven leagues into the sea, suffered shipwreck; yet did we find there the air so temperate, and the country so abundantly fruitful of all fit necessaries for the sustentation and preservation of man's life, that most in a manner of all our provisions of bread, beer, and victual, being quite spoiled, in lying long drowned in salt water; notwithstanding, we were there for the space of nine months (few days over) not only well refreshed, comforted, and with good satiety contented, but out of the abundance thereof, provided us some reasonable quantity and proportion of provision, to carry us for Virginia, and to maintain ourselves, and that company we found there, to the great relief of them, as it fell out in their so great extremities, and in respect of the shortness of time, until it pleased God, that by my Lord De La Warr's coming thither, their store was better supplied. And greater, and better provision we might have made, if we had had better means for the storing and transportation thereof. Wherefore my opinion sincerely of this island is, that whereas it hath been, and is still accounted, the most dangerous, infortunate, and most forlorn place of the world, it is in truth the richest, healthfullest, and pleasing land, (the quantity and bigness thereof considered) and merely natural, as ever man set foot upon: the particular profits and benefits whereof, shall be more especially inserted, and hereunto annexed, which every man to his own private knowledge, that was there, can avouch and justify for a truth.

Upon the eight and twentieth day of July 1609 (after the extremity of the storm was something qualified) we fell upon the shore at the Bermudas; where after our General Sir Thomas Gates, Sir George Somers, and Captain Newport, had by their provident carefulness landed all their men, and so much of the goods and provisions out of the ship, as was not utterly spoiled, every man disposed and applied himself to search for, and to seek out such relief and sustentation, as the country afforded: and Sir George Somers, a man inured to extremities, (and knowing what thereunto belonged) was in this service neither idle nor backward, but presently by his careful industry went, and found out sufficient of many kind of fishes, and so plentiful thereof, that in half an hour he took so many fishes with hooks, as did suffice the whole company one day. And fish is there so abundant, that if a man step into the water, they will come round about him; so that men were fain to get out for fear of biting. These fishes are very fat and sweet, and of that proportion and bigness, that three of them will conveniently lade two men: those we called rock-fish. Besides there are such abundance of mullets, that

might be taken at one draught one thousand at the least, and
pilchards, with divers kinds of great fishes, the names of
to me: of tray fishes very great ones, and so great store, as
been taken in one night with making lights, even sufficient
e company a day. The country affordeth great abundance of
hogs, as that there hath been taken by Sir George Somers, who was the first
that hunted for them, to the number of two and thirty at one time, which
he brought to the company in a boat, built by his own hands. There is fowl
in great number upon the islands, where they breed, that there hath been
taken in two or three hours, a thousand at the least; the bird being of the
bigness of a good pigeon, and layeth eggs as big as hen eggs upon the sand,
where they come and lay them daily, although men sit down amongst them;
that there hath been taken up in one morning by Sir Thomas Gates' men,
one thousand of eggs: and Sir George Somers' men, coming a little distance
of time after them, have stayed there whilst they came and laid their eggs
amongst them, that they brought away as many more with them; with many
young birds very fat and sweet.

Another sea fowl there is that lyeth in little holes in the ground, like
unto a coney-hole, and are in great numbers, exceeding good meat, very fat
and sweet (those we had in the winter) and their eggs are white, and of that
bigness, that they are not to be known from hen eggs. The other birds' eggs
are speckled, and of a different color: there are also great store and plenty of
herons, and those so familiar and tame, that we beat them down from the
trees with stones and staves; but such were young herons: besides many white
herons, without so much as a black or gray feather on them; with other small
birds so tame and gentle, that a man walking in the woods with a stick, and
whistling to them, they will come and gaze on you, so near that you may
strike and kill many of them with your stick; and with singing and hollowing
you may do the like.

There are also great store of tortoises, (which some call turtles) and those
so great, that I have seen a bushel of eggs in one of their bellies, which are
sweeter than any hen egg: and the tortoise itself is all very good meat, and
yieldeth great store of oil, which is as sweet as any butter; and one of them
will suffice fifty men a meal, at the least: and, of these hath been taken great
store, with two boats, at the least forty in one day. The country yieldeth
divers fruits, as prickled pears, great abundance, which continue green upon
the trees all the year; also great plenty of mulberries, white and red: and on
the same are great store of silk worms, which yield cods of silk, both white
and yellow, being some course, and some fine. And there is a tree called a

palmetto tree, which hath a very sweet berry, upon which the hogs do most feed; but our men finding the sweetness of them, did willingly share with the hogs for them, they being very pleasant and wholesome, which made them careless almost of any bread with their meat; which occasioned us to carry in a manner all that store of flour and meal we did or could save, for Virginia. The head of the palmetto tree is very good meat, either raw or sodden, it yieldeth a head which weigheth about twenty pound, and is far better meat, than any cabbage. There are an infinite number of cedar trees, (the fairest I think in the world) and those bring forth a very sweet berry, and wholesome to eat. The country (for as much as I could find myself, or hear by others) affords no venomous creature, or so much as rat or mouse, or any other thing unwholesome. There is great store of pearl, and some of them very fair, round, and oriental; and you shall find at least one hundred seed of pearl in one oyster; there hath been likewise found some good quantity of Amber Greece, and that of the best sort.

There are also great plenty of whales, which I conceive are very easy to be killed, for they come so usually, and ordinarily to the shore, that we heard them oftentimes in the night a bed; and have seen many of them near the shore, in the daytime.

There was born upon the Bermudas, at the time of our being there, two children, the one a man child, there baptized by the name of Bermudas: and a woman child, baptized by the name of Bermuda: as also there was a marriage between two English people upon that island. This island, I mean the main island, with all the broken islands adjacent, are made in the form of a half moon, but a little more rounder, and divided into many broken islands, and there are many good harbors in it, but we could find but one especial place to go in, or rather to go out from it, which was not altogether free from some danger, where there is three fathoms water at the entrance thereof, but within, six, seven, or eight fathoms at the least, where you may safely lie land-locked, from the danger of all winds and weathers, and more to the trees. The corning into it is so narrow and straight between the rocks, as that it will with small store of munition be fortified, and easily defended, against the forces of the potentest King of Europe, such advantage the place affords.

There are also plenty of hawks, and very good tobacco, as I think, which through forgetfulness, I had almost omitted. Now having finished and rigged our ship, and pinnace, the one called the *Deliverance*, the pinnace which we built there, the *Patience*, we prepared and made ourselves ready, to ship for Virginia, having powdered some store of hog's flesh for provision thither, and the company thereof, for some reasonable time: but were compelled to make salt for the same purpose, for all our salt was spent and spoiled, before wee recovered the shore. We carried with us also a good portion of tortoise-oil, which either for frying or baking did us very great pleasure, it being very sweet, nourishing, and wholesome: the greatest defects we found there, were tar and pitch for our ship and pinnace, instead whereof we were forced to make lime there of a hard kind of stone, and use it: which for the present occasion and necessity, with some wax we found cast up by the sea, from some shipwreck, served the turn to pay the seams of the pinnace Sir George Somers built, for which he had neither pitch nor tar: so that God in the supplying of all our wants, beyond all measure, showed himself still merciful unto us, that we might accomplish our intended voyage to Virginia, for which I confidently hope, he doth yet reserve a blessing in store, and to the which I presume every honest and religious heart will readily give their Amen.

When all hinges were made ready, and commodiously fitted, the wind coming fair, we set sail and put off from the Bermudas, the tenth day of May, in the year 1610, and arrived at Jamestown in Virginia, the four and twentieth day of the same month: where we found some threescore persons living. And being then some three weeks or thereabouts passed, and not hearing of any supply, it was thought fitting by a general consent, to use the best means for the preservation of all those people that were living, being all in number two hundred persons. And so upon the eighth of June one thousand six hundred and ten, we embarked at Jamestown, not having above fourteen days' victual, and so were determined to direct our course for Newfoundland, there to refresh us, and supply ourselves with victual, to bring us home; but it pleased God to dispose otherwise of us, and to give us better means. For being all of us shipped in four pinnaces, and departed from the town, almost down half the river, we met my Lord De La Warr coming up with three ships, well furnished with victual, which revived all the company, and gave them great content.

And after some few days, my Lord understanding of the great plenty of hogs and fish was at the Bermudas, and the necessity of them to Virginia, was desirous to send thither, to supply himself with those things, for the better comforting of his men, and the plantation of the country. Whereupon Sir George Somers being a man best acquainted with the place, and being willing to do service unto his Prince and Country, without any respect of his own private gain, and being of threescore years of age at the least, out of his worthy and valiant mind, offered himself to undertake to perform with God's help that dangerous voyage for the Bermudas, for the better relief and comfort of the people in Virginia, and for the better plantation of it, which offer my

Lord De La Warr very willingly and thankfully accepted: and so upon the nineteenth of June, Sir George Somers embarked himself at Jamestown in a small barge of thirty ton, or thereabout, that he built at the Bermudas: wherein he labored from morning until night, as duly as any workman doth labor for wages, and built her all with cedar, with little or no iron work at all: having in her but one bolt, which was in the kilson: notwithstanding thanks be to God, she brought us in safety to Virginia, and so I trust he will protect him, and send him well back again, to his heart's desire, and the great comfort of all the company there.

Appendix V

A JOURNEY TO POKANOKET

A chapter from *A Relation or Journal of the Beginning and Proceedings of the English Plantation Settled at Plymouth in New England* (London, 1622).

A
JOURNEY TO POKANOKET
The Habitation of the Great King
MASSASOIT.
As also our Message, the
Answer and entertainment
we had of
HIM.

It seemed good to the company for many considerations to send some amongst them to Massasoit, the greatest commander amongst the savages, bordering about us; partly to know where to find them, if occasion served, as also to see their strength, discover the country, prevent abuses in their disorderly coming unto us, make satisfaction for some conceived injuries to be done on our parts, and to continue the league of peace and friendship between them and us. For these, and the like ends, it pleased the governor to make choice of Stephen Hopkins, and Edward Winslow to go unto him, and having a fit opportunity, by reason of a savage, called Tisquantum (that could speak English) coming unto us; with all expedition provided a horseman's coat, of red cotton, and laced with a slight lace, for a present, that both they and their message might be the more acceptable amongst them. The message was as followeth; that forasmuch as his subjects came often and without fear, upon all occasions amongst us, so we were now come unto him, and in witness of the love and good will the English bear unto him, the governor hath sent him a coat, desiring that the peace and amity that was between them and us might be continued, not that we feared them, but because we intended not to injure any, desiring to live peaceably: and as with all men, so especially with them our nearest neighbors. But whereas his people came very often, and very many together unto us, bringing for the most part their wives and children with them, they were welcome; yet we being but strangers as yet at Patuxet, alias New Plymouth, and not knowing how our corn might prosper, we could no longer give them such entertainment as we had done, and as we desired still to do: yet if he would be pleased to come himself, or any special friend of his desired to see us, coming from him they should be welcome; and to the end we might know them from others, our governor had sent him a copper chain, desiring if any messenger should come from him to us, we might know him by bringing it with him, and hearken and give credit to his message accordingly. Also requesting him that such as have skins, should bring them to us, and that he would hinder the multitude from oppressing us with them. And whereas at our first arrival at Pamet (called by us Cape Cod) we found there corn buried in the ground, and finding no inhabitants but some graves of dead new buried, took the corn, resolving if ever we could hear of any that had right thereunto, to make satisfaction to the full for it, yet since we understand the owners thereof were fled for fear of us, our desire was either to pay them with the like quantity of corn, English meal, or any other commodities we had to pleasure them withal; requesting him that some one of his men might signify so much unto them, and we would content him for his pains. And last of all, our governor requested one favor of him, which was, that he would exchange some of their corn for seed with us, that we might make trial which best agreed with the soil where we live.

With these presents and message we set forward the tenth June, about 9 o'clock in the morning[123], our guide resolving that night to rest at Nemasket[124],

---

[123]   The month of June for this travel is suspect, for numerous reasons; this expedition likely took place in April. First, June 10 was a Sabbath and the Pilgrims would not have sent out an expedition on Sunday. Second, Winslow later notes at Nemasket that they had abundance of shad spawning in the river, and shad spawn in April, not June. Winslow also mentions asking to trade for corn seed, but by June it would be too late in the season to plant. Additionally, the next voyage made by Plymouth men (to Nauset) set off on Monday, June 11, and it is unlikely Plymouth would have sent off so many men on several different expeditions simultaneously, given their weak state of defense. For more information, see Maurice Robbins, "The Path to Pokanoket: Winslow and Hopkins visit the Great Chief" (Massachusetts Archaeological Society, n.d.)

[124]   An Indian village near modern-day Middleboro.

a town under Massasoit, and conceived by us to be very near, because the inhabitants flocked so thick upon every slight occasion amongst us: but we found it to be some fifteen English miles. On the way we found some ten or twelve men, women and children, which had pestered us, till we were weary of them, perceiving that (as the manner of them all is) where victual is easiest to be got, there they live, especially in the summer: by reason whereof our bay affording many lobsters, they resort every spring tide thither: and now returned with us to Nemasket. Thither we came about 3 o'clock after noon, the inhabitants entertaining us with joy, in the best manner they could, giving us a kind of bread called by them *maizium*, and the spawn of shads, which then they got in abundance, insomuch as they gave us spoons to eat them, with these they boiled musty acorns, but of the shads we ate heartily. After this they desired one of our men to shoot a crow, complaining what damage they sustained in their corn by them, who shooting some fourscore off and killing, they much admired it, as other shots on other occasions. After this Tisquantum told us we should hardly in one day reach Pokanoket, moving us to go some 8 miles further, where we should find more store and better victuals than there: being willing to hasten our journey we went, and came thither at sunsetting, where we found many of the Namascheucks (they so calling the men of Nemasket) fishing upon a weir which they had made on a river which belonged to them, where they caught abundance of bass. These welcomed us also, gave us of their fish, and we them of our victuals, not doubting but we should have enough where ere we came. There we lodged in the open fields: for houses they had none, though they spent the most of the summer there. The head of this river is reported to be not far from the place of our abode, upon it are, and have been many towns, it being a good length. The ground is very good on both sides, it being for the most part cleared: thousands of men have lived there, which died in a great plague not long since: and pity it was and is to see, so many goodly fields, and so well seated, without men to dress and manure the same. Upon this river dwelleth Massasoit: it cometh into the sea at the Narragansett Bay, where the Frenchmen so much use. A ship may go many miles up it, as the savages report, and a shallop to the head of it: but so far as we saw, we are sure a shallop may.

But to return to our journey. The next morning we broke our fast, took our leave and departed, being then accompanied with some six savages, having gone about six miles by the river side[125], at a known shoal place, it being low

---

[125]   Taunton River.

water, they spake to us to put off our breeches, for we must wade through. Here let me not forget the valor and courage of some of the savages, on the opposite side of the river, for there were remaining alive only 2 men, both aged, especially the one being above threescore; these two espying a company of men entering the river, ran very swiftly and low in the grass to meet us at the bank, where with shrill voices and great courage standing charged upon us with their bows, they demanded what we were, supposing us to be enemies, and thinking to take advantage on us in the water: but seeing we were friends, they welcomed us with such food as they had, and we bestowed a small bracelet of beads on them. Thus far we are sure the tide ebbs and flows.

Having here again refreshed ourselves we proceeded in our journey, the weather being very hot for travel, yet the country so well watered that a man could scarce be dry, but he should have a spring at hand to cool his thirst, beside small rivers in abundance: but the savages will not willingly drink, but at a springhead. When we came to any small brook where no bridge was, two of them desired to carry us through of their own accords, also fearing we were or would be weary, offered to carry our pieces, also if we would lay off any of our clothes, we should have them carried: and as the one of them had found more special kindness from one of the messengers, and the other savage from the other so they showed their thankfulness accordingly in affording us all help, and furtherance in the journey.

As we passed along, we observed that there were few places by the river, but had been inhabited, by reason whereof, much ground was clear, save of weeds which grew higher than our heads. There is much good timber both oak, walnut tree, fir, beech, and exceeding great chestnut trees. The country in respect of the lying of it, is both champaign and hilly, like many places in England. In some places it is very rocky both above ground and in it: and though the country be wild and overgrown with woods, yet the trees stand not thick, but a man may well ride a horse amongst them.

Passing on at length, one of the company an Indian espied a man, and told the rest of it, we asked them if they feared any, they told us that if they were Narragansett, men they would not trust them, whereat, we called for our pieces and bid them not to fear; for though they were twenty, we two alone would not care for them: but they hailing him, he proved a friend, and had only two women with him: their baskets were empty, but they fetched water in their bottles, so that we drank with them and departed. After we met another man with other two women, which had been at rendezvous by the salt water, and their baskets were full of roasted crab fishes, and other dried shellfish, of which they gave us, and we ate and drank with them: and gave each of the women a string of beads, and departed.

After we came to a town of Massasoit's, where we ate oysters and other fish. From thence we went to Pokanoket[126], but Massasoit was not at home, there we stayed, he being sent for: when news was brought of his coming, our guide Tisquantum requested that at our meeting, we would discharge our pieces, but one of us going about to charge his piece, the women and children through fear to see him take up his piece, ran away, and could not be pacified, till he laid it down again, who afterward were better informed by our interpreter.

Massasoit being come, we discharged our pieces, and saluted him, who after their manner kindly welcomed us, and took us into his house, and set us down by him, where having delivered our foresaid message, and presents, and having put the coat on his back, and the chain about his neck, he was not a little proud to behold himself, and his men also to see their king so bravely attired.

For answer to our message, he told us we were welcome, and he would gladly continue that peace and friendship which was between him and us: and for his men they should no more pester us as they had done: also, that he would send to Pamet, and would help us with corn for seed, according to our request.

This being done, his men gathered near to him, to whom he turned himself, and made a great speech; they sometimes interposing, and as it were, confirming and applauding him in that he said. The meaning whereof was (as far as we could learn) thus; Was not he Massasoit, commander of the country about them? Was not such a town his and the people of it? And should they not bring their skins unto us? To which they answered, they were his and would be at peace with us, and bring their skins to us. After this manner, he named at least thirty places, and their answer was as aforesaid to every one: so that as it was delightful, it was tedious unto us.

This being ended, he lighted tobacco for us, and fell to discoursing of England, and of the King's Majesty, marveling that he would live without a wife. Also he talked of the Frenchmen, bidding us not to suffer them to come to Narragansett, for it was King James his country, and he also was King James his man. Late it grew, but victuals he offered none; for indeed he had not any, being he came so newly home. So we desired to go to rest: he laid us on the bed with himself and his wife, they at the one end and we at the

---

[126] Pokanoket, home of Massasoit, was in the vicinity of modern-day Warren and Barrington, Rhode Island.

other, it being only planks laid a foot from the ground, and a thin mat upon them. Two more of his chief men, for want of room pressed by and upon us; so that we were worse weary of our lodging than of our journey.

The next day being Thursday, many of their sachems, or petty governors came to see us, and many of their men also. There they went to their manner of games for skins and knives. There we challenged them to shoot with them for skins: but they durst not: only they desired to see one of us shoot at a mark, who shooting with hail-shot, they wondered to see the mark so full of holes. About one o'clock, Massasoit brought two fishes thathe had shot, they were like bream but three times so big, and better meat. These being boiled there were at least forty looked for share in them, the most ate of them: this meal only we had in two nights and a day, and had not one of us bought a partridge, we had taken our journey fasting: very importunate he was to have us stay with them longer: but we desired to keep the Sabbath at home: and feared we should either be light-headed for want of sleep, for what with bad lodging, the savages' barbarous singing, (for they use to sing themselves asleep) lice and fleas within doors, and mosquitoes without, we could hardly sleep all the time of our being there; we much fearing, that if we should stay any longer, we should not be able to recover home for want of strength. So that on the Friday morning before sunrising, we took our leave and departed, Massasoit being both grieved and ashamed, that he could no better entertain us: and retaining Tisquantum to send from place to place to procure truck for us: and appointing another, called Tokamahamon in his place, whom we had found faithful before and after upon all occasions.

At this town of Massasoit's, where we before ate, we were again refreshed with a little fish; and bought about a handful of meal of their parched corn, which was very precious at that time of the year, and a small string of dried shellfish, as big as oysters. The latter we gave to the six savages thataccompanied us, keeping the meal for ourselves, when we drank we ate each a spoonful of it with a pipe of tobacco, instead of other victuals; and of this also we could not but give them so long as it lasted. Five miles they led us to a house out of the way in hope of victuals: but we found nobody there, and so were but worse able to return home. That night we reached to the weir where we lay before, but the Namascheucks were returned: so that we had no hope of anything there. One of the savages had shot a shad in the water, and a small squirrel as big as a rat, called a neuxis, the one half of either he gave us, and after went to the weir to fish. From hence we wrote to Plymouth, and sent Tokamahamon before to Nemasket, willing him from thence to send another, that he might meet us with food at Nemasket. Two men now only remained with us, and it pleased God to give them good store of fish, so that we were well refreshed. After supper we went to rest, and they to fishing again: more they got and fell to eating afresh, and retained sufficient ready roast for all our breakfasts. About two o'clock in the morning, arose a great storm of wind, rain, lightning, and thunder, in such violent manner, that we could not keep in our fire; and had the savages not roasted fish when we were asleep, we had set forward fasting: for the rain still continued with great violence, even the whole day through, till we came within two miles of home.

Being wet and weary, at length we came to Nemasket, there we refreshed ourselves, giving gifts to all such as had showed us any kindness. Amongst others one of the six that came with us from Pokanoket, having before this on the way unkindly forsaken us, marveled we gave him nothing, and told us what he had done for us; we also told him of some discourtesies he offered us, whereby he deserved nothing, yet we gave him a small trifle: whereupon he offered us tobacco: but the house being full of people, we told them he stole some by the way, and if it were of that we would not take it: for we would not receive that which was stolen upon any terms; if we did, our God would be angry with us, and destroy us. This abashed him, and gave the rest great content: but at our departure he would needs carry him on his back through a river, whom he had formerly in some sort abused. Fain they would have had us to lodge there all night: and wondered we would set forth again in such weather: but God be praised, we came safe home that night, though wet, weary, and surbated.

Appendix VI

THE FIRST THREE GENERATIONS
OF STEPHEN HOPKINS' DESCENDANTS

Stephen Hopkins had 10 children, 37 grandchildren, and about 330 great-grandchildren. Today, we are roughly 10-15 generations removed: so Stephen has a *lot* of descendants living today, no doubt hundreds of thousands, if not more.

This brief genealogy showing the first three generations of Stephen Hopkins' descendants is intended only for quick reference, and is not a substitute for a "real" genealogy. I have chosen not to go into any great detail, just providing the bare minimum. Anyone wanting a more detailed (and source documented) genealogy should consult the 600+ page book, *Mayflower Families Through Five Generations: Stephen Hopkins* (Volume 6), by John D. Austin, FASG., published by the General Society of Mayflower Descendants.

Unlike the aforementioned work, I have chosen to include the great-grandchildren of highly probable (but not fully proven) lines, and have designated them as such in the listing.

STEPHEN HOPKINS was bp. 30 April 1581 at Upper Clatford, Hampshire, England, son of John and Elizabeth (Williams) Hopkins, and died between 6 June and 17 July 1644 at Plymouth. He married (1) c1602, presumably in Hampshire, to MARY (—), perhaps from the Machell family. She was buried 9 May 1613 at Hursley. He married (2) ELIZABETH FISHER, 19 February 1617/8, St. Mary (Matfellon), Whitechapel, co. Middlesex, England. She died sometime between 1639(?) and 1644, at Plymouth.

Children from Mary, all baptized at Hursley, Hampshire:

1. Elizabeth, bp. 13 March 1604/5; living in 1613 when mother died; apparently dead by the time of the *Mayflower's* voyage in 1620.
2. +Constance, bp. 11 May 1606
3. +Giles, bp. 30 January 1607/8

Children from Elizabeth:

4. Damaris, born c1618, probably in London. Died sometime before 1627, perhaps the first winter at Plymouth.
5. Oceanus, born onboard the *Mayflower* during the voyage, in 1620. Died sometime before 1627, perhaps during the first winter at Plymouth.
6. Caleb, born about 1622 at Plymouth. Died at sea near Barbados sometime between 1644 and 1651, never married.
7. +Deborah, born about 1624 at Plymouth.
8. +Damaris, born about 1627 at Plymouth.
9. Ruth, born about 1629 at Plymouth. Died unmarried sometime between 1644 and 1651.

10. Elizabeth, born about 1631, at Plymouth. Apparently suffered from some sort of medical condition that kept her weak and sickly. Unmarried when she disappeared about 1659, and was not seen again.

2. CONSTANCE HOPKINS was bp. 11 May 1606 at Hursley, Hampshire, England, daughter of Stephen and Mary Hopkins, and died in October 1677 at Eastham. She married NICHOLAS SNOW, c1626, at Plymouth. Nicholas was bp. 25 January 1599, St. Leonard's, Shoreditch, London, England, son of Nicholas Snow; and died 15 November 1676 at Eastham.

Children (first nine probably born at Plymouth, last three probably born at Eastham):

11. Mark, b. 9 May 1628. Married (1) Ann Cooke, and had dau. **Anna**; married (2) Jane Prence, had children: **Mary, Nicholas, Elizabeth (died young), Thomas, Sarah, Prence, Elizabeth (again) and Hannah.**

12. Mary, b. c1630. Married Thomas Paine, and had children: **Mary, Samuel, Thomas, Eleazer, Elisha, John, Nicholas, James, Joseph, and Dorcas.**

13. Sarah, b. c1632. Married William Walker, and had children: **John, William (died young), William (again), Sarah, Elizabeth, and Jabez.**

14. Joseph, b. c1634. Married Mary (—), and had children: **Joseph, Benjamin, Mary, Sarah, Ruth, Stephen, Lydia, Rebecca, James, Jane, and Josiah.**

15. Stephen, b. c1636. Married Susannah (Deane) Rogers, and had children: **Bathshuah, Hannah, Micajah, Bethiah, Mehitable, and Ebenezer.**

16. John, b. c1638. Married Mary Smalley, and had children **Hannah, Mary, Abigail, Rebecca, John, Isaac, Lydia, Elisha, and Phebe.**

17. Elizabeth, b. c1640. Married Thomas Rogers, and had children: **Elizabeth, Joseph, Hannah, Thomas (died young), Thomas (again), Eleazer, and Nathaniel.**

18. Jabez, b. c1642. Married Elizabeth (—), and had children: **Jabez, Edward, Sarah, Grace, Thomas, Elizabeth, Deborah, Rachel, and Mercy.**

19. Ruth, b. c1644. Married John Cole, and had children: **Ruth, John, Hepzibah, Hannah, Joseph, Mary, and Sarah.**

20. Constance, b. c1646. Although there is no conclusive record, it is very probable that Constance, wife of Daniel Doane (c1636-1712) of Eastham was the daughter of Nicholas and Constance (Hopkins) Snow. Daniel and Constance had nine children: **Joseph, Constant, Israel, Daniel, Nathaniel, Constanta, Rebecca, Abigail, and Ruth.**

21. child, name unknown, probably died young.

22. child, name unknown, probably died young.

3. GILES HOPKINS was bp. 30 January 1607/8 at Hursley, Hampshire, England, son of Stephen and Mary Hopkins, and died between 5 March 1688/9 and 16 April 1690 at Plymouth. He married CATHERINE WHELDON, dau. Gabrial Wheldon, on 9 October 1639 at Plymouth. She died after 1688 in Eastham.

Children (first four born at Yarmouth, last six at Eastham):

23. Mary, b. November 1640. Married Samuel Smith, had children: **son (died young), Samuel, Mary, Joseph, Grace, and Rebecca.**

24. Stephen, b. September 1642. Married Mary Merrick, had children: **Elizabeth, Stephen, Ruth, Judah, Samuel, Nathaniel, Joseph, Benjamin, and Mary.**

25. John, b. 1643. Died at three months.

26. Abigail, b. October 1644. Married William Merrick, had children: **Rebecca, William, Stephen, Benjamin, Nathaniel, John, Joshua, Ruth, and Samuel.**

27. Deborah, b. June 1648. Married Josiah Cooke, had children: **Elizabeth (died young), Josiah, Richard, Elizabeth (again), Caleb, Deborah, Joshua, and Benjamin.**

28. Caleb, b. January 1650/1. He married (1) Mary Williams, and had children **Caleb, Nathaniel, and Thomas**; and he married (2) Mary (—), and had daughter **Thankful.**

29. Ruth, b. June 1653. Possibly (but unproven) married Samuel Mayo. If so, they had children: **Hannah, Sarah, Samuel, Jonathan, Rebecca, and Mercy.**

30. Joshua, b. June 1657. He married Mary Cole, and had children: **John, Abigail, Elisha, Lydia, Mary, Joshua, Hannah, and Phebe.**

31. William, b. 9 January 1660. Apparently died unmarried.

32. Elizabeth, b. November 1664. Died December 1664.

7. DEBORAH HOPKINS was born about 1625 at Plymouth, daughter of Stephen and Elizabeth (Fisher) Hopkins, and died probably before 1674. She married ANDREW RING, 23 April 1646, at Plymouth. Andrew was born c1618 in Leiden, Holland, son of William and Mary Ring; and died 23 February 1690/1 at Plymouth.

Children (all born at Plymouth):

33. Elizabeth, b. 19 April 1652. Married William Mayo, and had children: **John, Hannah, Thankful, and Deborah.**
34. William, b. c1653. Married Hannah Sherman, and had children: **Deborah (died young), Hannah, William, Elizabeth, Eliazar, and Deborah (again).**
35. Eleazer, b. c1655. Married Mary Shaw, and had children: **Eleazer, Andrew, Phebe, Samuel, Andrew, Deborah, Mary, Jonathan, Susanna, Elkanah, Elizabeth, and Lydia.**
36. Mary, b. c1658. Married John Morton, and had children **Mary, John, Hannah, Ebenezer, Deborah, and Persis.**
37. Deborah, living 1691, no further record.
38. Susanna. Possibly (unproven) married William Walker. If so, had children: **Susanna, John, William, and Mehitable.**

8. DAMARIS HOPKINS was born about 1627 at Plymouth, daughter of Stephen and Elizabeth (Fisher) Hopkins, and died sometime between January 1665/6 and 18 November 1669. She married JACOB COOKE, about June 1646, at Plymouth. Jacob was born c1618 in Leiden, Holland, son of *Mayflower* passenger Francis Cooke and his wife Hester; and died between 11 and 18 December 1675.

Children (all born at Plymouth):

39. Elizabeth, b. 18 January 1648/9. Married John Doty, son of *Mayflower* passenger Edward Doty. Had children: **John, Edward, Jacob, Elizabeth, Isaac, Samuel, Elisha, Josiah, and Martha.**
40. Caleb, b. 29 March 1651. Married Jane (—). Had children: **John, Mercy, Ann, Jane, Elizabeth, Mary, Caleb, James, and Joseph.**
41. Jacob, b. 26 March 1653. Married Lydia Miller, and had children: **William, Lydia, Rebecca, Jacob, Margaret, Josiah, John, and Damaris.**

42. Mary, b. 12 January 1657/8. Married John Rickard, and had children: **John, Mercy, John, Mary, Esther, Elizabeth, and James.**

43. Martha, b. 16 March 1659/60. Married Elkanah Cushman, grandson of *Mayflower* passenger Isaac Allerton, and had children **Allerton, Elizabeth, Josiah, Martha, and Mehitable.**

44. Francis, b. 5 January 1662/3. Married Elizabeth Latham, granddaughter of *Mayflower* passenger Mary Chilton, and had children: **Susannah, Robert, Caleb, Francis, Sarah, and Elizabeth.**

45. Ruth, b. 17 January 1665/6. Probably (but unproven) married Hezekiah Tinkham. If so, had children: **Helkiah, Mary, John, Jacob, Caleb, Sarah, Ebenezer, Ruth, and Peter.**

46. Sarah, b. c1671. Married Robert Bartlett, and had children: **Hannah, Thomas, John, son (died young), Sarah, James, Joseph, Elizabeth, William, Ebenezer, Robert, and Samuel.**

47. Rebecca, b. c1673. Living 1675, no further record.

Appendix VII

WILL AND ESTATE INVENTORY OF
STEPHEN HOPKINS (1644)

The last Will and Testament of Mr. Stephen Hopkins exhibited upon the Oathes of mr Willm Bradford and Captaine Miles Standishat the generall Court holden at Plymouth the xxth of August Anno dm 1644 as it followeth in these wordes vizt.

The sixt of June 1644 I Stephen Hopkins of Plymouth in New England being weake yet in good and prfect memory blessed be God yet considering the fraile estate of all men I do ordaine and make this to be my last will and testament in manner and forme following and first I do committ my body to the earth from whence it was taken, and my soule to the Lord who gave it, my body to be buryed as neare as convenyently may be to my wyfe Deceased And first my will is that out of my whole estate my funerall expences be discharged secondly that out of the remayneing part of my said estate that all my lawfull Debts be payd thirdly I do bequeath by this my will to my sonn Giles Hopkins my great Bull wch is now in the hands of Mris Warren. Also I do give to Stephen Hopkins my sonn Giles his sonne twenty shillings in Mris Warrens hands for the hire of the said Bull Also I give and bequeath to my daughter Constanc Snow the wyfe of Nicholas Snow my mare also I give unto my daughter Deborah Hopkins the brodhorned black cowe and her calf and half the Cowe called Motley Also I doe give and bequeath unto my daughter Damaris Hopkins the Cowe called Damaris heiffer and the white faced calf and half the cowe called Mottley Also I give to my daughter Ruth the Cowe called Red Cole and her calfe and a Bull at Yarmouth wch is in the keepeing of Giles Hopkins wch is an yeare and advantage old and half the curld Cowe Also I give and bequeath to my daughter Elizabeth the Cowe called Smykins and her calf and thother half of the Curld Cowe wth Ruth and an yearelinge heiffer wth out a tayle in the keeping of Gyles Hopkins at

Yarmouth Also I do give and bequeath unto my foure daughters that is to say Deborah Hopkins Damaris Hopkins Ruth Hopkins and Elizabeth Hopkins all the mooveable goods the wch do belong to my house as linnen wollen beds bedcloathes pott kettles pewter or whatsoevr are moveable belonging to my said house of what kynd soever and not named by their prticular names all wch said mooveables to be equally devided amongst my said daughters foure silver spoones thatis to say to eich of them one, And in case any of my said daughters should be taken away by death before they be marryed that then the part of their division to be equally devided amongst the Survivors. I do also by this my will make Caleb Hopkins my sonn and heire apparent giveing and bequeathing unto my said sonn aforesaid all my Right title and interrest to my house and lands at Plymouth wth all the Right title and interrest wch doth might or of Right doth or may hereafter belong unto mee, as also I give unto my saide heire all such land wch of Right is Rightly due unto me and not at prsent in my reall possession wch belongs unto me by right of my first comeing into this land or by any other due Right, as by such freedome or otherwise giveing unto my said heire my full & whole and entire Right in all divisions allottments appoyntments or distributions whatsoever to all or any pt of the said lande at any tyme or tymes so to be disposed Also I do give moreover unto my foresaid heire one paire or yooke of oxen and the hyer of them wch are in the hands of Richard Church as may appeare by bill under his hand Also I do give unto my said heire Caleb Hopkins all my debts wch are now oweing unto me, or at the day of my death may be oweing unto mee either by booke bill or bills or any other way rightfully due unto mee ffurthermore my will is that my daughters aforesaid shall have free recourse to my house in Plymouth upon any occation there to abide and remayne for such tyme as any of them shall thinke meete and convenyent & they single persons And for the faythfull prformance of this my will I do make and ordayne my aforesaid sonn and heire Caleb Hopkins my true and lawfull Executor ffurther I do by this my will appoynt and make my said sonn and Captaine Miles Standishjoyntly supervisors of this my will according to the true meaneing of the same that is to say that my Executor & supervisor shall make the severall divisions parts or porcons legacies or whatsoever doth appertaine to the fullfilling of this my will It is also my will that my Executr & Supervisor shall advise devise and dispose by the best wayes & meanes they cann for the disposeing in marriage or other wise for the best advancnt of the estate of the forenamed Deborah Damaris Ruth and Elizabeth Hopkins Thus trusting in the Lord my will shalbe truly prformed according to the true meaneing of the same I committ the whole Disposeing hereof to the Lord that hee may direct you herein

June 6th 1644

Witnesses hereof By me Steven Hopkins

Myles StandishBradford

An Inventory of the Goods and th Cattells of mr Steven Hopkins taken by Captaine Miles Standishmr Thomas Willet and mr John Done the xviith of July 1644. xx° Cal. Re.

	£	s	d
Inpris one brod horne Cowe	05	10	00
it Mottlis Cowe	05	10	00
it Damaris heiffer	05	00	00
it Red Cowe	05	05	00
it Curld Cowe	05	05	00
it Symkins Cowe	05	00	00
it brod Hornes calf	00	12	00
it white faced calf	00	15	00
it Cooles calf	00	14	00
it Symkins calf	00	12	00
it a great Bull	08	00	00
it a mare	06	00	00
it a yeong bull	01	05	00
it a yearling heiffer wthout a tayle	01	05	00
it a yok of oxen	15	00	00
it 2 pigges	00	04	00
it poultry	00	10	00
it a bed & boulster & one pillow	03	10	00
it another bed & boulster & pillow	03	10	00
it another feathe bed & pillow	03	00	00
it another bed & bouster wth an old straw bed	02	00	00
it 3 white blankets	01	00	00
it one covering	00	12	00
it one covring	00	04	00
it a yellow Rugg	00	08	00
it a greene Rugg	00	06	00
it 2 checkr blanketts	00	14	00
it curtaines & vallence	00	10	00
it a scarfe	00	06	00
it a pair of flanell sheets	00	07	00
it one old paire of sheets	00	05	00
it one paire of sheets	00	08	00
it one paire of sheets	00	08	00

it 3 sheets	00 10 00
it 4 pillow beares	00 12 00
it 5 napkins	00 03 06
it 1 diapr napkins	00 02 06
it 3 table clothes	00 04 00
it 4 dymothy caps	00 02 00
it 2 white capps	00 03 00
it 2 wrought caps	00 02 06
it 2 shirts	00 12 00
	86 06 06
it two paire of shooes	00 06 00
it prs of cotton stockings	00 02 06
it 4 spoones	01 08 00
it in money	00 00 06
it claspes	00 00 02
it a pair of garters	00 00 04
it 2 Ruffe	00 07 00
it a paire of drawers	00 00 04
it a moheire petticote	01 15 00
it a petticote of phillip & cheny	01 00 00
it a grogorm coate	01 00 00
it a prpetuam coate	01 00 00
it a cloth coate	01 00 00
it a cloake	01 10 00
it a gray cloak	01 10 00
it suit of cloth	00 08 00
it a pair of breeches	00 03 00
it an old coate & jerkine	00 10 00
it a muffe	00 06 00
it 3 cusheons & a pair of breeches	00 04 00
it a chest	00 08 00
it a chest	00 06 00
it a case & bottel & box	00 03 00
it a hogshead	00 01 00
it an old warmeing pann	00 02 00
it a frying pann	00 01 00
it 6 porringers	00 05 00
it 2 porringers	00 01 00
it 4 wine measures	00 06 00

it 3 quart potts	00 06 00
it chamber potts	00 02 00
it 2 laten candlesticks	00 01 00
it 1 puter candlestick	00 01 00
it a pestell & morter	00 03 06
it a beere bowle & wine cup	00 01 06
it a beaker	00 00 06
it a salt seller	00 01 00
it 2 funnells	00 01 00
it 2 basens	00 06 00
it a great dish	00 05 00
it 6 dishes	00 14 00
it a little dish	00 00 02
it earthen potts	00 00 06
it an Iron pott	00 05 00
it a bras pott	00 08 00
it a cast skellet	00 05 00
it a smale skellet	00 01 06
it a great kettle	01 02 00
it a lesse kettle	00 06 00
it a smaler ketle	00 04 00
it another kettle	00 07 00
it 5 spoones	00 01 00
it 1 dossen & half trenchers	00 01 00
it two graters 2s	00 02 00
it a shooeing horne	00 00 01
it a paire of bellowes	00 01 00
it 4 paire of old pothookes	00 03 00
it a fireshovell & tongs	00 04 00
it two spitts	00 03 06
it 3 paire of links	00 07 06
it a peece of a bar of Iron	00 01 06
it a gridiron	00 01 00
it 9 trayes	00 09 00
it a churne	00 04 00
it 2 chees fatts	00 01 00
it a old Cullender	00 00 02
it 2 payles	00 01 04
it wodden Mo	00 01 06

it 2 wheeles	00 07 00
it 2 chaires	00 08 00
it 2 stooles	00 02 00
it latten pans	00 00 06
it a tubb & forme	00 12 00
it a cheane	00 06 00
it a sive	00 00 06
it old chest	00 02 00
it a bakeing Tub	00 02 00
it old tubbs	00 01 00
it feathers	00 03 00
it 3 hoopes of Iron	00 01 06
it 1 sawe	00 01 06
it a cheese rack	00 04 00
it 4 skins	00 03 00
it an axe	00 01 06
it a prcell hemp	00 02 06
it scales & weights	00 05 00
it Debts	16 05 00
it Divers bookes	00 12 00
it more in Debts	01 01 00
it a hatt	00 01 00

Index

Made in the USA
Lexington, KY
18 May 2015